To Alex,
#1 Son,

Could not have done this without you. What I wrote in the acknowledgments is not just complimentary, not exaggeration but straight-up truth. Your proofreading to make it better made all the difference. And no-one encourages me more than you. If this book is successful, it is partly your fault.

Thy Son,
Dad

THE ARROGANCE OF RELIGIOUS THOUGHT

Information Kills Religion

WILLIAM A ZINGRONE

Copyright © 2016 William A. Zingrone.

All rights reserved. No part of this book may be reproduced, stored, or transmitted by any means—whether auditory, graphic, mechanical, or electronic—without written permission of both publisher and author, except in the case of brief excerpts used in critical articles and reviews. Unauthorized reproduction of any part of this work is illegal and is punishable by law.

This book is a work of non-fiction. Unless otherwise noted, the author and the publisher make no explicit guarantees as to the accuracy of the information contained in this book and in some cases, names of people and places have been altered to protect their privacy.

ISBN: 978-1-4834-5873-1 (sc)
ISBN: 978-1-4834-5872-4 (e)

Because of the dynamic nature of the Internet, any web addresses or links contained in this book may have changed since publication and may no longer be valid. The views expressed in this work are solely those of the author and do not necessarily reflect the views of the publisher, and the publisher hereby disclaims any responsibility for them.

Any people depicted in stock imagery provided by Thinkstock are models, and such images are being used for illustrative purposes only.
Certain stock imagery © Thinkstock.

Lulu Publishing Services rev. date: 10/4/2016

DEDICATION

"Yet again it is demonstrated, that monotheistic religion is a plagiarism of a plagiarism, of a hearsay of a hearsay, of an illusion of an illusion, extending all the way back to a fabrication of a few nonevents"

Christopher Hitchens

To Hitch, the incomparable Christopher Hitchens, whom I never met but like thousands of others, I felt like I lost a good friend and possibly the most eloquent and vociferous, upfront, defender of the New Enlightenment when he died; and to all the wonderful women of this world, past and present, who have suffered...still suffer, many horribly, and more than any other group...from the arrogance of religious thought.

TABLE OF CONTENTS

Introduction i
Chapter 1:   Divisiveness 1
Chapter 2:   Mysogyny and Homophobia 18
Chapter 3:   Eternal Damnation and the Afterlife 34
Chapter 4:   Creationism 43
Chapter 5:   Evangelizing and Moralizing 55
Chapter 6:   Conservatism 69
Chapter 7:   Child Indoctrination 87
Chapter 8:   Denial of Knowledge 101
Chapter 9:   Information Kills Religion 122
Chapter 10: The New Enlightenment 140
Acknowledgments 163
References and Recommended Reading 165

INTRODUCTION

I am a non-theist. I don't care if someone needs to believe in a Creator Being of some kind. I think however, it to be highly unlikely that any such being ever existed. I put the idea of a god or spiritual entities in the same boat as ghosts, fairies, Bigfoot, UFO's, Osiris, Wodin, Zeus, or any of the other supposed imagined things such as gods or spirits, which humans have dreamed up and claimed to exist through all time, and for which there has never been any evidence. If you believe some person-like intelligent agent must have started the whole universe, go for it, you won't bother me or any of our fellow men and women. As Thomas Jefferson, deistic sort that he was, said: *"It neither picks my pocket nor breaks my leg."* But if you then tell me you know what He (your god, a stern male persona for over 3 billion believers of Xianity and Islam for example) is thinking, and what this God of yours intends for our behavior, my behavior, your fellow man's behavior, especially woman's behavior, then I think you have been sold the most destructive set of ideas man has yet invented. I detest theism for this reason, because it is those ideas, more precisely, that kind of arrogant thinking that claims to know what it cannot and then forces such ideas on your fellow man, that this book is about: The Arrogance of Religious Thought.

Arrogant in its claims to know things with no evidence, arrogant in its demand for the right behavior and beliefs of others, arrogant in its condemnation to eternal torment of others who do not conform, arrogant in its smug grasp of children's minds through coercive indoctrination, arrogant in its treatment of others, especially women, and lastly, arrogant for its demand for respect and a "free pass" to do all these things we would not allow in other realms of human interactions. Religious thought, with no basis in reality, and precious little tolerance, is the most destructive of fashions ever adopted by mankind. We can lose it like the bad habit that it is. That is the purpose of this book: to help facilitate the demise of religious thought and free ourselves from the divisiveness, delusion, cruelty, and arrogance it promotes.

I was not always a militant non-believer. Even as an activist in the secular movement, I was a reluctant participant in the Culture Wars. I operated solely from the response side, not the aggressor, a passive defender of the New Enlightenment, promoting free-thinking, reason and tolerance, but not attacking religion itself. In fact, usually making excuses for, and excusing religion for its faults. As a freethinker, as a humanist I saw my role as merely righting the misconceptions about non-belief, defusing religious claims in response mode only. But merely defending free thought and promoting tolerance is not enough. Always being on the defensive, merely cleaning up after the Creationist attacks on science for example, or countering Christian and Islamic attacks on woman's and gays' rights is not sufficient to stop the bad habit of religious thinking.

We must go to the heart of the problem, and not just after any one religion, but the fuel that drives all religions: religious thought. Unquestioned, unfounded, arrogant religious thought. The uncritical acceptance and repetition of religious thinking by modern society is the root of many, if not most of our evils. We must educate ourselves as to the ludicrousness and cruelty of religious claims and free ourselves of the sense of false necessity that religious thought has too long enjoyed. Millions of people over the centuries have lived fulfilled, compassionate, fully human lives without need of religion. A billion or two or more alive today, live free thinking lives, fully empathetic to their fellow human's rights, without religious thinking's roadblocks to lucid reasoning and compassion. These billions of non-believers, prove that religion and religious thought are wholly unnecessary to a rewarding, successful human life. The billions more who have suffered, and those who still suffer today, some horribly under religious rules, prove in fact, that religion is detrimental to human existence. Each chapter in this book provides a number of examples of religious arrogance from different areas of human interaction. This book is different in not offering the usual religion bashing examples (though there so many to choose from) like the Catholic priest child-rape scandal or Evangelical TV preachers bad behavior, but rather more mundane everyday examples of the insidious perfusion and blind acceptance of religious thought throughout our modern culture.

What if your neighbor said?

"Hey I just joined this really great organization, it's awsum, has huge resources, weekly meetings, a lot of support, a real sense of community, well organized, branches all over the place, a long history, well-funded and really stable."

Wow, sounds great!

"Yeah, even chance for advancement!"

Hey, that's fantastic, congratulations!

"Yeah, as long as you are not a woman"

What?

"Well yeah, women can't be in supervisory positions."

What?

"They can't be supervisors, managers, executives or president."

And you like this place?

"Oh, yeah it's great, I mean it is in their charter that women can't be in authority positions, it has always been that way, that's just how it is, goes way back, no big deal."

You wouldn't be too impressed with your neighbor and his admiration for this company, nor would you think too much of any corporation, charity organization, social club or government office if it operated like that. In fact, the outrage by most would be palpable in today's day and age if any organization blatantly and un-apologetically tried to get away with a discriminatory policy such as that. Yet, that is exactly the situation with the Catholic Church and many Xian denominations: the only thing female in Holy Mother Church isn't the church or its management, just the line workers, the nuns.

They can never be priests, bishops, cardinals nor Pope. They are barred from management of the operation, and can never be members of the executive level from which the head of the association is elected. I've always told my daughter never to join any organization of which she couldn't become the leader. We wouldn't allow such primitive, demeaning discriminatory practices in any other entity or function in our modern society, but if it is within a religion, then somehow it is OK. Religion gets a free pass. This is a classic example, and but one of far too many, of the arrogance of religious thought. We will explore far too many more, all of which we can do without, throughout the rest of this book. Religious thought is built upon arrogance, giving one the feeling however false, of superiority over other humans:

"We are chosen, you are not"

"We're on the path of righteousness, you're not"

"We worship the real god, you don't"

"We're elect and will be raptured, you won't"

"We will go to heaven, you will burn in hell"

"We practice right morals, you do not"

"We are saved, you are damned"

"We are the true believers, you are heretics, infidels"

"I suppose that one reason I have always detested religion is its sly tendency to insinuate the idea that the universe is designed with 'you' in mind or, even worse, that there is a divine plan into which one fits whether one knows it or not. This kind of modesty is too arrogant for me."

Christopher Hitchens

end religion now
waz
1/1/16

1

DIVISIVENESS

"Religion has ever been anti-human, anti-woman, anti-life, anti-peace, anti-reason and anti-science. The god idea has been detrimental not only to humankind but to the earth. It is time now for reason, education and science to take over."

Madalyn Murray O'Hair

"I think that religion is the most dangerous and divisive ideology that we have ever produced. It is also the only ideology that is systematically protected from criticism, both from within and without."

Sam Harris

"I am absolutely convinced that religion is the main source of hatred in this world."

Christopher Hitchens

For me, it really hit home about 10 years ago. Returning to graduate school in my 50's, I was a founding member of a newly formed secular group, the Northern Illinois Atheists, Agnostics and Freethinkers (AAFT). In 2006 we were roughly the 75th college campus organization to join the Secular Student Alliance (SSA). Now, there are in the neighborhood of 300 such groups nationwide including more than a few in high schools. One of our other founders had put together a meeting for the different religious groups on campus to get together and open a dialogue among them to promote religious tolerance. He had done a tour in Iraq as an 18 year old Army private assigned to a security force in Baghdad and had seen firsthand, up close and personal, the effects of sectarian violence that we were only beginning to understand were so commonplace in the Middle East, such as the mutilated bodies of someone's family members who had disappeared and were found weeks later in a ditch.

Doing whatever he could to diminish religious division, hatred, and violence was his sincere and heartfelt mission. His descriptions of the sectarian atrocities he witnessed were horribly similar to the atrocities I saw from another Middle Eastern country in a YouTube documentary years later: bodies floating down the river in a Syrian city in the midst of their sectarian fueled civil war, sent from the wrong end of town and washed back down to loved ones at the other end. Muslims killing Muslims, the most common terrorism they commit. About 40 of us assembled on a circle of couches facing one another, Christians, Muslims, atheists, agnostics, with one or two kids exploring other faiths such as Buddhism and even paganism. Truly a diverse bunch. We went around the room introducing ourselves as to what faith, or lack thereof, we identified with. We'd covered about half the group when after one young man told of his Evangelical Christian background the next guy in line said something to the effect, *"Yes, I'm Christian too, I'm a Catholic and I grew up...."* Before he could finish his sentence the evangelical kid turned to him and said plainly almost matter of fact: *"You're not a real Christian."*

I was floored. Here I am, a fucking godless unbelieving scum assumed by most Xians to have no moral basis of any kind, and I wouldn't dream of being so goddam rude to another human being, certainly not in front of a bunch of strangers. Even if I thought someone was utterly out to lunch in their beliefs (something I vehemently, wholeheartedly feel about Evangelical Xiansanity), I wouldn't have the 24 karat chutzpah, the abject arrogance to diss someone to their face in front of a group, much less a group of strangers assembled to exercise our common humanity in working together to overcome religious intolerance. Un-fucking-believable.

Since then of course, while living below the Ohio River down south in rural Kentucky for 5 years, I experienced that sort of religious arrogance on nearly a daily basis. I was born and raised in the liberal North and despite being raised Catholic, a member of the *"one, true, holy Catholic and apostolic Church,"* we were never instilled with the attitude of superiority inherent in that quote. We had a vague understanding that our Protestant friends were practicing a slightly altered if not diminished version of our original Xianity, but we were never made to view them as inferior. They were, after all, Xians too, saved by Christ and all that jazz. We, as Catholic kids, didn't give it much thought. But down south was a whole different world, and it still is. Baptists viewing Catholics as not really Xians and kids witnessing to other Xians, even in grade school: *"You're gonna burn in Hell, you're not a real Xian"* were regular occurrences you heard or read about often enough down south. Such is the arrogance that religious thought can bring forth.

I'd been irreligious most of my life, an agnostic/atheist since 8th grade/freshman year. Growing up in a very liberal Catholic household (my Dad got away with being an Easter-Xmas Catholic, mom took us to church mostly), we went to mass not quite every Sunday and attended Catholic grade and high school, but belief was never a big issue in our home. Religion was just something we did. Although I'd left any practice of faith behind, (not sure I ever really believed, just went thru the motions), and often asked probing questions in religion class, I was certainly no firebrand, no budding young activist by any means. Early in my adult life I was pre-occupied with running a small business and thereafter just trying to stay gainfully employed, and keep the family fed. I still read voraciously during those times, mostly science, some philosophy, including Bertrand Russell and his very influential *Why I am not a Christian*. It planted the first seeds that religion might not be so harmless as portrayed in the detailed but detached anthropological works of comparative religion such as Joseph Campbell's *The Masks of God* or Weston LaBarre's *The Ghost Dance*.

I had no bad experience with religion, despite what my later Evangelical acquaintances and adversaries in print and on Facebook would instantly assume when they discovered I was an ex-Catholic. The depredations I must have endured surely explained to them my vociferous non-belief. How wrong they were. My teachers, many of them nuns and priests, were friendly, dedicated educators. We had no rulers smacked across our knuckles nor experienced any unwanted advances. This book is an explication of the actual and far too many reasons why I work so hard now for the end of religion; all of them, and as soon as possible.

Years later, reading Richard Dawkins' staggeringly blunt and clear attack, *The God Delusion*, was the beginning of my call to action against religion. Then of course, the incomparable Christopher Hitchens' *God is not Great* demonstrated the destruction of lives all over the planet due to religion and the ridiculous illogic of all faith. My first reaction to both books was *"Damn, can they say that?"* Like, wow. Similarly, as the five of us students met for the first time to form the NIU SSA group in 2006, we all showed up one by one asking timidly *"Are you here for the...meeting?"* No-one would use the "A" word out loud. "Atheist" was not to become mainstream, discussed everywhere, uttered out loud daily and appearing in all media for a few more years. I'd never experienced the ugliness of religion personally, only it's obvious absurdity. It wasn't until reading Hitch, experiencing the NIU AAFT meetings and later the immersion in the thickly religious culture of Western Kentucky, the American Biblical South that I saw how obnoxious religious thought could make an otherwise normal human being. After reading Hitch, Dawkins, and then Sam Harris, Dan Dennett, the religious studies of Pascal Boyer and Scott Atran, the Biblical analyses of the Internet Infidels and the New Testament scholar Bart Ehrman, and then daily scouring Richard Dawkins' RDFRS *(Richard Dawkins Foundation for Reason and Science)*, and Jerry Coyne's *Why Evolution is True* websites for everything on religion and its absurd cruelties, did I realize how lucky I had been growing up relatively free of religious thought. Nearly everything I read demonstrated how so many worldwide led cramped, stifled lives if not outright ruined ones, due solely to the crippling idiocies of religious ideas. These things made me the activist that I am today. It is all so ludicrous, so unnecessary. No-one's life should be diminished by any religious thought anywhere, anytime, any more.

Religious Pluralism

There are well over 700 different religions in the world today, all with their special claims to knowledge about a spiritual realm, unique origin myths, beliefs how the world really works and, of course, guidelines or outright demands for right behavior, especially restrictive for women. This estimate doesn't include the hundreds more religions of earlier times such as those of ancient Egypt, Greece, Rome, etc., or the many tribal religions that have come and gone. The largest religions of today are each subdivided by dozens, hundreds, even thousands of different sects that reflect minor differences in doctrine and practice or represent irreconcilable differences in interpretation of their holy scriptures. Xianity today is estimated to contain tens of thousands of individual sects alone.

The "Big 2" as I'll call them here; Xianity and Islam and the "Karma 2" the reincarnation religions of Hinduism and Buddhism comprise roughly 4.5 billion or nearly 2/3 of the just over 7 billion humans on the planet today. Xianity has the largest number of adherents estimated at around 2 billion, with Islam second at over 1.5 billion and the reincarnation religions close to 1 billion members combined. All religions claim they have the goods for right living and the correct knowledge of which god to worship, or not, and are certain in their different versions of the afterlife awaiting the human soul when a person dies. Two things stand out:

1. Their claims are mutually exclusive and contradictory.

2. Religious affiliation is mostly an accident of birth locale.

The Buddhists are unconcerned with the necessity of a creator god, the Hindus have gods enough for everybody, and the Xians and Muslims of course, are unquestionably certain their Creator is the sole god and the only one to be believed in, worshiped properly, or else. Many theologians have waxed poetic in trying to explicate the old truism that "we all worship the same god", but the Muslims certainly won't stand for that and a brief analysis of Xian and Muslim dogmas negates that futile attempt at reconciliation rather quickly. "There is but one god Allah and Mohammed is his prophet" and "Allah neither begets nor is begotten", doesn't wash with Yahweh being one of a Trinity, having begotten a Son and their relationship spawning the ephemeral Holy Spirit, or not, depending on which sort of Trinity doctrine your church adheres to. To a Muslim that is such ridiculous and abject polytheistic blasphemy that to believe it one may as well be an atheist.

The fanciful idea of the reincarnation religions; that the soul re-animates into another body after a believer's death instead of winding up either in heavenly union with god, or doomed to eternal and appropriately excruciating hellfire punishment, is utter heresy to the Xian as well as the Muslim. It is perfectly reasonable to believe, in Islam for example, in fact one is compelled without exception to accept that a soul will regenerate new skin in Hell to re-burn again and again, in perpetual agony, but certainly not that one could come back for another go at it as a different human being, or a cockroach, or a steak.

One could go on for hours analyzing the doctrinal differences that make up the absurdities of religious claims. Those claims divide us all over absolute illogical fantasies, to no benefit whatsoever. In the vast majority of cases, someone only believes whatever religion they do, because it was the dominant religion within a mile or so of their birth and upbringing as a child or adolescent. The predominantly Xian West, the East's adherence to the Reincarnation religions and the Middle East's near monopoly by Islam and its lateral extensions across central Africa and eastward to Indonesia, dictate by and large what religion you will later "believe" to the exclusion of all others. You believe what you were born into, mostly by being indoctrinated as a child. As Richard Dawkins has pointed out, religious belief is largely a function of geography. So much for eternal truth.

An example of this same phenomenon in microcosm is displayed so well in the American South. A child could be born properly godly on one side of a crossroad in a hamlet of no more than a few dwellings into the ultra-conservative Church of Christ. Should they have had the misfortune of leaving their mother's womb on the opposite side of the road, they might have wound up only marginally Christian (to the Church of Christer's at least) as a First Baptist. Worse still, should they have been born but a mile or two down the road in the decidedly wrong direction, they may have (god forbid), wound up Catholic and been looked down upon by both the good Baptists and rock-solid Church of Christ members with certain disdain as damn near atheists, and reminded as early as elementary school: *"You're not a real Christian."*

The secular world would like all religionists to consider those facts before making any noise whatsoever about how their religion is "the one." Additionally, please remember that even if you belong to any one of the "Big 2" or "Karma 2" religions, 70-80% of the rest of us alive today do not belong to your religion, never will, will never read your damn book, get along just fine without it, and don't need nor want to hear about how sure you are of your arbitrary brand of nonsense. Religion doesn't unite, it divides all across the spectrum, over wholly arbitrary cultural myths taught to children as truths. We can do better.

Arrogant but Accepted Religious Divisiveness

This from the bottom of the Statue of Liberty:

"Give me your tired, your poor,

Your huddled masses yearning to breathe free;

The wretched refuse of your teeming shore,

Send these, the homeless,

Tempest-tossed to me

I lift my lamp beside the golden door!"

Boy, how that attitude has been compromised by the so-called "religion of love". For a pathetic example, in a video from 2012 which garnered over 200,000 hits on YouTube, the Reverend Dennis Terry, Baptist minister from Louisiana, while introducing then Republican presidential candidate Rick Perry to his flock lets the world know just what he thinks about folks different from him and what we should do with them. Does he welcome with open arms the poor huddled masses? Hell no. This man of Christ, deacon of the religion of love has but two words for anyone who believes in some other god or religion and doesn't believe with him that *"there's only one god, Jeezus"*, and those two words are *"Get out!"* You heard right: *"Get out."*

Whatever happened to the Golden Rule Xians are always bandying on about? You know: "love thy neighbor, do unto others, turn the other cheek, Jesus taught us to love one another, all men are brothers", and the like? These are not so prominent to many like Dennis Terry. He knows better. Bullshit, get out. This action and attitude shared by so many within Conservative Xiansanity, just epitomizes for me the arrogance of religious thought. You can all leave his America forthwith. Isn't that just special? Get out of his America if you don't believe what he believes.

When did old white Xians, mostly from the South, take over this country? Since Reagan and both Bushes I guess, with a boost from the liberal Evangelical Carter, who also legitimized the Religious Right to rise to prominence and hijack the Republican Party over the last 30 years or so. Who says it's his (Rev. Terry's), country anyway? Baptists didn't found and lay claim to America, they never had first dibs. In fact, the Baptists, who didn't believe exactly what the New England Puritans and other sects did about Xianity, suffered discrimination, even persecution as immigrants who dared differ from the Xians already established in the colonies. Baptist might lose their property, be run out of town on a rail, or worse. How quickly one forgets.

Thomas Jefferson's 1801 letter to the Danbury Baptists about their persecution, suffered at the hands of other Xians, reiterated this was a secular country, not a Xian nation, despite Rev. Terry's revisionist attitude to the contrary. In it Jefferson used the words *"building a wall of separation between church and state"*, in referring to the 1st Amendment guaranteeing religious freedom. Rev. Terry as an American, as a Baptist especially, should know this. This is a prime example of the arrogance (and smug delusion), that religious thought promotes. Tell you what, let's have some old time Enlightenment thought, promoting tolerance as ensconced in those words at the bottom of the Lady Liberty, not any more "old time religion", which only divides us all.

Dennis Terry of course, still had his job. He was no doubt a respected member of his community, and would be held in high regard immediately almost anywhere he might go in America, just for being a reverend, and for all anyone knows he may be a swell guy otherwise, a good father, grandfather and husband, a true friend, a giving, hard-working minister sincerely interested in and dedicated to his congregation. For all I know he's most likely an honest guy, taxpayer and citizen, like the majority of us walking around this country, or any country for that matter, regardless of what we were taught to believe.

And Reverend Terry, while smugly standing up there waving his finger with his audience applauding really pumped up the crowd with *"There's only one god, there's only one god, and his name is Jeezus!"* I'd be willing to bet huge sums that at the moment he was pontificating on his one true religion, on the other side of the world, all over the other side of the world, there were countless imams exhorting their fervent crowd of worshipers by reciting the Shahada, you know, the inscription in Arabic that runs across many Islamic countries and organization's flags, including ISIS: *"There is but one god, Allah, and Muhammad is his prophet."* And one can also be assured they are every bit as certain and smug as our good Baptist reverend.

So how do otherwise reasonable people adopt such an obnoxious arrogant attitude, one that is given a free pass and is almost expected and excused away? Religion. Religious thought tells us we are superior in our thinking, that we are right, eternally, unquestionably right and one has every right to demand non-believers to straighten up and fly right and practice religion the right way or they can leave. Or all too often in the case of Islam today, and with Xiansanity in its uglier past, die. Unbelievable. Religion divides us all.

One Species, One tribe: Science Unites, Religion Doesn't.

Flashbulb memories are those few incredibly significant events, usually of such a national or international impact that they remain forever etched in our memories. We know exactly where we were, what we were doing, how we found out, and how we felt when we first learned these events happened. We will never lose the vividness of those personal episode details, ever, no matter how old we get. Most of us have one or two per lifetime, but I'm lucky enough to have four. Two aren't pleasant but infamous, one is trivial but extremely satisfying, and the other is global and beyond one of a kind. For much of my teaching career in the early 2000's when I would present this topic to my Intro to Psychology freshmen, I knew what their flashbulb was going to be, it defined a generation; 9-11. They all know when they first heard, how they found out, what they were doing at the time, and exactly where they were and who they were with. Frozen into memory, forever we think. I tell them I have 9-11 burned in my brain just as they do, and then I tell them of my other three.

1. *The JFK assassination.* The class tries to remember the date. These young'uns often get the early 60's right, it takes a bit of prompting to get '63 and November out and finally the 22nd. And I tell them I remember being in Mrs. Calhoun's 4th grade class in St. Mary's grade school. Being a Catholic school it was an especially big deal with Kennedy being a Catholic so we heard constantly what a great man he was as a president, practicing Catholic, intellectual, statesman, and family man. The nuns I'm sure were blissfully unaware of his prowess in other areas (think Marilyn Monroe and others).

So at first when we heard the President was shot, it didn't sink in right away, at least for me, it was like, "what"? There was no TV to turn to, to make it instantly real and surreal like with the burning Twin towers, the second hit, the listing upper floors, *"is that really leaning?" "Oh no!"* No, we heard about Kennedy from someone who came in the room and then we heard radio reports, not TV, not reporting if he was dead or not for some time long after he was really gone. Very confused, very sketchy, but flashed into memory all the same.

2. The Moon Landing. July 20th 1969. This was the flashbulb of the century. I remember watching the live b/w feed from the moon with my parents, sophomore summer of high school, going back and forth from the TV in the living room out the back door thru the garage to the driveway to look up at the moon and back. Unreal, but it was real, and exhilarating, and very unlike the out-of-nowhere suddenness, tragedy, and impossibility of 9/11 or the Kennedy assassination. No, this was planned for months, years of buildup. We'd been watching the astronauts for nearly a decade. Their every move, every liftoff, every splashdown was part of our nearly daily routine every few months for almost ten years. The moon landing was unique as a flashbulb memory for those reasons, and it was nothing but a creator of positive emotions. It was truly opposite the horror of a mostly well-loved president, taken in his prime, with a fatal gunshot to the head, or the abject horror of fearing thousands of people may be dying before your eyes in real time when the World Trade Center towers burned and collapsed. No, the moon landing was exhilarating and so awe-inspiring it still brings tears to my eyes whenever I read about it or watch the films. It was unique among your average flashbulb memories that cognitive psychologists study and tell us about in the Introductory Psych textbooks.

But there was a far greater aspect of the moon landings uniqueness as an internationally awaited event. It was a flashbulb for all of mankind, maybe the only one, ever. It was ours, all of ours. Maybe it was our first (and last, so far) global, species-wide event that united us like never before and never since. It was an accomplishment of NASA, of the US to be sure, a fulfillment ahead of schedule to Kennedy's challenge made in May, 1961, given just over two years before he was to die. But to most everyone on the planet it was so much more than that. *"WE DID IT."* So read signs around the world.

A flashbulb memory is not merely novel or just unexpected, nor necessarily tragic but it is powerfully emotional. The moon landing tapped an unparalleled emotional response in people all over the globe. Over 50 million households in the US had their TV's on for the moon landing and it is estimated that 125 million in the US watched the moonwalk, and another 600 million humans may have watched worldwide. For example, in Japan, with a population in 1969 of 100 million, around 70 million of them witnessed the events live on TV. All over the world, streets were less busy, if not deserted, as people crowded into bars and hotels to watch. When Mike Collins, the commander of the service module that stayed in orbit while Armstrong and Aldrin landed, visited Italy sometime after wards he was labeled "the Roman" for having been born there. Italians took delight in that one of their own went to the moon.

"It's said science will dehumanize people and turn them into numbers, that's

false, tragically false. Look for yourself, this is the concentration camp and crematorium at Auschwitz, this is where people were turned into numbers. Into this pond were flushed the ashes of some 4 million people. And that was not done by gas, it was done arrogance, it was done by dogma, it was done by ignorance. When people believe they have absolute knowledge with no test in reality this is how they behave. This is what men do when they aspire to the knowledge of gods."

Jacob Bronowski

Religions, and political ideologies dehumanize people, not science. Science tells us we are all the same, we use the same DNA, genes, proteins, tissues, organs, bones and limbs. We think and feel with the same neurons, neurotransmitters and brains. And working together with our intellect, passion for knowledge and our highly evolved empathy we unite with each other in the myriad and multiple daily accomplishments in the lab, however minor, and in the grandiose and hugely co-operative endeavors of imagination like the unparalleled moon landing.

The second marvelous thing about science is that it is the most universal and democratic of undertakings; egalitarian and accessible to all, not dogmatic, not authoritarian. Einstein was wrong about wanting quantum physics to be deterministic. Despite his unparalleled theoretical advances in establishing modern physics, his view of sub-atomic physics was incorrect and was not automatically accepted just because he was stupendously right in other ways, (no scientist is infallible like the Pope, nor unquestionable like Chairman Mao). Pick up any textbook, in any science domain: chemistry, physics, biology, psychology, history, paleo-anthropology, etc., etc., and peruse through the few dozen pages of references in the back (usually numbering in the thousands) and check out the names of the thousands of researchers that produced and published that science. Male, female, black, white, yellow, brown, every nationality, every ethnicity will be represented there, from all walks of life, from all levels of scientific accomplishment. The lowliest grad student can refute the findings or challenge the hypotheses of loftiest professor. Anyone from anywhere can and does undertake science. And we arrive at the same data and theory precisely because science is a description of the world as we all find it.

3. Appropriately, the last flashbulb memory I tell my students I have was sophomore summer of college this time, June 1973, planting shrubs and bushes around a house for the nursery I worked for. Inside a couple of teenage girls were loudly playing their stereo with the widows wide open to the early summer warmth. That was the first time I heard Pink Floyd's "Dark Side of the Moon", released just a few months earlier. "All that you touch, All that you see, All that you taste, All that you feel…" Roger Waters' lyrics united us 'round the world then, and still do.

Ideologies, religious or political that completely ignore any attempt at correction from reality and dehumanize others, drive our inhumane behavior, not science. Science says we are all the same and does not tell us to kill anyone, bomb anyone, gas anyone, behead anyone, or burn anyone at the stake. That takes ideology, as Jacob

Bronowski so poignantly demonstrated. He was the intellectual godfather to all our excellent, modern science educators: Sagan, Attenborough, Nye, Krauss, Dawkins, and DeGrasse-Tyson. All these dedicated men, thoroughly invested in their work are fine communicators, but none, save possibly Sagan, could convey the level of passion that Bronowski routinely displayed. Tyson and Krauss come close. I've read that Bruno (as he is affectionately referred to), walking into the pond at Auschwitz, to deliver those lines quoted previously from his classic 1973 BBC series "The Ascent of Man", was unscripted. I miss this guy. We miss this guy. The link to the YouTube video of Bruno is listed in this chapter's references. Do watch it.

Science unites us like no ideology can. It is a shared endeavor of our intellects and of our tolerance and fallibility, ideals which political and religious dogmas collectively ignore in service to untested, often untestable ideas. Like Water's lyrics and the phenomenal global success and lasting popularity of "Dark Side of the Moon", science transcends all boundaries of geography, nationality, ethnicity and ideology. As the writer Sam Harris puts it: *"We all generate our electricity the same way."* There is no Muslim physics, Christian chemistry, Jewish biology, Buddhist paleontology. Science unites as a species. It epitomizes the reason and tolerance that so characterizes the New Enlightenment.

Science Rules, Religion Drools.

Consider this from a lovely sign seen here in the good ole US of A, down in Kentucky, in the heart of 'Murica, proudly displayed in the back window of a pickup truck by a member of the religion of love:

Calling an illegal alien an "undocumented immigrant" is like calling a drug dealer an "unlicensed pharmacist," Gun-loving, Bitter, Bible-thumping, White Person.

Touching in its breathtaking outreach to humanity isn't it? Right. Seeing this expression of blatant divisiveness and anger might be a novel enough event for it to become a flashbulb moment, it certainly is tragic enough. But unfortunately the arrogant attitude it displays is not novel, but all too common, almost expected and accepted as a normal aspect of religion. Moderates excuse it away as being another example of extremism that most don't adhere to. But it is not fringe. There's plenty of extremism promulgated by every religion. And even in its moderate expression, religion does not unite us. It divides people into us and them, worse than the most extreme of nationalistic tribal fervor, as it can create hatred and dehumanization not only among competing religions, but within any religion itself between deadly competing sects, arguing over wholly imaginary constructs, or competing interpretations of same. On the other hand, science unites us as no other human endeavor can. It allows us to extend our already extraordinarily expanded capacity for empathy to total strangers all over the planet. Instead of making ourselves busy with figuring out how to condemn those on the other side of the world to hell, science lets us feed them, clothe them, provide them fresh water and freedom from disease. *We are One Species.* We could be *One Tribe.* We *Should* be "One Tribe".

Religion is Like...

People who practice it regularly tend to be somewhat fanatical about it and will adamantly claim that it is altogether an indispensable part of the human condition, as much an integral part of human nature as family or the need for social interaction and acceptance. It will never go away. Of course I'm talking about...bowling. Roughly 15% of the US population bowls on occasion, some but once a year, while others wouldn't ever dream of missing their weekly stint at the alley. Bowling can be really, really important to some, an integral, even central part of their life they wouldn't dream of living without. To many it looks like a silly and inconsequential diversion, but to others its importance is unquestionable. A tad over 15 % of the earth's inhabitants practice Islam and most believe their faith is an absolutely central and indispensable part of their life as well. The dictates of the Koran and hadith openly endorse bringing about the imposition of Islamic custom and law over the entire globe. Everybody is born Muslim and we all will be better off to acknowledge that indisputable fact and follow Islam as the faithful do. Sharia to the Muslims would solve all of their, and all of the world's problems. A return to the caliphate is also an essential part of the religion. Most do not work openly, nor as disastrously toward the imposition of the caliphate like our friends from ISIS or the Taliban, but all Muslims are taught the answer to all the world's problems reside in following their scripture, and most couldn't dream of living without their religion.

Some of the Shi'a Muslims in particular, believe that the ritual flagellation done during the day of Ashura in remembrance of the murder of Husayn ibn Ali by fellow Muslims, is a perfectly normal practice and a significant part of their lives. There is certainly nothing strange or barbaric about it to them. The males gather out in the streets, cut their foreheads with sharp objects and whip themselves with chains, knives, or other sharp implements in mourning and remembrance of the outcome of the battle of Karbala. They are intensely emotionally invested in this as a consequence of their upbringing within this form of Islam. The other 7 billion or so of us who don't believe in an ounce of Shi'a Islam of course, find this practice utterly foreign and unnecessary, barbaric, and ghoulishly foolish, and would never partake in this ghastly ritual, despite how much it means to the Shi'a. The Shi'a refuse to forget the fact that Husayn, Muhammad's grandson was killed by other Muslims nearly 1,500 years ago in the power struggle for the control of Islam after Muhammad's death. Ninety per cent of the world's Muslims are Sunni Muslims, not Shi'a, and this extreme ritual, this fervent rehash of ancient rivalry does nothing to bring the factions closer, but is one of many examples of the huge and often fatal division within Islam itself. A bizarre, arbitrary ritual that splits otherwise normal humans from the rest of the world, and the Shi'a from their fellow Muslims. Despite its claims to the contrary, this is what religion does. It never forgets the past to move on to reconciliation and real forgiveness. It always looks backward, wallowing in original sin, innate depravity, the revering of old dead gods and martyrs or ancient and hopelessly wrong outdated sages and scriptures, even bloody sacrifices past and present. Insanity.

Only 3% of the world's population, approximately 280 million people are Xians who also identify as Pentecostals, and indulge in their own unique and bizarre ritual, much weirder than bowling to be sure. Speaking in tongues and handling snakes in worship of the Xian god seems pretty far out to most of us, at least as unnecessary and nonsensical as the Shi'a Muslim's ritual of emotional frenzy and self-mutilation. But I'd wager that both the Shi'a and Pentecostals are equally sure that they got it all down, they are doing it right, more right than anyone else, and that what they do is unquestionably holy, totally sacred and without a doubt what all of us should do to properly follow god given scripture, to worship the right god, the right way. I'd wager also that what each sect does is viewed as completely insane and blasphemous to the other. This is what religions do to people. They divide us all over ridiculous fantasies and absurd rituals. This is not good.

I often wonder how many of the Pentecostals have a clue, that the first mention of speaking in tongues is in the writings of Paul, and is open to quite a few interpretations as to what it actually means. The later Gospel passages which justify the practice of glossolalia, the handling of snakes and drinking of poisons to no harm, are to be found in the Gospel ascribed to someone named Mark (no-one knows who actually wrote it). Tellingly, these verses appear only in later manuscripts, added to the very end of Mark: Chapter 16, verses 15-18. The earliest manuscripts of Mark end at 16:8. No tongues, no snakes, no poisons. That was all added centuries later along with other details from the other Gospels to make Mark more in line with the later written Gospels stories. So the practice of speaking in tongues is derived from an addendum, a pasted on addition to the end of an anonymous Gospel written centuries before. This fact makes it even more difficult to maintain that speaking in tongues and handling snakes are unquestionable revelations from the Xian god.

But to the Pentecostals brought up in their fringe Xian tradition, they are as certain that what they do is as bona fide as any Shi'a Muslim is of their equally absurd ritual. They believe they have superior, godly knowledge and practice worship the right way, the only way. Which is as arrogant as it gets. This is what religious thought promotes and makes possible. It separates normal humans into arbitrary and ridiculous unnecessary groups. These two rather odd rituals from the "Big 2" illustrate the breadth of religious practices that divide us. But even the moderate practices of taking communion or heading to the prayer mat 5 times a day, with head bowed in absolute submission, do nothing but make us look at one another as different, while enmeshed in nothing but handed down delusional rituals that have no external validity whatsoever.

Religion is just like bowling; unless you were brought up to think it was *really, really, keen*, you'd probably never gravitate to it. The church, mosque, temple, sweatlodge, or shrine is no more or less sacred than the bowling alley and no less an arbitrary place to spend ones time. And if you weren't brought up being told that going to the mosque or church or to babble like a madman or rip your flesh open is a normal and righteous thing to do, you'd never gravitate to it on your own any more than bowling. Interestingly, bowling might fill all the social needs that religious worship and ritual do without being delusional, divisive, repressive, occasionally ridiculous and all too often violent. So, go bowling next Sunday instead of attending church, temple, or mosque and have a good time. It is just another silly human affectation that has no external validity whatsoever, beyond making you feel engaged or enraged, joyful or sad. It sure is a lot less harmful and divisive, and no-one will condemn you to hell for it.

Religions Inflame Xenophobia, and Kill Normal Human Empathy

Thanks to the wonders of the internet, we can get to know people from anywhere around the globe, and share their experiences and their feelings almost instantly. Books were once the main vehicle of stepping outside oneself and learning of other lands and other people. But now, with the instant connection and infinite content of the net, we can learn of others who may live different from us, in far-away places eating strange foods and practicing odd customs, yet truly discover how much we are all the same. A young couple I read of on an ex-Muslim website, displays the inane divisiveness we take for granted all religions promote:

"Our very existence as a couple shakes the very foundations of Islam; I, a Muslim Pakistani, being with a Hindu Indian."

And her mother's reaction when she found them out?

"'He's Indian? He's...a...Hindu?' I explained to her that, just like me, he was an atheist, but I couldn't deny that he had been raised in a Hindu household. That's all my mother needed, to shower him with hatred and disgust for each time she would encounter him. I had heard it all growing up: "Hindus are our enemies, we don't mix with them, we don't eat at their house; if they offer you meat, don't eat it, who knows what God they sacrifice their meat to; Hindus are dirty and they are all going to hell; you are a kaafir if you choose to be with a Hindu, etc. etc." When I was with him, I was free, I was away from all the toxic hatred that my family would try to fuel in me towards him and towards anyone else who was not like us - Pakistani Sunnis from Lahore."

One of my former coworkers, a Sikh from Burma once told me her grandfather would say, *"If you come upon a Muslim and a cobra on the road, kill the Muslim first."* The Sikhs and Muslims are adversaries that go way back. Religions provide reasons to see others as different, denigrate them, hate them, or kill them. This young couple had heard it all before, all their young lives; from their parents, their relatives, their neighbors, their imams and priests, their culture. That the other was wrong, dirty, non-believers (kafir), going to burn in hell, blah, blah, blah. Like the Reverend Dennis Terry we met at the beginning of this chapter, this Pakistani Muslim girl's mom was equally convinced by her religious thinking, that those who didn't believe what she did were less than deserving of equal treatment and respect as other human beings. Yes, these kids have heard it all before, and they know it is all bullshit. Reverend Terry's audience, at his Louisiana Baptist church, was mostly old white people, very few were under 50. Young people all over the world today are catching on that religious claims to superiority are bullshit. They understand instead that we are all the same.

Getting to know unbelievers and folks of other religions, personally contributes to the acceptance as well. We do live in unprecedented times of instant information exchange, access to higher education and daily dialogue through social media, podcasts, email, internet video, even TV and print news sources. The discussion of religion is constant and everywhere. Traditional religious ideas that promote division, repression, even hatred around the world are being questioned and jettisoned due to the spread of information and connection with our fellow humans all over the globe. This connectedness prompts us to extend our circle of compassion to all, to exercise our normal human empathy for others which religion tends to destroy. Let me give you a simple thought experiment to demonstrate.

As a teacher, I speak for a living, and have done a lot of speaking at secular group meetings like the one I described at the outset of this chapter. Let's say, at that meeting of kids of different faiths, I was up at the podium giving a talk, and as I leaned over to one side and rested my arm on the dais, some exposed electrical wiring there shorted out onto my arm giving me a 3- 4 inch long, severe burn, parts of it 2nd and 3rd degree with the accompanying nearly unbearable pain. The folks closest to me rushed to my aid, regardless of their particular faith (and my complete lack thereof), and helped me down to sit on the floor while others administered some first aid and called the paramedics. Others, again of varying religious backgrounds, stood around groaning and watching in sympathy, realizing how bad the burn was, sincerely feeling my pain and expressing sympathy for my injury. A normal human response that transcends all national, ethnic and wholly arbitrary religious boundaries. For the moment we were all just fellow humans, sharing the plight of another.

I'm in my 60's, and have a family history of heart disease. Despite being in relatively good health, what if the shock of the electricity and the pain of the burn itself proved to be too much for me, and I went into cardiac arrest? Despite the heroic efforts of those immediately around me and the later attempts of the paramedics to revive me, what if I died on the spot? Not an altogether unlikely scenario. I'm dead, and I was an unabashed non-believer. There was no god to me, no faith, and no belief in a religion of any kind.

According to both Xianity and Islam, the "Big 2" religions that represent nearly half of the world's population, I am now burning in one (or both?), of their hells for sure. Not just suffering a paltry 4 inch, 2nd degree burn on my arm, but burning in unquenchable to the bone fire over every square inch of my body. And not just for the few minutes until emergency medical help arrived with some skin numbing analgesic salve, and a powerful narcotic injection to deaden the pain completely, but for eternity: untold minutes, hours, days, weeks, months, years, decades, centuries, millennia upon millennia of unimaginable suffering. The Muslims are even taught to believe that infidels like me will regrow new skin in hell, just to ensure the suffering is maximized over and over. Where once believers of whatever stripe stood around going: *"Eew, ouch", "Damn, that's gotta hurt", "Oh, that poor man"*, while I suffered for a few minutes with my severely burnt but minimal patch of skin, they now are taught by their religion to believe I am frying over 100% of my body in unspeakable agony for all time and beyond, and I deserve it. *"Where's Bill now?"* one could ask the Xians and Muslims. *"Burning in hell forever, it is his own fault, the atheist bastard." "We tried to tell him, oh well."*

Whether I was a good man or not, a loving husband and father, honest taxpayer and good citizen, charitable and polite, a dedicated teacher, good friend, good listener, reliable employee, considerate and kind, none of that matters. I deserve to burn in hell for not accepting Jesus Christ as my personal savior, or had every chance throughout my life to submit to the will of Allah, and didn't.

Fuck religious thought. It teaches us to ignore our normal human empathy and create a whole humanity of deserving dead, suffering for all eternity, because not only they didn't behave like us, but they didn't think like us, the ultimate sin. This barbaric holdover of early primitive civilization has got to go. We are outgrowing it all over the world, many have come out, but I suspect legions more have fully realized the insane cruelty and absurdity of their religion's demand for eternal punishment for the "others", but dare not speak up. There is no good reason to carry on this despicable delusion any further. There is no good reason to teach one more generation of children to assimilate such barbarism. We would be better humans without it in so many ways.

Religion Sucks… and Then You Die.

PEW research reported in 2014, that religious strife is on the increase in many parts of the world, while overall deaths from wars have been declining, and more people in more societies worldwide are experiencing less violence than ever before. The PEW website presents clear data on how charming (violent), religion, any religion can be anywhere, anytime. More disturbing is the fact that increasing hostilities in many countries are directed at the *minority* religion(s), by those of the *majority* faith. Isn't religion just wonderful? And it is not just Muslims persecuting everyone else or mostly each other. Although you will notice Islam pops up regularly as one of the combatants in nearly every instance, it seems whoever has the upper hand, the majority, whether its Buddhists or Muslims or Hindus or a new state religion (Vietnam), or a majority sect of a religion (Sunni vs Shi'a Islam), or in a specific location like Northern Ireland, it appears the divisiveness of any and all religions fuels the anger that says the minority non-believers wherever they reside are worthy of persecution and violence. *Isn't that just special?* Whoever has the power of the majority, they tend to use it. So much for the moralizing power of religion.

You will also notice Xians (and Jews), for the most part are victims and not aggressors. Xianity was responsible for the Inquisitions, witch hunts, beheading and burning one other at the stake over doctrinal differences. Once very common, Xian violence has been relegated to the dustbin of recent history. Most Xians are also inhabitants of the secular West, where the influence of religion was significantly moderated by the first Enlightenment. Bolstered by the New Enlightenment emphasis on reason, tolerance and personal freedoms it is difficult to backslide into medieval behaviors. For the most part *"extremist"* Xians are quite tame and civilized compared to the religionists of many other denominations whose violent acts PEW reports. But then of course there's Uganda, and other African countries, where the homosexual minorities in residence get to experience a return to the *"good old time religion"* of past Xianity, and suffer under the repressive and violent religious behaviors promoted by Evangelical Xiansanity, whose pious members appear to yearn wistfully for a return to the Dark Ages. They can't make that happen in the US itself, but they can promote the persecution and murder of homosexuals elsewhere on the planet. Ain't that just special? Liberal Xians will claim it is not their fault of course, they are not the extremists who have hijacked the religion. Sorry folks, but as Sam Harris points out, moderates in any religion legitimize the same book as the extremists follow, albeit just a bit more closely, as the word of some god which must not be ignored. You asked for it. You grease the wheels.

Makes you nod your head in salute one more time to our Founding Fathers, especially Thomas Jefferson who strove to keep church and state separate for that very reason, to avoid letting any one sect obtain the upper hand:

"I am for freedom of religion, & against all maneuvers to bring about a legal ascendancy of one sect over another." "Millions of innocent men, women, and children, since the introduction of Christianity, have been burnt, tortured, fined, and imprisoned; yet we have not advanced one inch toward uniformity. What has been the effect of coercion? To make one-half the world fools and the other half hypocrites. To support roguery and error all over the earth."

One could substitute the name of any religion or any sect within a religion into TJ's quote above in place of "Christianity." I find it incredibly ironic that the PEW Research Center, a division of the Pew Charitable Trusts begun by a Presbyterian, the founder of Sun Oil Co., Joseph Newton Pew, is the primary source of this excellent information on religious violence worldwide. Presbyterianism was established largely on the charming ideas of everyone's good buddy John Calvin, who hated Jews, thought his enemies deserved beheading and burning at the stake, was convinced the Pope was of course the Antichrist and spearheaded the doctrine that most Xians however pious they were, were hopelessly doomed to eternal torment regardless. What a swell guy, huh? Fortunately, modern Presbyterians have long since enlightened themselves and jettisoned many of Calvin's medieval views. Modern Presbyterians thankfully, are demonstrably less religious than Calvin and the original members of their sect. If Pew Research had been launched in the 16th century, they could have included their own patriarch in their religious violence report.

Despite all this, I am optimistic. There are horrible occurrences all over the world, plenty of problems to be fixed, and we have a long way to go to extend the modern lack of violence and fear of immanent warfare to so many others, who live in these religion-torn countries. More people on earth enjoy a rejection of barbarism now more than ever before, when, for most of our existence, humans lived under the very real threat of it at any given time. We can change the world. We have changed the world. We can extend more peace and less violence to those who haven't experienced those changes yet. The biggest roadblock to that reality? Religion. In the words of Sam Harris:

"We have to get out of the game of defining ourselves tribally based on imaginary and fictitious ideas and we have to realize that the way forward is recognizing our common humanity, we're a single species on a single planet, trying to build a single, viable global civilization and there are a thousand different ways we can screw this up and not so many ways where we can build paradise over-nite on earth which should be our common project."

Thanks to the New Enlightenment, the critical examination of religion is ongoing everywhere; in the many secular books published just in the last decade and the innumerable blogs, videos, columns, articles, debates, movies…across all media; books magazines, TV, newspapers, and the ubiquitous internet. We can concentrate on the better angels of our nature and continue to make this life better for all, finishing the job of the first Enlightenment in throwing off the shackles of religious ideas. One needs only to look at the worst, most violent, backwards, undeveloped, least educated parts of the world and witness medieval levels of strife remaining, where life is miserable for so many, yet in the grip of religious thinking. Religions divide us into artificial and unproductive factions of believers and non-believers, imaginary groups of "us and them" based in primitive, horribly outdated outlooks on the human condition, and silly myths. In stark contrast, the New Enlightenment perspective unites us all in our hard-earned shared body of knowledge: science, and our formidable, evolved and expanding capacities for empathy and tolerance. Religions pay lip service to uniting humanity while dividing us into believers and non-believers, the pious and the heretic, the righteous and the infidel. We can do better.

2

MYSOGYNY AND HOMOPHOBIA

"We ignore what the Bible says about slavery because the Bible got slavery wrong. If the Bible got the easiest moral question that humanity has ever faced wrong, what are the odds that the Bible got something as complicated as homosexuality wrong?"

Dan Savage

"The whole tone of Church teaching in regard to women is, to the last degree, contemptuous and degrading"

Elizabeth Cady Stanton

One of the more lovely passages in the Bible appears in Judges, a particularly nasty chapter in a particularly nasty little book. It is a violent set of stories relating how the Old Testament god Yahweh is ready to smite the Israelites the moment they dare stray from proper behavior, like forgetting to worship him exclusively, or His commanding them to slaughter their enemies without mercy whenever the big guy says it is the right thing to do. Burning villages down with men, women and children in them, eye-gouging, head bashing: Judges has it all. The "Good Book," yeah, right

Besides all the ultra-violence at god's command, there's a story at the end about an old man and some fellows outside his door who insist on getting to know his daughters in the Biblical sense. Instead, he sends his concubine out for their entertainment. They literally rape her to death, and he finds her dying on his doorstep in the morning. Throughout Judges, the minute the Israelites did anything wrong, Yahweh would smite them mightily in an instant. For their enemies, punishment was every bit as swift and unmerciful. Whenever something improper was done, God's wrath was unavoidable and immediate. So one might think when anything as heinous as an innocent slave woman getting raped to death by a mob should occur, the retribution would be ugly, immediate and unavoidable, right? What does God do? Nothing. The mob gets off clean, as does her master. Then her body is cut up in twelve pieces and distributed across Israel. God is utterly silent. God doesn't lift a finger. God is nowhere to be found. Even if the story is a purely metaphorical one portraying a transgression against the twelve tribes of Israel or some such interpretation, and wasn't meant to describe a historical event, it remains a very telling, and particularly ugly example of the blatant misogyny inherent throughout the Bible. Women are second class citizens. They are property. They are unclean. They are temptresses. They are the cause of The Fall. Rape is common, and un-condemned, throughout the Bible. There's no 11th commandment, proclaiming "Thou shalt not rape", handed down from the mount. JC, later on, never says a word about it. God gets quite irate over worship of a golden calf or anyone who dares oppose his "Chosen People", but does absolutely nothing when a woman is raped, even raped to death. Shit happens.

Women and gays take it especially hard from most religions. Even the supposedly less nasty religions, the reincarnation faiths of Buddhism and Hinduism, are not all that enlightened when it comes to women's rights, gays, rape, and sexual behavior in general. Fundamentally, they are as patriarchal, archaic and repressive as any. For example, with the publicizing of one violent gang rape after another, the horrific rape culture endemic throughout India has come to light. For most of this chapter, however, I will concentrate on stories related to the "Big 2" Xianity and Islam, and the treatment of women and homosexuals all over the world. There are people all over the world in chains, both literally and metaphorically, due to religious thought. Most of them are women and homosexuals. Some suffer the chains of cultural repression; restrictions on behavior, and ridicule, however minimal and concealed. Some suffer undeniably obvious and crushing discrimination. Many endure regular physical abuse, even death, all for religious ideas. Let's look at misogyny first.

Christianity and Women

Women can't be priests. Did Jesus say that somewhere? Many liberal Xian sects of course, say *"No, he didn't"*, and allow women to become ministers and pastors. In most religions, however, they are relegated to being second class citizens. Judaism, Xianity, even the supposed spiritually "enlightened" and somewhat less repressive Buddhist religion has its positions of authority exclusive to men. It is said by some the Buddha claimed women aren't capable of reaching nirvana. In some Buddhist sects, the thinking is as primitive as any found in the Old Testament. They will not let women near the temple during their "unclean" menstrual period lest they somehow defile it. Anything but heterosexual sex for procreation is "unnatural", including homosexuality, masturbation, oral, or anal sex. Only religion allows, upholds, and propagates this base level of ancient, crude and ignorant thought. People sometimes take exception to my use of the term "arrogance" of religious thought. It is *arrogance* that allows religion to continue to dwell in absurd primitive, tribal, millennia-old wrong ideas, usually to the denigration of some group, women and gays in particular.

Women, of course, are responsible for The Fall, and it is really just best for men to do without them altogether, according to the rants of Paul. Read any of the New Testament writings of Xianity in the Epistles ascribed to Paul of Tarsus (I refuse to call that son-of-a-bitch a "saint"). His shitty attitudes toward women, written nearly 2,000 years ago, have set women back ever since; the most influential of which are found in Paul's Epistles to Timothy which Biblical scholars, both secular and conservative, agree he didn't even *write*. The fact that we even read these primitive, uninformed, and oppressive authoritarian writings for guidance is ridiculous in the modern age, given this knowledge. Every Xian should be told they are forgeries, and thereby temper any respect for what they say. The benefit to women would be immeasurable. These musings have no basis in reality, and no business being revered in our modern world. Even liberal Xianity glorifies this monster whose writings, whether actually his or merely those in his name, continue to set woman's freedoms back 2,000 years.

An Arizona Street Preacher

"Brother" *Dean Samuel* (aka Dean Saxton) is a lovely man. A swell guy. A God-fearing man. A righteous man, schooled in the ways of the Lord. Everything he says is in the Good Book. This is what real Xiansanity is all about. He's just following what's in his book. He wasn't born a sexist homophobe. It was taught to him. Dean made an internet You Tube sensation of himself in 2013, street preaching at Arizona State. If a woman wears provocative clothes she invites rape. Yoga pants are sinful. To guys like Dean (and the very same Muslims he preaches against), it is the woman's fault if she is raped for dressing like a whore, having pre-marital sex, or watching porn. She asked for it. Someone raised him to believe the stuff in his Bible by buying into the insane and completely false basis of all religions: revealed scripture.

"This book here says what god wants. This book here is god's own words. Don't doubt it. Live by it and tell others. God wants you to, compels you to, commands you to. You are righteous and have the capacity to decide others are sinners and are sanctioned to tell them." How much more arrogant can it get?

"The gays have an agenda, the feminists have an agenda," "I believe there are certain qualities that may be worthy of rape." Where did Brother Dean learn to say those words? Where did this soft-spoken young guy who truly thinks he will help others, change the world and save some souls, get his thinking? He quotes Paul from Ephesians, *"wives submit unto your husbands"* when answering to why he thinks that women attending the university where he preaches (or any university), is a complete waste of time. Women don't need to be educated to submit to their husbands. In the short time I spent teaching in Kentucky, I met two middle-aged women who had divorced their Baptist husbands (who still couldn't fathom why they got dumped), primarily because both women were discouraged or prevented from going back to school. To their Baptist brainwashed husbands, there was no need for school. Why weren't they satisfied with their chosen lot of taking care of their families and husband? It wasn't their final decision anyway, being women, expected to submit to their husband's opinion on such matters. According to their Conservative Xian thinking, itself largely a product of not-Saint Paul and his forger's writings, there was no need for education as a women belonged in the home. Our good Brother Dean repeats the whole package from Evangelical Xiansanity on women and other subjects including

"Evolution is a lie." Some passing students flip him off and he warns *"You will burn in Hell for that"* or pointing at another student *"that guy watches too much pornography."* To the masses *"you need to turn off the rockn'roll right now."* Oh my, my.

Our Brother Dean is not so soft-spoken when wielding his megaphone out on the street, on a righteous roll, cooking with that feeling of superiority he exudes when he's calling someone out for being a whore or looking like a homo. The arrogance of religious thought knows no bounds. *"All Muslims are going to hell," "Just because they are going to hell doesn't mean I hate them."* He sincerely believes he's going to save some souls from eternal punishment by getting them (Muslims, women, gays, Catholics, etc.), to behave according to his Book.

And Dean slips from mere arrogance to abject delusion: *"I am a living sign from god...that's what you guys need."* His religion taught him that, his parents, his minister, his Book. To paraphrase Jacob Bronowski: *"This is what happens when you aspire to the knowledge of gods."* More liberal religionists, moderate Xians especially, like to point out that *"extremists,"* like Brother Dean and so many others, take the book too literally and they just don't interpret it right. The problem is there is no way to know what any god really wants... no way to ever know who is doing the interpreting right: who is being extreme and who is merely following the book. So, in one sense we can excuse Brother Dean for just doing what mommy and daddy and Pastor *"what's-his-name"* and his surrounding rather theocratic culture told him to do: *"Believe this Book. It is the Good Book. You can't go wrong. It is the inerrant word of God and you have every right to condemn sinners as spelled out in the Book."*

On the other hand, in this day and age of the secular revolution and the internet, information to the contrary is everywhere and Brother Dean Saxton easily could, and should, know better. He is not a stupid man. But he has been hosed by people he trusts. The delusion of *"revealed scripture"* has created a lot of hatred, misery and death all over the world for women and gays and non-believers for millennia now, at the hands of bamboozled young guys like Brother Dean, and the millions more who don't stop at mere street preaching. Al Qaeda, Boko Haram, the Taliban and ISIS all come to mind.

Second Class Females: Mother Teresa

Renowned world-wide, by Catholic and non-Catholic alike as a wonderful religious icon, spiritual leader, caregiver to the poor, a selfless model of piety and charity, Mother Theresa is the epitome of a devout, devoted Catholic. To many Catholics she was a fricking saint already. Undoubtedly, there are thousands more such devoted females: nuns, sisters, laypeople who dedicate their lives to the Catholic faith in as deep and committed a fashion as Anjeze Bojaxhiu, her real name. There is one other thing all these true-blue faithful Catholic women have in common. No matter how good and exemplary a Catholic they may be, they could never, ever be pope. Not even Mother Teresa. Not pope, not cardinal, nor bishop, not even a priest. And why?

Because they have the wrong genitals between their legs. Period. Full stop. Do not pass go, do not collect the $200. Absurd? Cruel? Ridiculous? Commanded by scripture? Ordained by God? Outdated patriarchal interpretation? Complete bullshit? A classic example of the arrogance of religious thought? All of the above. Not even Mother Teresa, the quintessential Catholic of our time, whose publicity was a significant boon to the Catholic Church, every bit as much as her formidable fund-raising, couldn't even be a parish priest and deliver the sacraments because she was a woman. Limited, inferior, second class. Born with the wrong genitals. And from what we know of her life, she probably never even used them! WTF? This reasoning is absurd, insane, yet accepted as a normal aspect of religion. Nearly all faiths are misogynistic in some way, declaring women as inferior in some fashion or another. It is claimed the Buddha said women can't reach nirvana. Hindus won't let a menstruating woman near a temple, Muslims believe a woman's testimony is worth half of a man's. *"Well that's just good ole time religion for ya."* As I've said, I tell my daughter never to join a club she can't become president of, never join an organization where she cannot rise to become the leader, where you are defined from the outset as a second class citizen. All because you have the wrong sexual apparatus between your legs. How's that for arrogance the world accepts as normal from religion?

There Oughta Be 50

We have 20 female US Senators. A beautiful thing really, up from the traditional handful, but still 30 short of the 50 or 51 needed for equal representation. And we need 25 or 26 female governors instead of just the 5 there are at present. As of Jan. 2013 with nearly 317 million US residents, with the percent of females in the US at a bit more than half (50.8%) of the population, that's roughly 161 million females to 156 million males. Accordingly, half the seats in every state and federal Senate and House, half of the governors, and half of the Supreme Court, should be women. Fifty female Senators and a couple hundred Representatives. That's what we oughta have. As of early 2015 less than 20% of House seats were filled by women, only 45 out 435. We don't, however, need half the world's religious leaders to be female. We don't need religious leaders at all, or religion period. And that is the expressed goal of the courageous women from Russia of Femen.

These women perform well organized, well-rehearsed guerrilla street theater protests, by going topless all across Europe, even into Islamic countries. Besides breasts these females have balls. They are calling for nothing short of the end of patriarchal...everything! Their platform is no less than the end of religion, and thereby the end of repression of women, and the end of the sex trade. They draw huge publicity (and hatred), baring their chests. It works. It shouldn't matter in the 21st century whether a woman has no shirt on any more than a man, or breastfeeds her child in a public place and God forbid!... we see her naked breast. That is the point. Check out their campaign at femen.org. I'm safe writing my blog and books from the comfort of my home or office. I haven't been beat up, arrested, jailed, fined, harassed or received any deaths threats, yet. These ladies got stones. They invite such treatment to bring to light the plight of women all over the world, who suffer various levels of maltreatment from religion, solely due to their bodies and genitalia.

I am insanely glad my wife, daughter, sister, mom, female friends and acquaintances were born in developed countries, where repression of female behavior, while pervasive, has been minimized compared to the more patriarchal and religious parts of the world where misogyny is rampant and often violent. We still have a long way to go, even in the developed world, and the biggest roadblock is, as always, religion. That, unfortunately, is nothing new.

"The greatest block today in the way of woman's emancipation is the church, the canon law, the Bible and the priesthood."

Elizabeth Cady Stanton

I don't think Cady Stanton would have considered protesting topless to underscore the point that a woman's body is not property, dirty, or obscene, but I suspect she would wholeheartedly agree with the reasoning and courage of the women of Femen. Think about it. Modern science, particularly psychology, says women are capable intellectually of everything a man a can do. The sciences of history, sociology and anthropology show that fact is true throughout the ages and across cultures where women have accomplished themselves in nearly every endeavor. We have women as heads of state, Nobel Prize winners, writers, scientists, educators, business entrepreneurs and executives. It is only patriarchal religious thought that relegates women to lesser status. Get rid of religion and most, if not all, misogyny disappears.

The Education of Women

William James, one of the early pioneers of American psychology whose heyday was also the late 1800's, didn't appear to be much of an offending kinda guy. He looked like the mild-mannered bookish academic type, and he was a Harvard professor, publisher of one of the first textbooks in psychology, who did important work in philosophy as well. Suffering from a number of lifelong ailments, he was also given to serious bouts of depression. From his profile he hardly seems to have been an *"in your face"* offensive sort of person like the Femen women. Yet one incident in his life really stands out in that regard. He had the balls, the 24 karat chutzpah, to bring a woman into his Harvard psychology class, to admit a woman into graduate studies. This was late 19th century America. Education wasted on a woman? Ridiculous. Barefoot and pregnant and subservient to her husband, just as not-St. Paul said, was the unquestioned order of the day. A woman's place was in the home, raising children. A complete waste of money to provide education to a woman, an insult and against the Bible. That was the norm back then. That was the thinking. So James had the audacity to bring a female into class when Harvard refused to admit her. The story goes his 12 male grad students promptly walked out.

I tell my students nowadays, just how much times have changed. Today, 120 years later, roughly 65% of the PhD's awarded in Psychology are to women. What if James had said to himself: *"no that's too controversial"* or *"some people will be really offended and just shut me out if I do something as drastic as admit a woman to a grad program, so I better not."* What if he, and the other more noted champions of equality for women, like Elizabeth Cady Stanton, Susan B. Anthony and others, had caved in to the idea that they were being too radical, too challenging of their culture's long held *"truths"* and were offending people's religious based beliefs and should just stop? They certainly were directly challenging religious based beliefs. The main source of all misogyny in America then, and across the world today, is religion. Cady Stanton could not have been clearer in observing that the main obstacle to woman's rights, the most vehement opposition, was from the clergy. What if James and Cady Stanton had listened to that sort of advice, the kind of reprimand I keep hearing, and which has been oft-repeated in different atheist-bashing articles?

"You will just offend and lose the very audience of whom you are trying to change their minds."

"Attacking their religious beliefs is just offensive, you should stop it."

"You should be nice, and more respectful of their beliefs... even if they are wrong and hurting someone."

Really? How does society change peacefully without challenge of ideas? How did James get the ball rolling in psychology to become an equal opportunity course of study and career path for women but by challenging entrenched cultural beliefs? Beliefs that were predominantly, if not solely, upheld by religion, Xianity in particular. Challenging those ideas really pissed a lot of people off. As far as woman's rights, slavery, civil rights, homosexuality, and let's not forget science denial, the religious and their ideas are and were just plain wrong. Are we supposed to cave in to repression, absurdities, and outright cruelties solely because it is part and parcel of someone's religious belief? Repression can be exposed, ridiculed, protested, and attacked so long as it does not have a religious justification behind it, then it is off limits to criticism and ridicule? Religion gets a free pass?

In September 2014, a particularly lame call for just this sort of *"hands off"* treatment was offered up in the form of a *"challenge"* to us Unbelieving Scum, by Steve Neumann, a contributor to Salon magazine; *"Cut it out atheists, Why it is time to stop behaving like Bill Maher and Richard Dawkins."* The upshot was we shouldn't offend anyone. We should stop attacking religious absurdities and calling folks out on them. It hurts their feelings. His pitch in a nutshell:

"I'd like to challenge all atheists, myself included, to refrain from posting disparaging commentary about Christian news-makers on Facebook and other social media sites — including blogs — for one month. Let's call it The Atheist Positivity Challenge, or the APC for short. The purpose of this challenge is to draw attention to two things: The fact that gloating about the lunacy and misdeeds of specific Christians is not only unnecessary, but probably counterproductive; and the need to

rehabilitate the reputation of atheism in America."

Yup. Cady Stanton should have quit calling out the insane repression of women prevalent in her 19th century culture which was enmeshed in, and emboldened by Biblical attitudes towards females. According to Neumann's reasoning, Cady Stanton and William James should have been more "*positive*" and refrained from pointing out and challenging the "*lunacy and misdeeds of Christians*" because well, it was making them angry. They could have been so much nicer then and for us non-believers today it "*will make us look less arrogant and therefore less aversive*", if we just refrain (Neumann is evidently an atheist as well). So Stanton and James should have kept quiet, backed off, should have been nicer? And today we should be nicer too, back off and be less strident, lest we offend the religious and allow their absurd and repressive practices to continue to dominate our culture now, as they did then? Bullshit. I'm with the Femen ladies on this one. Turn up the volume.

Malala and Muslim Women

In 2012, Malala Yousafzai was riding on a school bus when she was shot by the Taliban. Though severely injured, she survived and has become a symbol of peace, reason and forgiveness throughout the world. Her father, Ziauddin Yousafzai, was featured not long after-wards in a very moving and informative TED video. Throughout his TED talk he repeatedly refers to tribalism and patriarchal culture, but never once makes any mention of religion in general, or Islam in particular. He is a Sunni Muslim, and TED is known for its rather soft and accommodating treatment of religion. According to the Wiki article on Malala, 50 imams issued fatwas condemning her shooting by the Taliban. A small step in the right direction, to be sure, but it avoids the real problem: religious thought itself.

Illiteracy runs nearly 70% in Islamic women worldwide. The figure for the entire globe is closer to only 16%. Restriction of women's education is common in Islamic countries. It is not exclusive to the Taliban and is not merely a local, tribal occurrence. Malala's dad is an exception to mainstream Islamic thinking and practice. The plight of women in Islamic countries ranges from the extreme repression and violence at the hands of the Taliban, the restriction from driving a car in Saudi Arabia, female genital mutilation sanctioned by Sunni Islamic schools of thought and practiced in many Muslim countries and Islamic enclaves in non-Muslim countries, to honor killings, acid attacks, kidnapping, rape and being sold into slavery by Boko Haram and ISIS. Along with the control of women's dress with the burqa, abbaya, hijab and the like, the Muslim religion dictates every aspect of a woman's life.

The hijab. The headscarf. No big deal, right? It's just a scarf, right? Some Muslim women freely choose it and are offended by arguments or restrictions against it. OK. Try to take it off and see what happens. This excerpt from the "ex-hijabi journal" is unfortunately all too typical of reports from the Muslim world. This from a woman who describes her Islamic upbringing as "moderate":

"My parents' reactions were also more intense than I expected. There are wom-

en in my family who took it off as well and some who never wore it at all so I thought it wouldn't be that bad. My mother said she would kill herself, she wouldn't let me graduate high school but instead take me to Turkey, leave me there at a Quran school. My father told me to fuck off and never come back home and my brother threatened to kill me. So my only option was to put it back on the next day."

From the same website, this from another of the millions of females stuck in an Islamic culture:

"This is exactly how Kurdish girls are treated as well. They are expected to do as they are told always. The girl does not only have father, uncle and brother to obey anymore; now she's got; father, brother, uncle, husband, father in law and brother in law to obey. Cleaning and cooking are her duties. Having this sort of picture in my mind of marriage all my life, it hit me once when a friend of mine referred to her wedding as the best day of her life. Because for me, marriage was something I had to do. To satisfy my parents. To make them happy. That day, I struggled to sleep at night because I was feeling so upset about the fact that I had NEVER viewed marriage as something that would benefit me or something joyful. After some time, I met a guy. He understands me, he loves me, he listens to me when I need to be heard, he, respects me. I can with the whole of my heart say that I truly love him. There is no one in this world that I rather spend the rest of my life with. However, he is British. I fear talking about him to anyone because of the risk comes with me dating a guy that is not Muslim. My mum have many times prayed to god that I will never end up with someone who isn't Kurdish and Muslim. This hurts every part of my body because I feel so restricted in my own life. I need to be able to make such a major decision myself. To choose who I want to spend the rest of my life with. To choose who I want to have children with. To make my own life choices."

For the vast majority of Muslim women, there just is little "choice" regarding the veil, or the abbaya, or the burqa. Some women may like to wear it. Some Islamic women even get indignant being asked about it, in that they choose to wear it without compulsion. Well good. Then I'd suggest any such woman try taking it off one hot day just because she suddenly felt like it. Maybe walk around without it for an hour, a day, a week. The immediate backlash from family and everyone else within 100 yards of her would be worse than that received by a Baptist kid who up and decided one Sunday morning *"Mom and Dad and Grandma and neighbors, I'm not going to go to church today."* Good fucking luck with that, huh? Religions by nature are intolerant, some are stricter than others, but all coerce to different degrees. From the extremes of honor killings, beatings, shaming, and shunning, to milder forms of intimidation such as being condemned to hell or *"Well, you will be living beyond the grace of god, I'll pray for you."* Even the "meek and mild" Buddhist doctrines consider women inferior and anything other than heterosexual vaginal sex to be "sexual misconduct." Another not-so-subtle example of trying to control behavior, control women. We accept this as a normal part of religious practice and we therefore shouldn't point out the cruelty, deceit and coercion, 'cuz "*Well, it is their religion*" Bullshit.

Religion as practiced today is an historical accident, it is not an integral, unchangeable part of human nature. Billions of the non-religious, non-believers have proven it is wholly un-necessary, and unless one is indoctrinated into one, the vast majority of us won't gravitate to one. Make all Muslim men wear a hijab too, all day, every day in public and make them find a female relative to accompany them whenever they venture out. I saw a meme once in which a veiled, Islamic woman took umbrage at a reporter for asking her if she was repressed having to wear the hijab she had on. She replied words to the effect that he should take his ugly dogshit-like face and veil it merely for asking her if she might be repressed. Gotcha. As a follow-up to her retort the reporter might have replied:

"Well, yes, and I can take my ugly dog-shit face out wherever and whenever I want without having to cover it with a veil because Allah in his infinite wisdom and mercy, unlike you, chose to give me a dick. Furthermore, I don't have to find a male relative to accompany me everywhere lest the neighbors and my older brothers and parents brand me a whore. And if I was not such a nice guy and had taken offense to your remark about my face and impulsively slapped or punched you, I wouldn't have needed to worry about you prosecuting me as your testimony is worth 1/2 that of mine and you'd need 3-4 witnesses to even attempt to bring a case against me. I'm so glad you enlightened me as to the condition of my face and your religion's tolerant and relaxed rules for women."

I'd like to see any man volunteer for this duty. Religion sucks in a lot of ways, but mostly for women. From the femen.org website:

"We live in the world of male economic, cultural and ideological occupation. In this world, a woman is a slave, she is stripped of the right to any property but above all she is stripped of ownership of her own body. All functions of the female body are harshly controlled and regulated by patriarchy. Separated from the woman, her body is an object to monstrous patriarchal exploitation, animated by production of heirs, surplus profits, sexual pleasures and pornographic shows. Complete control over the woman's body is the key instrument of her suppression; the woman's sexual demarche is the key to her liberation. Manifestation of the right to her body by the woman is the first and the most important step to her liberation. Female nudity, free of patriarchal system, is a grave-digger of the system, militant manifesto and sacral symbol of women's liberation. FEMEN's naked attacks is a naked nerve of the historic woman-system conflict, it's most visual and appropriate illustration. Activist's naked body is the undisguised hatred toward the patriarchal order and new aesthetics of women's revolution. FEMEN's Goal: Complete victory over patriarchy."

Can you blame them? Would any man not protest over the same treatment?

Gays

Gays are not an abomination. Homophobia is. Our buddy Brother Dean, the "expert" on provocative clothing and deserved rape, again: *"It's not OK to be gay, it's not OK to be a homo, God didn't design you that way."* Sorry, pal that's not what the science says. Dean is once again repeating the Conservative Xian storyline. A classic example of such is found in the writings of a guy from a little town in Kentucky, Richard Nelson, who set himself up as the *"Commonwealth Policy Center."* What a hi-falutin' name, but a quick search revealed no physical address. He is probably just at home and using a P.O. Box. He calls himself *"Director"* which makes me think of *"Il Duce,"* kinda self-proclaimed importance, ya know? He then proceeded to write letters to the editor a few times per semester to our college newspaper down there in the Bible Belt, to expound on Creationism and other conservative-with-a-capital-"C" concerns, like the *"Defense of man/woman marriage."* Uh, oh, here we go. What pissed off Herr Direttori enough to write his *"Defense"* was the failure of the Kentucky Attorney General (AG) to defend the Commonwealth's marriage law that prevented gay marriage. It really frosted his ass. It seems the good AG figured out he'd backed that horse just long enough to get elected and since there was no constitutional basis for Kentucky's marriage law, and states with similar laws had dropped them like dominoes all over the US, there was no good legal or political reason for him to fight for a dead issue.

But what really got our pal from the Commonwealth Policy Center incensed was in jumping off the *"Good Ship DOMA"* the KY AG dared to profess Kentucky's marriage law wasn't all that important in the grand scheme of things. According to the AG's statement: *"redefining marriage doesn't affect anyone else's marriage."* Whoa, Nellie! Talk about your frost-bitten gonads! In his editorial the Director set the AG and us all straight with this line right out of the local Baptist pulpit: *"How human beings order themselves in the most intimate of ways has everything to do with the success or demise of their civilization."* Really? Let's unpack that rascal, shall we? So if two guys fuck each other in the ass the cosmic order is a bit unbalanced but can somehow recover and still proceed, but if we dare let them wear a wedding band while they're doing it, Holy Fuck! Civilization will come crashing down around us like cutoffs in a bathhouse. Can anyone spell YMCA? Can't you just hear it? *"It's bad enough we have to live with fruits and dykes and their unnatural acts against god, but if we let the goddam faggots and carpet-munchers git married on top of it, Well Jumpin' Jehosophat everything will be ruined!"*

This guy truly worries that civilization will come to a grinding halt if we let gays marry. It is what he's been taught. He's probably as clear-headed and logical in much of what he does in his daily life tasks as any other human being, but when it comes to religious ideas, reasoning goes out the fucking window. Religious thought is not merely arrogant, it promotes ignorance and illogical thinking as well. He then quotes someone deemed a *"Marriage Advocate"* who tells it like it was: *"sex makes babies,* society needs babies, and babies need mothers and fathers." And there you have it. We won't have any babies, or mommies or daddies for babies, if we let gays and lesbians get married. Somehow they will take over the world *if we let them marry*, and convert, or out-compete, or somehow eliminate the 92% of the population who are heterosexuals and bring about the end of society. Mr. Director, the Marriage Advocate, and their ilk never quite explain that last part though: like exactly how all this destruction of society is going to happen thanks to a few gays and lesbians trying to lead normal lives in peace. So let's look at some data on the subject shall we?

Homosexuals of either gender combined, tend to make up around 5-8% of the population in any country, any culture, now, or in the past. This low incidence of same sex preference appears in hundreds of other species. In sexually reproducing species, the variance in sexual orientation shows a minimum of same sex behavior, with most of the species individuals reproducing just fine heterosexually and producing plenty of offspring. Humans are no exception and despite same sex behavior going back thousands of years, we surely have had no problem as a species making and raising plenty of babies. From a few million (or less), on the planet for much of our existence we now have a population of over 7 billion, and growing. So having some gay folks around has never slowed us down one bit. The experiment has been done, and Conservative Xians couldn't be more clueless or more wrong. Yet, they are so sure if we let the gays marry, then surely, somehow this will insure our demise. As I said the mechanism whereby this would be accomplished is never quite explained in Mr. Director's newspaper rant, nor in any other Xian warning, that the gay agenda will tear apart the very fabric of our society, ruin the family, and end the species.

I imagine because one tenet of Conservative Xiansanity's absurd anti-gay propaganda is that homosexuality is a "*lifestyle choice*," a learned behavior, that it could somehow take over the world and turn us all gay if we dare give it one more sanction, just one more ounce of legitimacy such as allowing them to marry. Right. This is what happens when you get your science from a church. Just like Creationism, you get bullshit and denial of reality. What he (and other commentators), are really pissed off about is this, in the Director's words again:

"Redefining marriage is incompatible with religious freedom – the ability to live in a society according to one's moral convictions" and *"We are actually talking about a covenant that Christians, Jews, and Muslims believe is a sacrament that God ordained."*

This to me is downright laughable except these folks really believe it. So two things come to mind about their religious freedom concerns:

1. They have the religious freedom to not like gays, to consider it an abomination in their church, but no freedom to make the rest of us follow their "moral convictions." The vast majority of us do not go to their church. Making anyone else follow the dictates of your religion is not religious freedom but religious imposition, and we are damn tired of it.

2. The second part is really hilarious. Most Muslim countries teach that Jews are descended from monkeys and pigs and some are up front about calling for the total destruction of the Jews and Israel, but somehow Jews and Muslims "share a covenant with god" and are all buddy-buddy as far as keeping the gays from marrying.

Just who does the *"Commonwealth Policy Center"* speak for in America, away? Twenty-three percent of us declare ourselves unaffiliated with any religion: the "Nones." Of the others who are religious, 5% are of non-Xian affiliation. Of the 70% that do identify as Xians, the more liberal sects like United Church of Christ, Unitarians, and others don't have any problem with gay marriage. According to the Barna Group: *"Nearly half of practicing Protestants under 40 today support changing laws to enable more freedoms for the LGBTQ community, while just one-third of their parents' and grandparents' generation feel the same."*

Similarly, Pew Research in 2013 said: *"Americans' opinions on same-sex marriage have changed markedly since 2001,"* when 57% of the overall U.S. population said they opposed the practice. Now, the tide has shifted so that half of Americans favor the practice and only 43% do not." The "Nones," the liberal Xians, and 1/2 the Protestants under 40 don't have an issue with it, so that leaves the Catholic Church and the Conservative Xian denominations like the Baptists, Pentecostals, and Church of Christ. However, as with the issue of birth control, the majority of Catholics do not buy the party line. This from the Public Religion Research Institute: *Catholics are more supportive of legal recognitions of same-sex relationships than members of any other Christian tradition and Americans overall. Nearly three-quarters of Catholics favor either allowing gay and lesbian people to marry (43%) or allowing them to form civil unions (31%). Only 22% of Catholics say there should be no legal recognition of a gay couple's relationship."*

So that leaves the older Conservative Xians and a few old Catholics who generally oppose it, maybe 10-15% of the population. And they can oppose it all they want, but none of the rest of us have to go along with any of their religious ideas anymore. That's real religious freedom, which includes freedom from religion as well. USA TODAY published an Op-Ed on 5/30/14, in their weekend edition entitled *"Modern Family in High Court"* It suggested that the effect of images, video and grass-roots activism was a significant mediator of social change, exemplified in the then dramatic turnaround in US courts and public acceptance of gay and lesbian marriage: marriage equality. In it, Michael Dorf, a law professor at Cornell, discussed the impact of media. He suggested that the over-the-top reaction of the religious right undermined their quest for stopping gay marriage: *"the vitriol of the homophobic right, which opposed same-sex marriage, thus energizing the movement for the very institution it feared."*

Read that "homophobic *'religious'* right" as I'm not aware of any secular groups opposed to marriage equality or who preach "love the sinner, hate the sin" or some such nonsense. I don't recall having seen anyone from a secular organization carrying multicolored signs proclaiming: *"Reason Hates Fags."* It's a good bet it is predominantly, if not solely, Conservative Xiansanity that's to blame for the homophobia and same-sex marriage opposition that remains in the US. The above polls have shown the majority of Americans do not oppose marriage equality, evidently not buying into the various Biblical based, illogical (isn't that redundant?), arguments offered by Xiansanity. Just three pages before this Op-Ed, another article in USA Today's Nation section discussed the tidal wave of victories at the state level legalizing same-sex marriage:

"Victories Propel Gay Marriage" From the text: "Advocates for same sex marriage count 19 consecutive victories since the high (Supreme) court ruled that the federal government must recognize same-sex marriages performed in states where it is legal."

As of this writing, 37 states allow gay marriage and the Supreme Court decision legalizing gay marriage for the US had been delivered. So much for folks like the Commonwealth Policy Center's director Biblical based ravings about the end of society. Through images, TV, movies, and just knowing some gay folks personally, the consciousness raising efforts of gay-lesbian activists over the past 2-3 decades, and the internet's role in disseminating information: all these combined have educated the average American to realize that sexual orientation is nothing to get excited about. When people are educated, when they know better, bullshit ideas lose their power. Information kills religion.

Uncle Dan and that Asshole, Paul

I have a gay *"uncle"* now, "Uncle" Dan Savage. What an upfront no-nonsense guy. I once had a gay cousin who died of AIDS many years ago, back when we were just beginning to figure out what the hell HIV even was. He was in the closet quite a while before he came out. An AAU diver, college athlete, spoke 3 languages, Army Intelligence officer, served in 'Nam, hot little wife and beautiful daughter. Lily white, all 3 of them. Frickin' Republicans nowadays woulda loved this guy, except for one thing... *he was gay!* Now I have 3 close gay friends and a dozen other gay-lesbian friends/acquaintances, and of course, Uncle Dan, my new hero. And they all put up with a raft of shit thanks to that nasty little book; the Bible, the *"Good Book"*, and that asshole: *"Saint"* Paul. Good Book, my ass. And calling that prick a saint? Give it a rest. Cultural inertia keeps us all repeating that nonsense in this day and age when we all know better. Well, people, we can do better. We can drop this reliance upon trying to run our lives on this 2,000 year old mish-mosh of primitive tribal musings, fabricated history, and just plain old repressive ideas.

If you are a Xian, what part of what Dan Savage says in his quote at the beginning of this chapter don't you get? What part is incorrect? The Bible couldn't be clearer. When folks like our Brother Dean, the ASU street preacher spews his nonsense, he's following exactly what the Good Book says, and telling us it is the unimpeachable word of god we all must follow. He's not making anything up nor watering it down. And Dan Savage is repeating the same message and exposing it for the primitive hateful bullshit that it is. Dan talks plainly, pulls no punches, doesn't conform to social norms, and lives by compassion, tolerance, and knowledge. One famous incident in 2012 where a number of high school students at a Seattle journalism convention walked out on Dan as he talked plainly of the Bible's homophobia and support of slavery, is chronicled at the website Citizen Link, an affiliate of the conservative Xian "Focus on the Family" organization. According to one student:

"The first thing he told the audience was, 'I hope you're all using birth control!' she recalled. Then "he said there are people using the Bible as an excuse for gay bullying, because it says in Leviticus and Romans that being gay is wrong. Right after that, he said we can ignore all the 'B.S.' in the Bible." As Savage continued the student related; "I was thinking, 'This is not going a good direction at all." Then he started going off about the Bible. He said somehow the Bible was pro-slavery. I'm really shy. I'm not really someone to, like, stir up anything. But all of a sudden I just blurted out, 'That's bull!' "

The Citizen Link report goes on to say he called the kids who walked out "*pansies*" which is incorrect, he called them "*pansy-asses*." The good Xians just couldn't repeat the "asses" part. I'm still laughing. So the kids that walked out on his talk because he dissed their Bible, were "hurt", or "offended"? Dan is himself offended that folks like him are ridiculed, discriminated against, beat-up, imprisoned, commit suicide and are even killed outright all over the world, because of that nasty little book. I'd say it is well worth offending a few folks to try to end this insanity. People don't die because of any other "Good" book. Yup, not-Saint Paul, and the Old Testament, say Dan deserves death, along with my gay/lesbian friends, acquaintances, and my cousin. And as we have seen Paul wasn't so keen on women either. So thank you Uncle Dan for your phenomenal courage and clarity. The New Enlightenment movement would love to ditch religion right now, but until that happens we follow Uncle Dan's lead and campaign vociferously for religionists to keep their repressive ideas to themselves. We want all believers to be like the Amish and the Mennonites. Believe what you will but kindly keep it to yourselves.

Death to the Fornicators and Sodomites

Rick Wiles is a Christian commentator with his own TRUNEWS media blog and radio show. He is a happy guy now that the Ebola virus has come to town. Filling the void left by the irascible Jerry Falwell, and following in the footsteps of the likes of Pat Robertson, Rick is just waiting for God's wrath to assert itself in the form of the hemorrhagic and often fatal viral infection, to rid us all of the faggots and unbelieving scum and other undesirables (you know, like people that just like to have sex). And all this from a man of the religion of love. Like Brother Dean, he is a classic example of what the arrogance of religious thought can produce at a number of levels:

1. Believing you have revealed scripture in your hands.

2. Being certain YOU know how to interpret it best.

3. Thinking you have the god-given right to moralize and make the world conform to your religion's ideas of purity and proper behavior.

4. Being obnoxious enough to hope people die if they don't follow your religion's dictates.

All of the early Church leaders: Aquinas, Augustine, Calvin, Luther, the Popes, modern day preachers and self-anointed guardians of the Word, like our friend Rick and all his contemporary Xian bombasts, wish for death of those who don't conform. Just like ISIS, Al-Qaeda, and all the Islamic groups who wish for death to infidels. Unfortunately the Muslim death-wishers, stuck in a medieval level of arrogance, carry out their fervent hopes for the gay and unbelievers in horrific reminders of what religious thinking can still promulgate. This is what religious belief does when taken seriously and scripture is followed, all without any need for "*extreme*" interpretation. Leviticus, Paul, the Suras, and hadith are crystal clear about faggots and fornicators and heretics. Rick is just reading his book and following what it says, just like the Taliban fellas and their pals in Al Qaeda, ISIS, and any number of Islamic organizations. The arrogance and the danger, is in those first three assumptions in the list above. It can turn otherwise reasonable humans possessing normal human empathy, into sanctimonious bastards who readily sidestep that empathy by living out that fourth level of arrogance, literally wanting people to die if they don't comply. And it turns a righteous few into monsters, who carry it out.

The Gay Agenda

The Spanish Catholic Church is especially concerned about homosexuality, as much as Holy Mother Church herself. During his Boxing Day sermon, the Bishop of Córdoba, Demetrio Fernández, said there was a conspiracy by the United Nations:

"The Minister for Family of the Papal Government, Cardinal Antonelli, told me a few days ago in Zaragoza that UNESCO has a program for the next 20 years to make half the world population homosexual. To do this they have distinct programs, and will continue to implant the ideology that is already present in our schools."

In the face of nonsense like that, is it any wonder that young people today don't take religion seriously? Young people have gay friends, and accept them, and love them. Young people know that sexuality spans a wide spectrum of preferences, and is not a 'choice', any more than eye color is a choice. Young people don't care what anyone's sexual preferences are. Does anyone really wonder why young people laugh at the idiocy of the good Bishop's fears? So when some clueless minister, or priest, or self-annointed street preacher, out to save all of our fornicating, rock'n rolling, gay souls says something as stupid as this, they laugh, they know better, they may even lose all interest in religion and its ignorance and intolerance as a result. Information kills religion and the kids have got all the information they need. Women and gays are not second class citizens, and there is no fucking agenda. They know better. We know better.

3

ETERNAL DAMNATION AND THE AFTERLIFE

"Nothing proves the man-made character of religion as obviously as the sick mind that designed hell..."

Christopher Hitchens

Suppose you thought of something really clever about the world, a true insight possessing intricate detail and explanation. Stop at that point of purely rational thought and wholly un-empirical conjecture and ask yourself, as clever and as highly plausible as your idea may well be, how can it be knowledge without an empirical test of some kind? Until you find your idea actually describes or maps onto the real world, you have only an idea at that point, maybe a good hunch, but nothing more.

Consider the legendary story of discovery of the benzene ring structure by the chemist August Kekule, where he allegedly daydreamed of a snake biting its own tail and it dawned on him that a circular chain structure would finally explain the properties of this aromatic compound. That structure has been confirmed, his dream was correct, it fits, it maps onto the real world; the actual arrangement of carbon atoms in benzene. His idea exists in the real world as a real thing. But if it hadn't, it would be but one more plausible and clever, however ultimately wrong, idea, and not an instance of new knowledge. You gotta collect the data, do the empirical test and verify that some thing or process truly exists or there is no knowledge, just speculation. Now consider Hell.

An Amazon search will get you over 30,000 titles on Hell alone! This listing may not include a multitude of theological works not having Hell in their titles, which may also have weighed in on the subject. Possibly, tens of thousands more? Generations of authors have written on the subject, most profoundly, most authoritatively. But there is no data, there is no knowledge. No-one has ever been there. There is no evidence at all of such a place. No such torturous realm has ever been discovered. No-one has visited and come back with any evidence of the afterlife. A few authors have gotten rich describing what was, in all probability, a hallucination induced by oxygen starvation of their brains. Despite their pleadings, this is not evidence. Most claim to have been to heaven and back, and not the other place. Be that as it may, any discussion of hell should have disappeared from our modern 21st century conversation. Yet is hasn't. Other than as a speculative and wholly imaginary idea, there is nothing to talk about.

There is no evidence whatsoever that anyone's conception of hell throughout human history, in any given set of cultural myths, describes a real place. It's like talking about Never-Never land. Religion keeps this fantasy going solely by lying to successive generations of children that such a place surely must exist, and that many of us deserve to go there for not participating in the correct religion or religious practices.

Theology has this problem with any and every thing it professes to investigate or discover. Without any empirical test, one person's speculation remains as unfounded and imaginary as another, all equally unprovable. Unlike the example of Kekule's dream of the benzene ring, there is no empirical test to determine what is really real or merely an idea. This conundrum explains why there are, according to Pew Research, around 40,000 denominations of Xianity alone, each with its own untestable interpretations of Scripture, such as musings about Hell, God's attributes, angels, original sin, etc., etc., ad infinitum, ad nauseum. There is no empirical test of theological musings to decide who is right or wrong, because all of the imaginary ideas don't describe or map onto the real world. Any one of the 7 billion plus of us on the planet could go in the lab and confirm the structure, the reality, of Kekule's benzene ring. But not one person on earth can verify anyone's claims of hell or the afterlife. Such is the continued arrogance of religious thought that we blindly pass on to our children.

Child Indoctrination and Condemnation

How dare we teach children it is perfectly normal and acceptable to condemn someone to eternal suffering in some god's totally imaginary Hell. No-one is born hoping others will burn forever in some dastardly conception of unspeakable agony. You have to teach people to think that's a real good thing, a necessary consequence, a righteous idea, an inescapable reality. You have to con them, convince them while they're young. If you wait until they are adults to try to peddle that shit, they will probably tell you to *"go to Hell."* We non-believers are thinking: *"You teach your children that nasty crap? You should be ashamed of yourself! You perpetuate that hatred in the name of some frothy deity so you can claim to have faith?"*

This is but one reason many of us secularists the world over are incensed, angry, and fed up. It is but one reason why I write, definitely one of my main motives. We are not *Homo religicus* by design. That is an ugly historical accident of cults and conquest, dominance through the Dark Ages, and a social respectability that is so ingrained it remains entrenched, though not intractable, in the modern era. The Renaissance thinkers pulled away from religion, the Enlightenment thinkers dared to question and reject it, and the New Enlightenment movement attacks it and calls for its further decline and marginalization, if not its end. And that's all religions and not merely Xiansanity.

I have this bumper sticker on my car along with a few others, and boy do they get the looks:

"IF you are worried about burning in someone's Hell, thank a religion"

Think about it, is this incredibly obnoxious or what? A common practice in the world's main religions is to condemn the rest of humanity to eternal gruesome punishment for not believing or behaving in a precise manner they claim is pleasing to their god. There is no better example of the arrogance of religious thought than believing you are superior enough in your thinking and behavior that you can suppose, or demand, or feel certain, or be smugly satisfied, even downright pleased another human will spend an eternity suffering in some omnipotent prick's fiery medieval torture chamber. What an asshole idea, whose time has come to be relegated forever, as Hitch would say, "to the dustbin of history." Merriam-Webster defines *"arrogant"* thusly: *"having or showing the insulting attitude of people who believe that they are better, smarter, or more important than other people: having or showing arrogance."* How more arrogant can anyone get?

How dare any missionary, any youth minister, any preacher, any priest or imam sell the phony, cruel idea of eternal damnation; burning in some god's hellfire to anyone, much less to children. Children, who are cognitively immature, emotionally vulnerable, and coerced through uncritical respect for adult authority and likely behavioral sanction, from outright punishment to reprimand or parental disapproval. The concept that some god dictated or inspired some book of "Holy Scripture" and people will burn in hell if they fail to follow that book is absurd. Or that people will burn in hell if they never even heard about the book. Or better still, they will burn in hell even if they just have doubts about it. This is a primitive, ugly fantasy we should no longer foist on defenseless children. Consider the standard Xian view as espoused by their hero, the inscrutable C.S. Lewis. They love to remind you what a swell guy he was:

"There are only two kinds of people in the end: those who say to God, "Thy will be done," and those to whom God says, in the end, "Thy will be done." All that are in Hell, choose it. Without that self-choice there could be no Hell. No soul that seriously and constantly desires joy will ever miss it. Those who seek find. Those who knock it is opened."

"Fuck you" is the response that immediately comes to my mind. How dare you claim to know anyone's ultimate fate, you pompous bastard. And to be smugly satisfied that any human may suffer unspeakable agony for an eternity? What an asshole. This is your brain on religion. My Xian friends just love this arrogant DB. More proper replies to this obnoxious stance have been offered by many a clear headed secularist, so in better words than I might hope to assemble:

"The doctrine that future happiness depends upon belief is monstrous. It is the infamy of infamies. The notion that faith in Christ is to be rewarded by an eternity of bliss, while a dependence upon reason, observation, and experience merits everlasting pain, is too absurd for refutation, and can be relieved only by that unhappy mixture of insanity and ignorance, called 'faith.'"

Robert G. Ingersoll

> "The infliction of cruelty with a good conscience is a delight to moralists. That is why they invented Hell."

Bertrand Russell

> "But I was very unwilling to give up my belief... Thus disbelief crept over me at a very slow rate, but was at last complete. The rate was so slow that I felt no distress, and have never since doubted even for a single second that my conclusion was correct. I can indeed hardly see how anyone ought to wish Christianity to be true; for if so the plain language of the text seems to show that the men who do not believe, and this would include my Father, Brother, and almost all of my friends, will be everlastingly punished. And this is a damnable doctrine."

Charles Darwin

> "To terrify children with the image of hell, to consider women an inferior creation—is that good for the world?"

Christopher Hitchens

Hell is an asshole idea whose time has come to die a quick death itself. Let's quit teaching children of so many faiths that this bullshit is true.

The Fantasy of Hell

Now just imagine a conversation between you and your next door neighbor, out on the deck, during a leisurely summer afternoon's barbeque. As the conversation about the yard or your garden rambles on, your neighbor starts describing some obscure region of the world, some really remote place that he sounds like he knows something about, expounding on about it for some minutes in great detail: terrain, climate, flora and fauna, inhabitants, etc., in a fascinating, plausible, and coherent narrative, and so you comment:

Wow, sounds interesting, and you ask: Have you ever been there?
"Nope"
Oh, So you've read a great deal about it?
"A little"
Oh, from like explorers or anthropologists, biologists who have been there?
"Nope"
So, from just someone who has visited there?
"No, no-one's ever been there"
What?

"Yeah, but a lot of people have thought about it a lot, and so have I, and I read some of their books and some Scripture about it so I wrote a whole book on it."

What?

Sounds silly, doesn't it? Those 30,000 Amazon search titles on Hell which have authoritatively weighed in on the subject over the centuries, are all as completely imaginary as your neighbor's musings about some supposed place on the earth, somewhere that no-one has ever been to. There is no data, no observations, and no information. There is no knowledge. No-one has ever seen it, there is no evidence of any real place such as Hell whatsoever. Hell is no more real than Middle Earth or the Land of the Jedi. But that fact hasn't deterred many thousands of the pious from penning entire books on the subject, as if they knew something about it.

Rob Bell and Hell

One prominent and recent example is Pastor Rob Bell's 2011 *Love Wins*. From the advertising blurb: "A book about heaven, hell and the fate of every person who ever lived." The arrogance of that byline from his publisher is astounding. How the fuck would Rob know about any human, their life, their deserved ultimate fate, much less every human that ever lived? This is your brain on religion. It is not built in, it must be taught. It must be indoctrinated to sound so plausible, so right and righteous. Unbelievable. The absurdity and chutzpah is breathtaking. He wrote an entire book on something he has no knowledge of, only speculations on other speculations, which, in turn, are based on other speculations. It is speculations all the way down. Imaginary ideas piled upon imaginary ideas. Rob took a lot of heat from the Evangelical community as he skirted around but wouldn't commit to the idea of "universalism:" the proposal that everyone gets into heaven and no-one goes to hell. *"Love wins"* in the sense that Rob's god just might not burn everyone who didn't obey or believe. God is too nice a guy according to young Rob and maybe, just maybe universalism could be true or at least is a viable option for today's young liberal Xian to consider. That is Pastor Bell's swell, peachy keen message. I had to side with the Evangelicals on this one.

For me to agree with as lofty a church leader and theologian as Albert Mohler of the Southern Baptist Theological Seminary is one hell of a stretch, but logically I'm right with Uncle Al on this one. If everyone gets in to see god after death, and no-one goes to hell, what's the point of salvation through JC's death on the cross? If original sin doesn't necessitate our redemption, nor our evil, wicked, weak, putrid, sniveling, degraded, depraved, all too human ways which god finds so disgusting that he already has a dungeon of eternal torment all cooked up to punish us in, then what the hell is the point of Hell in the first place? The whole Xian edifice crumbles down like absurd house of cards that it is.

Rob Bell is considered an all-around nice guy and is a very influential mega church pastor catering to the more liberal younger evangelical Xians. He has written half a dozen books and has been featured in the top news magazines. His *Love Wins*, made the New York Times bestseller list. Oprah praises him and Young Xians dig what he has to say. He is I'm sure, a sincere hipster sorta guy, what with the spriggy hair, skinny genes and tennies. He's hip. But Rob, swell guy as he may be, is just trying to figure it all out like the rest of us. He knows nothing more about hell than you or I do. Or your neighbor. Or your goldfish for that matter. He knows nothing. Everything he muddles on about in his book concerning the fiery place and whether his god would give us a free pass on it or not, is utter speculation. Pure imagination. Any conclusions, however sincerely presented, are nonsense. When good writers make shit up and deftly craft entire worlds out of whole cloth we call it Harry Potter or Lord of the Rings. When pastors and ministers, popes, priests, gurus and imams, sages and sophists thru the centuries do it we call it theology.

Yet, it is all abject fiction. Sean Carroll the physicist, science educator, and author participated in a 2014 debate with Eben Alexander, the neurosurgeon author of *Proof of Heaven*, entitled, "Death is Not Final." Alexander claims that he was totally brain dead during a coma, and that he had the experience of visiting heaven and coming back. The experience was vivid and compelling to him, and therefore heaven must be real. It's like total proof, dude. Bill Maher and Lawrence Krauss, the physicist and secular speaker, took Newsweek's editor Tina Brown to task on Maher's "Real Time" show for featuring Alexander's book, and for presenting his absurd claim as much more than merely plausible, and not at all a hallucination, but probably for real! Newsweek printed a decidedly "isn't this proof?" credulous report.

As did Maher and Krauss, on "Real Time", Sean Carroll and Dr. Steven Novella, a neurologist from Yale, during the "Death is Not Final" debate, pointed out that vivid, life-changing hallucinations while in a coma are nothing new, and are no proof of going anywhere, much less visiting the ethereal realm. Sean Carroll nails the crux of this controversy and that of any and all religious claims, which all alike have no empirical basis. Despite the wishful thinking by the world's religions for millennia, there is no evidence of god, gods, angels, devils, souls, heaven, hell, etc. Here's Sean Carroll on the options regarding the existence of a soul and a heaven:

Either: *"Everything we think we understand about the behavior of matter and energy is wrong, in a way that has somehow escaped notice in every experiment ever done in the history of science. Instead, there are unknown mechanisms which allow information in the brain to survive in the form of a blob of spirit energy, which can then go start talking to other blobs of spirit energy, but only after death, except sometimes even before death."*

Or: *"Physics is right. And people under stress sometimes have experiences that seem real but aren't."*

Thanks, Sean. Information kills religion. We have to stop lying to our children that we know these things like souls and heaven and gods and devils to be real. Even some highly intelligent people who are smart enough to earn advanced degrees, edit national magazines, even practice medicine (where nothing but clearheaded empiricism is required or people die), just can't give up the ideas they were indoctrinated into as children.

More Afterlife Nonsense

Back to the casual barbeque conversation with your neighbor, who now mentions that he is the reincarnation of his great, great, (repeat 10x) grandfather, making him the 14th *"Joe Hodges"* in a long line of Joe's from Hodgetown, NJ. You might say:
"Oh, so you're descended directly from him, all of your ancestors had the same name? Wow, that's totally cool"
He replies: "No, I'm him. He's me."
"Well yeah, same name, I get it."
He replies further: "No, I am him, same soul, different body, I'm the 14th reincarnation."
"What?" "Oh, hey that's a good one, you had me for a second."

"And furthermore, I hate those scum in New York so I'm gonna make sure I get reincarnated again as number 15 somewhere right here in or near beautiful Hodgetown, definitely in Jersey and not across the river with those heathens in New York!"

You'd wonder what drugs he was on, or if he forgot to take some of his meds that morning. Yet, this is exactly what our good friend Tenzin Gyatso (his real name) the 14th Dalai Lama wholeheartedly believes. According to Tibetan Buddhism:

1. There is a soul.

2. It can be reincarnated.

3. He is the 14th reincarnation of the Dalai Lama soul.

4. He can control where his soul will be reanimated into another body.

No shit. This is as preposterous and delusional as it gets, and you would react accordingly if your neighbor spouted such absurdities. Tenzin is a swell guy to many, a revered spiritual leader to many more, thought of as a kind and learned, man, to be respected and listened to all over the world. And in many ways, for a religious person of some renown, he is rather enlightened in much of his thinking. He readily admits that the power of prayer is unreliable and a bit of a misnomer; it doesn't work. He further has expressed the realization that religion does not matter to morality. He has met too many good people of all religions, and especially of no religion at all, to repeat the cultural truism that one needs a religion to be good. Not bad for a religious leader. Damn progressive and secular in his thinking, one must observe.

Yet, he clings to the absurd four beliefs I posted above. Beliefs that if expressed by your neighbor, or a family member, would leave you flabbergasted and incredulous. But if it's a religious figure, a respected spiritual world leader expressing the exact same utterly absurd claims, we grant it a free pass and chalk it up to *"well, that's his belief"*. If your neighbor started spouting the same ridiculous fantasies, you'd rightly consider him half-nuts and grant him and his inanities little to no respect at all. The Dalai Lama may be a swell guy and a progressive thinker in many ways, but like all religious leaders he legitimizes the absurdity and arrogance of religious thought.

There's not a shred of evidence that consciousness survives the death of the brain, nor an ounce of evidence for any of the myriad and imaginative descriptions of an afterlife, offered from hundreds of cultures throughout history. That is the data from modern science. What makes the Lama so sure that the Tibetan Buddhist version of the afterlife is the correct one? Could it be that's what he was brought up to believe and nothing more? Sure sounds exactly like the same kind of absolute certainty that the Xians and Muslims profess about their undeniable heaven and hell, run by their god.

Maybe the Greeks were right, and you must cross the river Styx and Hades awaits you. Maybe the Muslims are right, and part of Allah's eternal punishment includes re-growing your own skin over and over for infinity so you can suffer anew his eternal fire that awaits you. Maybe the liberal Xians like Rob Bell are right, and nobody really goes to hell. Maybe the Mormons are right and it is Joe Smith, sitting beside Jesus who you will meet in heaven, instead of the Buddha and a whole host of other enlightened bodhisattvas, floating out there in some undefined celestial realm.

Yes, that's right, you heard right. As utterly absurd and ridiculous as it sounds, Mormons are taught to believe that Joseph Smith, the founder of Mormonism himself, the con man from upstate 19th century New York will be seated there with Yahweh the Almighty and our dear lord Jesus in heaven to await your final judgment. No shit. How's THAT for beyond far-out fucking arrogant? It is as bat-shit crazy as any belief out there, right up with the Dalai's insistence he will come back for the 15th time, maybe as a woman, but definitely not in dastardly Communist China. As I have said before, the Dalai Lama #14 is totally accepting of the lack of evidence for the efficacy of prayer. He is in full agreement with the strong evidence that one doesn't need a religion, any religion, to be a good person, but he draws the line at the soul and astrology and reincarnation, and divination, ideas every bit as ludicrous as the claims the Mormons are taught to believe.

From the Lama's treatise on reincarnation on his own website, he explains that the discovery of the next Dalai Lama can be verified by oracles, visions in sacred lakes, and especially by the dough ball divination method. Dough ball divination. No shit. I am not making this up. Google it yourself. One twirls 3-4 dough balls in a bowl, and the one that falls out has the name of the next Lama on it. Thus, you find out, directly from "the Beyond" if the next little Dalai is a pretender, or the real McCoy, 'er Lama. Try to reconcile this absurd belief with his realistic views on the ineffectualness of prayer and the ability to be moral without religion.

You might be surprised, to find that even the supposedly kinder reincarnation religions of Buddhism and Hinduism, relegate the unbelieving scum and sinners of this life to eternal pain and sorrow, through reincarnation of the soul into another round of suffering in this existence, if not directly into a full blown conception of hell. From the Wiki: *"Naraka (Sanskrit:नरक) is the Hindu equivalent of Hell, where sinners are tormented after death. It is also the abode of Yama, the god of Death. It is described as located in the south of the universe and beneath the earth."*

A shitty, bleak outlook if there ever was one. We usually think of Xiansanity and Islamania as the main promoters of the idea of sinners and apostates and heretics deserving of eternal torment, but along with the Hindu beliefs above, here's our all-around nice guy Dalai Lama himself on the subject:

"I really wish there were no suffering in this world and no suffering after death. I wish there were no hells or ghost regions. But it would not be wise to believe that these do not exist and to continue in the negative ways that draw the mind down to these realms. The distance between our present existence and the hells could be as short as a single breath." He continues:

"Some people doubt the existence of the hell realms. However, many independent cultures speak of these realms, and there are people with clairvoyant powers who can perceive them. In Buddhism it is said that through meditation we can develop certain extraordinary powers of memory ourselves and thus recollect some of our previous lives, in which case we would be able to remember our own experiences in hell."

Deepak Chopra himself could not have blathered it any better. I've taken a lot of shit from some folks on Facebook for daring to diss the Dalai Lama, cuz he is such a sweet guy (he does seem to be). I've critiqued his rather ludicrous beliefs on divination and reincarnation before and was amazed to find the depth of his delusions, but now clairvoyance and memory of past lives too? And tell me the bullshit above about hell he professes is any less ridiculous and delusional than any Muslim or Xian claim about the unbearable suffering in the afterlife that awaits us if we fuck up. It is incredible in its depth of delusion and especially its arrogance. No-one thinks like this unless indoctrinated by the pious into one religion or another. Arrogance, delusion, and fantasy repeated with the false certainty of religious sanction. We need to drop religious thoughts and behaviors such as there being an eternal, gruesome, and deserved suffering of others, who weren't indoctrinated into our set of cultural myths. Child indoctrination is the only thing that perpetuates this cruel nonsense. Like slavery, eternal damnation is one of humanity's worst ideas. Let's move on. It's time. We can do better.

4

CREATIONISM

"Unlike science, creationism cannot predict anything, and it cannot provide satisfactory answers about the past."

Bill Nye

"Evolution should be one of the first things you learn at school... and what do they [children] get instead? Sacred hearts and incense. Shallow, empty religion."

Richard Dawkins

Polls show year after year that belief in Creationism in the United States hovers around 40%. It is not because evolution is any harder to grasp than any other scientific concept, or that teachers and textbooks do a bad job of explaining it, nor is it due to a lack of excellent popular resources promoting it. There is one reason and one reason only: religion. In the US, its Xianity, and worldwide Xianity and Islam are the prime culprits for this abject denial of science. Denying evolution is uncritically accepted solely because somebody's minister or some "expert" their minister brought in to speak to the congregation, told them evolution cannot, must not be true. A brief and flimsy but plausible sounding denial of evolution is offered that is said to be drawn directly from Scripture, and that takes care of it. However, believing in Creationism and denying evolution is as preposterous as believing in a flat earth. Denying thousands of orbiting satellites, the moon landings, space probes, high altitude balloon and aerospace flights, the space station, GPS, etc., denying all of that science that demonstrates our spherical earth, all that data, all those experiments and millions of scientists, is just as absurd as denying evolution. We have as much data and proof of evolution as the earth not being flat. Evolution and the age of the earth are undeniable facts, as much as the earth is round and goes 'round the sun.

There is no religious promotion of "flat-earthism" and subsequently no-one in the US considers it for a second, despite multiple Bible verses from which one could easily make a case similar to Creationism. There is too much knowledge in the public's mind to even make the attempt. Yet, Creationism, in claiming evolution or the age of the earth for example just can't be true, is every bit as impossible as a flat earth in light of what we know about the world. Let's look at just the tip of the iceberg of the all the science one must deny.

Hugh Ross, "Old Earth" Creationist

An astrophysicist. A PhD. A swell guy. He's got credentials right? So he must know, right? Given that he's trained in physics and studied quasars and pulsars and such, it is impossible for him to deny the immense ages of the astronomical objects he has studied or the age of the 4.5 billion year old earth or the 13.5 billion year universe itself. But he readily denies evolution. It could not have happened. Period. It doesn't "fit" his interpretation of the Bible. Of course he is certain Ken Ham, Ray Comfort and all the other "Young Earth" Creationists are hopelessly deluded in denying the immense ages of everything we have discovered through science by claiming Biblical proof for a 6,000 year old earth, but he himself is not deluded in denying evolution for the exact same reason Ham and Comfort employ. It doesn't fit his interpretation of Genesis.

When Dr. Ross denies the part of science he doesn't like, he of course, in his mind has the science exactly right. Although he agrees with all the mountains of data, and millions of scientists, and thousands of textbooks that explain and confirm the undeniable immense age of things, he however knows better than the oceans of data, millions of scientists and thousands of textbooks that explain and confirm evolution. They're all wrong, he's right. Just because has a PhD, in astrophysics, a field wholly unrelated to evolutionary biology. Some of my Xian friends buy this. This is like letting someone with a PhD in art history tell you that all of set theory and all the mathematicians working on it within mathematics are hopelessly wrong.

"But he's got a PhD!" (ooh) "He's a physicist" (ooh wow!) "an Astrophysicist" (double ooh, double wow). He's gotta be really smart, no, really, really smart. So smart in fact that despite not being a biologist, an evolutionary biologist, an archaeologist, a paleontologist, a paleo-anthropologist, a geneticist, or any of a dozen other specialists who work in evolution related fields every day of the week, he knows better than all of them. Although science got the ages of things right, all of evolution must be wrong. I guess that PhD in astrophysics confers one with special powers of knowledge to overturn entire fields of discovery, entire disciplines of work, 150 years of painstaking research, ignore oceans of data and be smarter than those millions of scientists that explain and confirm evolution. The hubris of it is breathtaking. Hugh Ross may be a wonderful man, good neighbor, dad, husband, even a quite competent astrophysicist, but I strongly suspect he does not have the super-genius intelligence required to know for certain how completely deluded millions of other bright minds utterly are. The absurdity is as breathtaking as the chutzpah. This is not arrogance?

Creationism is the Biggest Lie Ever Perpetrated on the American Public.

Imagine if a cell biologist read the astrophysics literature and then declared the entire field, and everyone working in it, was hopelessly wrong. This biologist just knew better, despite never doing astrophysics. She knew better than every astronomer and physicist and cosmologist working in the field. They were completely wrong about how quasars and pulsars work, for example. Imagine. And all because it didn't comport with this biologist's idiosyncratic interpretation of select passages of a nearly 3,000 year-old set of religious writings, from a particularly un-progressive nomadic culture, from one tiny corner of the world. That's the reason. Not because she discovered something incredibly groundbreaking or developed a new theory that had phenomenal explanatory power. No, just because she didn't like that it didn't fit with her own personal interpretation of a tiny sample of the scripture from the particular religion she was raised in, raised in by pure accident. Would anyone in astrophysics take her seriously? Would anyone take her seriously? Would you get your astronomy from a biologist if it overturned everything the astronomers were telling you, what all the scientists in the field knew and were working on daily?

Check out the websites Science Daily, or Science News, any day of the week. Start with the new reports and see how many articles have to do with evolution, confirmation of evolution, or new data on evolution. Take a gander at all the people in all the different fields, working on and compiling more confirmatory data by the minute on evolution: comparative genomics, paleo-anthropology, evolutionary biology, genetics, paleontology, comparative anatomy, etc. Hugh Ross says he knows better. Each one of those research reports, every one of the thousands of researchers, they are all wrong. 150 years of work in all those fields is wrong. Hugh Ross says so. Evolution didn't happen, could not happen because of his culture's myths, or really, his interpretation of a few passages from his culture's myths. What bullshit. He's no better than Ham or Comfort in parlaying his absurd, impossible interpretations because he just doesn't like what we have found out about our world. And he's hiding behind the false credentials of a PhD and using "faith" as a shield. The arrogance of his stance is only made possible by the undeserved respect given to religious claims and beliefs.

Speaking of Ken and Ray, one day a year or two ago, I opened the Science Daily website and clicked on Fossils and Ruins and found this article on Appalachian orogeny (mountain building), and the geology of New England, hot off the press, not even a week old.

Here's a brief excerpt of the detailed geology, published in the science journal appropriately titled: GEOLOGY:

"The mountain-building period that affected most of modern-day New England, known as the "Taconic orogeny," is commonly depicted as a collision during the Ordovician period (435 to 500 million years ago) of a North American-derived arc (the Shelburne Falls arc) and the North American margin, followed by accretion of African-derived terranes (groups of rocks with geologic histories different from surrounding rocks) during the Silurian period (410 to 435 million years ago). It further describes the Iapetus Ocean that...separated continental fragments of ancestral North America and Africa more than 450 million years ago.

You could access hundreds, no, probably thousands of journal articles like this one, published in dozens of geology journals over decades, describing the ancient geology and formation of the North American continent, including the ancient seas and mountain building episodes of both the Appalachians and the Rockies, the formation of the Grand Canyon, and Yellowstone's repeated volcanism over millions of years. Besides being incredibly detailed, painstakingly researched and corroborated solid geological science about the continent we live on, all these papers would have one other thing in common: they must all be wrong because Ken Ham and Ray Comfort say so.

It took me maybe 15 minutes, thanks to the Internet, to access the Science Daily article, read it, and search Yahoo Images for photos and illustrations. Of course, once again, the hundreds of images detailing the Iapetus Ocean I found, and the movement of the continents and the Appalachian orogeny itself, must all be utterly wrong, according to our two buddies. Ham and Comfort know better, and insist on children being taught their extreme and completely fanciful interpretation of a few Bible verses that insist that the earth is only a few thousand years old.

When I last dared criticize Creationism in the university newspaper at Murray State University in Kentucky where I was teaching, the MSU News Facebook page zoomed to over a hundred responses. There was quite a heated exchange with Creationists from all over the US, absolutely incensed that I had the gall to diss the unquestioned truths of Ham and Comfort. Some questioned my credentials, saying a Developmental Psychologist can't know anything about evolution. I replied politely that my undergrad degree was in Anthropology with an emphasis in archeology and human evolution, that I had done graduate work in brain and behavioral evolution, and that my current research studies included Cognitive Evolution, so that maybe I have more than enough relevant education and experience to discuss the subject. That seemed to shut them up on that line of argument, but there is a larger and more crucial point to be made about my credentials, anyone's credentials and my stance on evolution versus those of Ken Ham's PhD employees at his Answers in Genesis (AiG) organization, who deny evolution.

When I discuss the age of the earth, the fossil evidence that makes humans and dinosaurs living together utterly preposterous, the genetic evidence that refutes any attempt at a literal interpretation of Adam and Eve, or the comparative genomics of dog evolution which confirms the symbiotic evolution of dogs from wolf ancestors tens of thousands of years ago, I am reporting the science, not interpreting it. I'm communicating and explaining the data and the consensus of hundreds of thousands of scientists, who work directly in those and related fields. I'm telling you what we know, because of what practicing scientists in the relevant fields know. I am acting as a reporter, a science journalist, a teacher who has enough education and familiarity to write accurately about what the experts in those fields know, and convey it accurately. I am not countermanding, nor refuting, nor denying the science. Conversely, Ken Ham's underlings, (and Hugh Ross), just because they have PhD's, whether theirs is in a related field or not, are insisting all those scientists and all that science is wrong. Ham contends that one or two people, with somewhat related degrees, who don't even work in these fields, can completely overturn what thousands of scientists know and work on every day of the week. Somehow Ham's employees know better than entire disciplines worth of scientists who actually do the research, solely because the revisions and denials of AiG employees must comport with Ham's extreme Creationist interpretations. That's the absurdity, the 24 karat chutzpah, the absolute arrogance of religious thought.

Consider this little thought experiment. If your brother in law, who took a mechanics course once, was a reasonably bright guy and had done a little work on his car on occasion, began telling you that every transmission mechanic in town was wrong, that they didn't know what they were doing and didn't fix transmissions right, you would want some reasons as to why he was so sure he knew better than all these experienced mechanics who seemed to be working knowledgeably every day of the week, fixing transmissions all over town just fine. If your brother in law admitted that no, he doesn't fix transmissions himself, but he has read about them and worked on one once, and he knows all those mechanics are wrong because what they are doing doesn't comport with his religious beliefs, how likely would it be that you or anyone else would take him seriously?

I teach courses in Developmental Psychology. My PhD allows me to be familiar enough with the subject and its research to lecture competently on the current findings from an up to date textbook, which contains the latest knowledge gleaned from thousands of studies, published by thousands of child development researchers. It would be absurd enough for me, even with a degree and research experience in the same field, to insist that all those scientists, all those studies were wrong: that an entire field was hopelessly incorrect and all its practitioners thoroughly deluded just because I said so. But that is exactly what Ham's hired hands do, and without relevant background in most of the fields they pretend to overturn all consensus on. All based on a very stretched and imaginative literal interpretation of Genesis. Ya gotta admit they got balls, if not brains. Just because you have earned an advanced degree doesn't mean you're a genius.

One of the brightest professors I ever had, possibly the smartest intellect I've had the pleasure of knowing, said a PhD guarantees only one thing: that a person has worked very hard at least once in their life. Ham's hired guns, although they may have an education related to some of the fields of study they obnoxiously claim are in error, and may have earned their degrees with a lot of hard work, possess absolutely no credentials, have no justification for claiming they know better than whole disciplines of working scientists. That goes for Hugh Ross too. Any scientist, any person is entitled to their opinion on given subjects, sometimes controversial. But if you claim to have special knowledge and with it have outwitted entire fields of science and equally bright legions of scientists, you better have more than the ancient musings of ignorant goat-herders in your hand. Stick to your astrophysics, pal.

The whole Creationist enterprise is bankrupt from the start. There's all the evidence that unequivocally supports evolution, supports it to the point it is absurd to deny it, like denying gravity. If there is anything Creationists are competent at, it is absurdity and denial. Creationism is one of the most striking examples of the conflict of religion and science in this country and around the world. What the average believer doesn't consider, is the sheer enormous volume of information that we use every day that must be hopelessly wrong in order for the deniers like Ham, Comfort and Ross to be correct in the slightest degree.

To give you a flavor of the mountains of scientific knowledge that must be hopelessly wrong to buy Ken Ham's "Young Earth" and other Creationist fantasies, let's look at just a few things we know about the world we live in, starting here in the good ole USA. I'm going to stick solely to famous places and their geology. Excellent reviews of the overwhelming fossil, genetic, and biological evidence for evolution can be found in the readings for this chapter. The examples I present are the merest tip of the iceberg that makes denying evolution even more ridiculous than denying gravity or proclaiming a flat earth. The descriptions and data come from the wikis on these sites.

Meteor Crater, Arizona

Beringer Crater, as it is also known, was formed by an impact roughly 50,000 years ago. At this time during the Pleistocence epoch, the Colorado Plateau area of the southwest US was not hot and dry desert as it is today, but a grassland where huge megafauna such as ground sloths and wooly mammoths roamed.

But, of course, 50,000 years ago is a lie according to Ham and Comfort, and the now-extinct woolly mammoths and ground sloths having evolved along with all the other mammals after the extinction of the dinosaurs, is a lie to them and to Hugh Ross and all the other evolution deniers as well.

Niagara Falls

The meltwaters of the last Ice Age, produced around 11,000 years ago, formed Niagara Falls as water flowing towards the Atlantic cut through the rock in the Niagara Escarpment. Geologists know this, as sure as they know how to find oil, water and minerals in the earth using the ages of different strata. All this knowledge ties together, despite the absurd pleadings of Young Earth Creationists that no geologic formation can be older than 6-10,000 years.

Mississippi River Delta

The delta formed in stages and at varying locations due to sea level change. During the last Ice Age when so much water was still tied up in ice, sea levels in the Gulf of Mexico were much lower and the delta silt deposits formed much further out than today's river delta. As the ice melted 10,000 years ago and sea level rose, the locations of the deposits receded to the more modern location we see today.

Yellowstone

The last eruption of the Yellowstone super volcano happened roughly 640,000 years ago (sorry, Creationists...yeah, you are a sorry bunch), blowing out in an explosion 1,000 times bigger than the Mt. St. Helens eruption in 1980. The caldera that was created is over ½ mile deep and covers nearly 1,300 square miles. An older eruption occurred at 1.3 million years ago, with the most violent one happening at 2.1 million years before present, ejecting nearly 600 cubic miles of rock and ash. This is not made up. This is solid findings, from a wealth of confirmed data uncovered over the years by hundreds, maybe thousands of geologists and other researchers. It is a travesty that Creationists deny the validity of this knowledge to children, based on absurd interpretations of myths borrowed from previous cultures which found their way into the Old Testament.

Grand Canyon

The Grand Canyon itself is the result of 40 million years of erosion by the Colorado River cutting thru layer upon layer of separate geologic strata all the way down to the 2 billion year-old Vishnu Schist at the bottom. Rocks along the rim of the Canyon date to 230 million years. About 65 million years before present, the entire Colorado Plateau experienced the beginning of a period of uplift further increasing the depth of the erosion by the river. The great depth of the canyon had been cut by a little over a million years before modern times.

Mt. St. Helens

Comparatively speaking, from a geological standpoint, Mt. St. Helens is a rather young feature rising from the base of the Cascades only in the past 40,000 years. The cone that existed at the summit before the cataclysmic 1980 eruption, had only developed in the past few thousand years.

Yosemite

Yosemite's characteristic U-shaped valleys were formed by the uplift of the Sierra Nevada mountains close to 10 million years ago, creating deep and narrow canyons cut by rivers and streams through the granite rock. As glaciers formed sometime after 1 million years ago, the typical glacial valley U shape was scoured out by nearly 4,000 feet thick ice moving slowly down through the existing canyons.

Great Lakes

Around 10,000 years before present, at the end of the Wisconsin Glacial, as the ice sheets retreated northward, the rushing meltwater formed basins which became the Great Lakes.

Devils Tower

Devil's Tower is volcanic intrusion, an "almost-made-it" volcano, an upwelling of molten rock that didn't quite make it to the surface, which cooled and solidified into the mostly 6 sided columns of igneous rock that now tower above the landscape. Formed just over 40 million years ago, subsequent erosion over millions of years of the surrounding much softer sandstone and other rock left it to stand as a monument to the power and majesty of geological processes.

Badlands

The deposition of the various layers that make up the Badlands in South Dakota, occurred over 47 million years which left visibly different layers of sediment which characterize the Badlands formations. Continued erosion does not proceed at a steady pace per year as is sometimes reported, but varies with the nature of the sediments and their interposition and exposure.

Hawaii

The Hawaiian Island chain formed over millions of years stretching from the oldest atoll to the northwest at approximately 28 million years of age to the youngest, Hawai'i and Lo'ihi at the southwest end of the chain being under 400,000 years old. Lo'ihi is yet underwater but growing and most of the world is familiar with the volcanic activity on the main island itself which has been erupting for the last 200 years.

These are just a dozen familiar US formations, of literally millions on earth one could discuss, where the geology has been worked out in great detail over the past 150 years, using dozens of dating methods and thousands of comparative geological, biological, paleontological, and archaeological studies. All of which have confirmed the age of these locations beyond any reasonable doubt. The isotope chemistry that give us the dates of all these formations isn't wrong. The same science runs the smoke detectors in your house, nuclear power plants for electricity, ships and submarines, and cancer detection machines like PET scanners used worldwide. Whole fields of technologies wouldn't work if these dates were all wrong. The data presented here were drawn from individual Wikipedia articles, easily accessed by anyone wishing to see excellent summaries of what we do know about our Earth. The wikis, and the thousands of original science articles they summarize, comprise merely a representative sampling of the voluminous references detailing our knowledge of the age and formation of these landmarks. For excellent reviews of the oceans of evolutionary data from the fossil record, comparative anatomy, and comparative genomics, which demonstrate the utter impossibility of Creationism, Young or Old Earth style, read Jerry Coyne's *Why Evolution is True*, Donald Prothero's *What the Fossils Say and Why it Matters* and, of course, Richard Dawkins' *Greatest Show on Earth*.

The average Xian, who has been sold the absurd fantasy of a *"Young Earth"*, only 6,000 years old, doesn't realize the enormity of the science that must be totally wrong for that insane lie to be true. Ken Ham and Ray Comfort count on the hope that anyone who buys their preposterous fantasy will never research the science of these 12 landmarks, and see it for themselves. Oh hell, let's make it a baker's dozen, shall we?

Eyjafjallajokul (Ayaf yal yokool)

Say that fast 10 times. The geology, the volcanology behind this Icelandic volcano that erupted in April 2010 isn't wrong, despite what Ken Ham and his "experts" say. Some of you may remember that the ash cloud from this month-long volcanic eruption disrupted air travel over much of Europe. Volcanologists (those folks who study volcanoes, not Spock's home planet), considered this eruption to be a modest event on the geology scale. They were more concerned at the time if Eyjaf's spectacular spewing might trigger a neighboring volcano to come alive with disastrous consequences. Larger volcanoes can leave enough ash in the atmosphere to significantly alter the amount of sunlight warming the earth and change the weather dramatically for years. We are reminded that we live on the very thin and relatively solid crust of the earth, which is comparatively cool compared to the seething, molten interior that makes up 99% of our earth, and which cooks at over 1,000 degrees C. Our atmosphere is even thinner. The fragile thin blanket of air covering our planet, is equivalent in thickness to that of the moisture on your eyeball in comparison to the size of the earth. We're talking thin. Phenomenal.

We know these things. They are not made up. They are not mere conjectures, not the product of armchair speculations, nor simplistic interpretations of some culture's "revealed" scripture. They are not the dictates of a competing worldview. This is knowledge, born of scientific inquiry, observation and experimentation guided by theory, of the world we find ourselves in. This is the real deal. Little eruptions can have devastating local impact, larger ones; temporary global impact and the biggest of all, the super-volcanoes can affect large swaths of the planet and its weather for many years. Thankfully, at present, no known super-volcanoes are active. The last one to erupt, Toba, in Sumatra, blew out 75,000 year ago. The consensus is that it didn't trigger the glaciation that was in process at the time, but may have accelerated or at least exacerbated the earth's cooling with the amount of ash and noxious gasses ejected. There is even some speculation that this eruption may have affected human evolution, as it coincided with the "bottleneck" in the human population, when our numbers may have dropped as low as 10,000 individual humans or less, around 70,000 years ago.

There is strong genetic and archaeological evidence for the bottleneck's population crash, with or without the influence of the Toba super-volcano eruption. But then, of course, all of this science, the genetics, the human evolution, the volcanology, the geology, the climatology, and the archaeology, all of it is hopelessly misguided and incorrect by many orders of magnitude because, according to our old friends Ken Ham and Ray Comfort, armed with their strained calculations and interpretations of Biblical genealogies, the earth can only be 6-10,000 years old! According to them, if Toba erupted, it was only a few thousand years ago and all of the corroborating evidence from dozens of disciplines and thousands of scientists using numerous dating methods that requires a 70,000 year time frame are just hopelessly deluded. Science can put a Rover on Mars, put a smart-phone in your hand, discover the Higgs boson, attack leukemia with genetically modified immune system cells, map the genomes of over 1,000 species, but it can't possibly get the dating of the earth, the sun, the solar system, the volcanoes or fossils and human ancestors or anything else right, because the Creationist peddlers know better. Fuck me.

Sorry boyz, you lose. All this stuff is as real as your smart-phone. We lose, if we let you continue lying to the American public and school students without a strident and continual challenge. Creationism lost the Texas textbook battle and has lost every court case in recent years. We know the age of the earth and the solar system (roughly 4.5 billion years). We have pretty good approximation for how many billions of years the sun and other stars have, and will continue, to burn. We know this stuff. Astonishingly, we recently extracted DNA from a 400,000 year-old human ancestor, from an excavation in Spain. Incredible. No lie. No denial. No mere "competing" worldview or alternate godless interpretation of the data. Just good corroborated, replicated, advancing science that isn't going away, isn't backing down because someone wants to hide absurd claims behind the arrogant and ignorant wall of faith.

One doesn't have to go to Iceland or Sumatra to learn about volcanism. We have our own super-volcano right here in our backyard, our favorite backyard: Yellowstone. It hasn't erupted in 640,000 years, the last in a series of major eruptions dating to 1.3 and 2.1 million years ago, as the Wiki excerpt above says. You can read the references it cites for hours about what we truly know. Read the original research. You can read for days actually, weeks even. Look up Toba, look up the age of the earth, look up human evolution, or volcanism, or the genetic bottleneck, any of it, all of it. You won't read any lies. Creationism denying all this very real science is the lie, and the churches should be ridiculed and slammed for spreading this shit in the name of faith. We secularists should be incensed, not them, over what is taught in our schools. Or rather, what is avoided in our schools as too many of our biology teachers are cowed into giving evolution the short shrift to preempt any hurt sensibilities on the part of Xian parents. I'm with Hitch on this one: *"Well, fuck that!"* should be our indignant reply. We should be strident about the incredible knowledge our schoolchildren don't learn in service to absurd interpretations of nearly 3,000 year old myths, defended under the false banner of faith.

Lastly, human evolution, the study of our origins: Paleo-anthropology, Biological Anthropology, Physical Anthropology. Whatever you want to call it, it's for real. This is not a competing worldview or a fantasy about apes and monkeys that weren't human, made up just to satisfy the demands of atheistic 'Evilution'. What we know about human evolution from the fields of archaeology, geology, paleontology, genetics and genomics, and paleo-anthropology itself, is not a lie, not a fantasy. It is the real deal, just like any other science. Thousands upon thousands of scientists from all those fields, have put in millions of hours of research, and published thousands of papers. Ken Ham and other deniers say they are wrong. That's the lie. The religionist's claim that *"the earth can only be 6,000 years old and our god made each species separately"* is the blatant lie. *"Living things cannot be related genetically, we did not evolve, evolution didn't and couldn't happen, and the entire field of human evolution must be a fantasy mistaking monkeys for human ancestors"* is the psychosis they preach. The arrogance of their claims are breathtaking. We should be outraged, and strident in our opposition.

We know that humans and chimpanzees evolved from a common ancestor roughly 6 million years ago. We are not over-evolved chimps, and chimps are in no way just undeveloped humans waiting to blossom into us. We are not the crown of creation, we are not the ultimate endpoint that 3.5 billion years of a god-directed evolutionary process was meant to bring about. We are but one tiny branch of life, appearing in our current modern form barely 200,000 years ago. If evolution has an endpoint, a purpose on earth (it doesn't appear to have one) it would be to produce bacteria and insects, not bipedal primates. Check out the *Interactive Tree of Life* website listed in the readings for this chapter and see for yourself.

I once had an interesting exchange on Facebook with a commenter on one my columns that took Creationism to task. This guy claimed he had the ultimate interpretation of the Genesis story that really told how god did it, which incorporated both the fossil record and an old earth, but contained his unique personal discovery of the REAL TRUTH (his caps) of the Evolution/Creationism debate as only he had been able to extract from the beginning verses of the Bible. (He used a lot of caps). Further he claimed that Ken Ham, Bill Nye, the National Center for Science Education (the evolution education organization) and even the Christian apologist and Young Earth Creationist Hugh Ross mentioned above, were all totally afraid to debate him. (Xians love debates, like they love wars). According to this guy, they have all run away from his challenge because they fear he's got the real facts, the real pipeline to god's mind and they must all keep him and his revelations suppressed lest he blow them all out of the water.

Just what the world needs, another asshole's re-interpretation of the almost 3,000 year old writings of an un-remarkable, primitive and rather barbaric culture from the Middle East, who borrowed their myths from other primitive cultures, and that through the vagaries of religious syncretism and historical accident (adoption by the Roman Empire), we are yet struggling to free ourselves from. We have to stop teaching children the absurd lie that everything we need to know is in some ancient book if we just decipher it right; whether it is the Koran, Bible, or Bhagavad Gita.

Instead, how about some real knowledge for a change? In addition to the facts of our hominid evolution occurring over the past 4-6 million years of being bipedal, with 2.5 million years of stone tool making, and subsequent brain expansion, and 40,000 years of cave art, harpoons, flutes, needles and other elements of modern human culture, here's a few examples from modern genetics, of more recent human evolution that make Ken Ham and his hired deniers, and Hugh Ross and all Creationists look as ridiculous as their absurd claims.

Humans adapted to eating dairy products by developing lactose tolerance over the last 7,000 years (sorry, Ken). The gene that makes the enzyme that allows infants to digest milk normally shuts off in childhood. Some populations evolved a mutation that keeps the gene turned on into adulthood. We know this. The genetic mutation for blue eyes arose between 6,000 and 10,000 years ago in Eastern Europe. Where malaria is endemic, red blood cells evolved to be resistant by way of the sickle cell mutation within the last 10,000 years. Some of these adaptations have evolved in different ways in different populations. We know all this to be true in just the last decade or two of genetic research. As Bill Nye related to the American public in his debate with Ken Ham: *"We have trees older than 6,000 years."* This is reality. The arrogance of knowledge-deniers like Ham, Comfort and Ross must continue to be exposed for the delusional ignorance that it is.

At the end of Ham-Nye debate a secularist from the crowd who now works for Hemant Mehta's Friendly Atheist site as a researcher and writer, Tracey Moody, sent up the hay-maker question of the evening, short, simple and to the point: *"What, if anything, would ever change your mind?."* Directed at Mr. Ham, he rather haltingly replied: *"Hmm...Well the answer to that question is...I am a Xian...I can't prove it to you but God has definitely shown me very clearly through his word, the Bible is the word of God...I admit that is where I stand from."* In short, "nothing." Nye responded with a few examples of possible findings among millions that could be imagined, such as discovering fossils out of place that might force us to rethink evolution (which has never occurred). In short, "evidence." There is nothing but evidence for evolution, and none at all for Creationism. Only claims to personal revelation maintain the fantasy.

5

EVANGELIZING AND MORALIZING

"The people who are regarded as moral luminaries are those who fore-go ordinary pleasures themselves and find compensation in interfering with the pleasure of others"

Bertrand Russell

In this chapter I will examine the unquestioned arrogance of both spreading one's religion and the obnoxious moralizing of the religious. Once again, rather than rehash the TV preacher's excesses or other already well-worked over examples of religious arrogance, I look to mostly everyday instances of pious folks declaring how we must live our lives according to their ideas of sanctity and right sexual practice.

Stealth Proselytizing

One of my colleagues was a regular at a local steak and potato grill, where despite the lack of a bar, they did serve alcohol along with dinner. How progressive for a Kentucky college town, where up until 10 years ago it was completely dry and one couldn't enjoy a glass of wine or a beer with dinner at any eating establishment. Only recently did this little bastion of Christian temperance, the likes of which one is not unlikely to still encounter down south of the Ohio river, despite this being the 21st century, go from "moist" to "wet." Now one can finally buy package liquors in local stores without having to drive to the next county. It took another ten years of lobbying by the university faculty and other progressives in town to achieve this privilege, added to being able to buy alcohol along with a meal in a restaurant. My colleague and her friends ordered their meal as usual. In her words:

"However, our meal had an unexpected twist. Our young male server was reluctant to serve me a glass of Chianti to go with my rare prime rib. The others did not order drinks. When I first ordered the Chianti to go with the meal, he warned me that he was likely to "forget" my order. So I promised to remind him. When he showed up to take our orders, he had prominently displayed, protruding from the order pad, the following: Ephesians 5.18. I had no idea of what he was up to, but one of my friends spotted the verse, presumably by Paul, as one probably against drink. So I Googled with my i-Phone and found the following: "And be not drunk with wine, wherein is excess; but be filled with the Spirit;" We found this offensive in a secular restaurant, so I Googled some other verses, such as "A little wine for thy stomach's sake," "Respect

your elders," "Judge that ye be not judged," and another pro wine one. My friend scribbled down the names of the Biblical books, chapters, and verses and gave the napkin to him. As I was going into the restroom, I told one of the women in charge about this guy. She apologized and said that he had already been warned about this and not to do it again. I hope that he gets his butt kicked hard for this."

And the end of the story is the guy was fired shortly thereafter. How's that for an obnoxious case of moralizing? If you are of some religious sect and you don't like alcohol (hard-core Xians and Muslims), or stimulants like caffeine (Mormons), or zippers (some Amish, Mennonites), or birth control (Catholic clergy, Catholics in undeveloped countries), Groovy! Goody for you! Don't use those things. Abstain all you want. But dig this: the rest of us do not need nor want your moralizing. Live your life however "pure" your religion dictates but leave the rest of us the fuck alone. Only religion, especially Evangelical Xiansanity and Islam, teach people like this poor horribly bullshitted schmuck of a waiter that he oughta impose his retarded beliefs on others, to "save" them from certain destruction, or just to make sure they conform to how he was taught the world should work to please his god. If there is one thing us secularists and many other religious folks would like to get across to y'all is, do what you will, live under whatever set of rules you were taught that make you feel correct and comfortable, just leave us out of it. If you must be religious, kindly keep it to yourself. From Steven Pinker's, *Better Angels of our Nature* comes a concise and clear definition of moralizing: *"Formulate universal principles and punish those who don't conform...maintain purity and remove contamination of a divine essence."*

This kid didn't know any better. It is what they taught him; his parents, pastor, or youth minister from the local Church of Christ or possibly one the Baptist churches in town. I feel sorry for him, for anyone losing their employment, but he'd been warned and made his choice. Somebody in this guy's life is responsible for not only the bullshit he believes, but for implanting the arrogance that compelled him to slyly and obnoxiously attempt to impose his ideas on others and get himself fired. He thought he was doing the Lord's work, saving souls by "maintaining the purity of the divine essence."

In his youth, Mitt Romney, the former Republican presidential candidate was a good Mormon missionary. Except Mitt of course, coming from privilege, didn't canvass the wastelands of western Kentucky, nor the slums of Cleveland. No, young Romney evidently wandered about Southern France, also attempting to persuade the local folks they shouldn't use alcohol either. Imagine a pre-pubescent Mitt, armed with the mighty Book of Mormon, out to reverse 27 centuries of exquisite viticulture all because some 1830's American conman decided he would outdo Muhammad and create his own religion right here in 'Murica, wherein he could have unrestricted access, in fact divine license, to pooch adolescent females. The insanity of religion's influence on human behavior sometimes boggles the mind, does it not? I contend this sort of obnoxious 'tude to push your view of morality on others is not natural.

Children will not naturally grow up to be imams, fire and brimstone street preachers, Popes, moralizing church ladies, or Mormon missionaries bent on telling everyone how they must behave to conform to some god's will. Or muddled headed waiters trying to save academics from the pleasures of Chianti with rare prime rib. Where my family hails from it's an infamnia not to have a dry red with rare beef. So unless you brainwash someone like that poor misguided waiter that proselytizing is a really keen idea, they won't grow up to tell others how they ought to live their lives. This is not natural.

When you are on your deathbed, what are the odds you think you'll convert to Islam? Think about it. Despite a 600 year head start for Xianity, Islam is up to nearly 2 billion adherents, the number 2 religion only a few 100 million or so behind Xianity, which is now estimated as having over 2 billion believers worldwide. The Muslim claim to priority is looking good to them. What if they had another 600 years, wanna bet they'd still be number 2? Islam passed up the number of Catholic believers a few years back to become the single biggest religion on earth, even though the One Holy and Apostolic Church (the only true one as well, according to Catholic dogma), had a 300 year jump on Islam and the benefit of the much wider and earlier spread of the Roman empire, as compared to the later and less extensive conquests of the Arab empire.

Furthermore, our Muslim friends assure us that we were all born Muslim. Since there is but one god, Allah, according to the Muslims everyone on the planet, from anywhere, anytime is a child of Allah and born a Muslim, some just don't know it. And when one "converts" to Islam or rather admits to the fact of already being Muslim, one takes an Arabic name to acknowledge the fact. All of us remaining infidels have had plenty of opportunity to submit to the will of Allah during our lifetimes, and since we knowingly chose not to convert, we will surely burn in the His hell for the glaring omission.

Now my Xian friends and I not only share a complete disregard for this obviously silly notion that we will burn in Hell for not buying into Islam, we also don't give it so much as a first thought, much less a second one. There is not a snowballs chance in anybody's hell that the vast majority of good Xians, or us Unbelieving Scum will ever convert to Islam, while alive or nearly dead. And my Xian friends please take note: that is exactly how all of us non-believers feel about Xianity. There is not a moment's thought of converting. So please get it out of your head you think you will somehow, someday, save us. Or that we will certainly see the light as it fades upon our deathbed. Whatever your minister told you about non-believers, forget it. It couldn't be more clueless, a hallmark of Xian apologetics in general. So no, we won't convert on our deathbeds any more than you will to Islam. So get over it. Hitch didn't, Darwin didn't, despite wishful thinking and obnoxious Xian propaganda to the contrary. Get over yourselves. And if you figure it out, if the light goes on, go tell the Muslims.

The Commandments

Most of you know that there's two versions of the Ten Commandments in the OT, first one in Exodus and then a different list in Deuteronomy. In addition, the various divisions of Xianity split those up further into at least seven different renditions some going well back before the reformers Luther and Calvin, all the way back to Augustine and Philo. And the believers wonder why us skeptical types won't take this stuff seriously? Somehow these Commandments are supposed to be from "on High" (yeah, somebody was high when they dreamed this whole scheme up). Accordingly, we must base our life upon them, or be relegated to an utter and complete lack of objective morals, as well as impending eternal fire. Yet, we are subject to the whims of interpretation and formatting by mere humans throughout the millennia on said Commandments, each with their own, quite different direct pipeline to God to know what He really, really meant. The absurdity of religious thought knows no bounds.

One often hears from liberal Xians how the NT superseded and softened the nastiness of the OT, how "Jesus changed all that." Well, where are the truly relevant missing Commandments that JC never seemed to supply nor comment upon? How 'bout:

11. Thou shalt not own other human beings.

That would have been a good one. Jesus or Paul had ample chance to right that wrong 1800 years before us lowly humans figured it out on our own that our brothers, our con-specifics, our fellow humans of any creed or stripe didn't really like a life in chains, and we shouldn't do that to one another anymore. Think of the suffering that tiny bit of enlightenment could have saved. Instead, Paul and the Gospels merely echo the 1st century perspective on the normalcy and operation of enslaving human beings.

12. Thou shalt not rape.

The god of the OT would have had to edit too much of his book, I suppose, if JC or Paul had weighed in on the heinousness of forcible entry of females. Patriarchal cultures, with their misogynistic religions from all over the world, could have used a shining example of how to consider the violation of women as a true abomination from the "religion of love" but no, eliminating or lessening a dozen or so centuries of the continued horrific degradation and suffering of women just wasn't on their agenda.

On Moralizing Vehemently

Religious conservatives. Why are they so pissed off? Let's concentrate on the "Big 2"; Xianity and Islam. We're stuck with them through nothing but historical accident. We are stuck with the "Big 2" mostly because of conquest. They are not primarily indigenous religions like Hinduism, Buddhism, Taoism, Confucianism, Shintoism or the bazillion tribal religions (like Mormonism, eh?), which are dominant in the cultures and geographic locations where they were dreamed up. Dreamed up. That's not a colloquialism nor demeaning hyperbole, but a purely descriptive term. All religions were dreamed up. Much of what modern Xianity is today is due to the visions of Paul. He never met Jesus. He had visions. Period. Full stop

Muhammad's one-man manufacture of the religico-political system that is Islam was all his own, solely from his own visions as well, like the classic dream where he was transported from Medina to Jerusalem and then whisked off to heaven on a winged horse (mule?), and chatted in Heaven with Moses and Adam, and whole host of heavenly denizens about mundane items such as how many times a good Muslim should pray daily. Joseph Smith managed much the same feat in America in the 1830's as did L. Ron Hubbard a century later... and they both said they intended to do it! They dreamed up a religion all by their lonesome: no corroborating gospels and epistles needed for Muhammad and his two American wannabe emulators. And we teach children their bullshit is true. *"Everybody else's prophet just heard voices in their head... but not yours."* Right.

So why are folks like Rush Limbaugh, Mark Driscoll, countless other preachers and imams, so-called spiritual leaders of the "Big 2" so pissed off? Quite often, because somebody somewhere is not behaving according to the rules of their religion. Most regular folks belonging to any given religion worldwide aren't that uptight and incensed over non-believers or others lack of adherence to their religion's rules. Most don't know shit about their own religion. If they did, they would be quite likely able to see it as if from the outside, as they do all other religions, and realize what a preposterous set of myths and repressive injunctions theirs really contains. Most former Xians will tell you it was because they took the effort to actually read their damn Bible in toto and view all its absurdities, contradictions, fantasies, cruelties, patriarchal intolerance and violence, that made them discard their faith.

It is the conservatives in each respective religion that lead the charge in moralizing, making sure we straighten up and fly right. Religionists the world over, especially those of the "Big 2", work real hard to make all of us conform to their ideas of right behavior. We are threatened at the very least, with pain of eternal fire in their god's hell, ridicule or exclusion from your family or social group, the limiting of your personal rights and freedoms, and sometimes violence, jail, maybe even death. All of this brought to you by the religions of love and peace. Isn't that just special? All because of somebody's dreams... are you kidding me? People, we need to outgrow this nonsense. And soon. We used to just have spears to skewer the infidels, or we could burn a few non-believers at the stake. Now, it is sniper rifles that can kill from a mile away, drones that kill from across the globe, explosives with carpet nails, chemical and nuclear weapons that can slaughter people in wholesale numbers.

People have their lives ruined or are killed every day, all over the world, by the aftereffects of religious dreams. Try being a woman, a gay, a non-believer, or a freethinker in an Islamic or Conservative Xian culture and then you'll really reap the benefits of Paul's or Muhammad's dreams. The moderates, the liberals within any religion are no help, they are not off the hook, they are not free of blame because they promote the legitimacy of their scriptures full of dreamed up ideas, that the conservatives take oh so seriously. Their religion is, of course, the true one, their prophet(s), really, really did talk to god. Uh huh. And the conservatives have a field day with it, demanding discrimination, even death to gays, women, apostates, sinners of all kinds, while the liberals claim *"that isn't my Xianity"* or *"the extremists have hijacked Islam."* But every word the so-called extremists follow, every idea the conservatives want adherence to, is in the scripture that liberals worship as well, whoever dreamed it up.

A buddy of mine, who happens to be gay, and from a rather conservative Xian area of KY, once experienced a charming little episode of real religious arrogance, courtesy of Conservative Xiansanity. Waiting in line at a retail store, a woman remarked to her daughter next to her, quite out loud and well within earshot of the rather obviously gay clerk: *"Well if this faggot would learn to do his job."* Ya gotta love it, right? It gets better. My friend, fed up, as most of my gay friends are of being a constant topic of discussion, as well as being constantly scrutinized and scorned by Xians in this country, just lost it and retorted something just as loudly to the effect that: *"Well lady, why is it you resemble something that just crawled out of the abortion bucket."*

Ouch! A double stab to the overtly Xian among us, yes? It must have been delicious to witness the look on her face. For everything else there's Mastercard. The manager came over and asked both parties to leave since they couldn't behave themselves. A few observations are in order:

1. At least being gay in the obnoxious American South is better than being gay in Uganda, where thanks to the pious and fervent evangelism of some US Conservative Xian groups, one can now get a life prison term for homosexual behavior. Homosexual behavior is illegal to some degree in 37 African Xian or Muslim countries. In another half a dozen or so Islamic countries, the penalty is death. So glad we have these religions of peace and love around to keep us in line, yes?

2. If you are offended by my friends clever remark about *"crawling out of an abortion bucket"* (I'm still laughing about it...the balls to say that out loud!), think of what the woman said. The gay clerk in no way provoked it. She shot her mouth off and got an instant retort which said loud and clear: *"You can't get away with that bullshit anymore."* She has the freedom of speech here in the US to be as bigoted and obnoxious as she pleases, but one can't hide behind religious justification anymore and get away with it. She got a powerful dose of equally free speech in response.

3. The lady in question may be an otherwise admirable human being. She may be a great mom, a terrific grandma, charitable to the poor, what have you. Maybe not a saint, but probably not a terrible person either, prolly just an average citizen,

usually polite and accommodating to kin and strangers, every bit as much as the rest of us are. And that's the point. Her religious beliefs are probably what motivated her to shoot her mouth off. It is plain as day in the Bible; faggots and their behaviors are abominable (OT) and deserve death (NT). So, as a real Xian, she was fully justified, right? Just following what she was taught, it's in the book. The Good Book. And I betcha she wasn't born homophobic. She learned it somewhere along the way. In western KY, there's a whole lot of folks that learned the same thing and they don't like behaviors that don't conform to the purity of their divine laws. Damn faggots!

4. Suppose she had said, *"Gook", "Nigger", "Spic,"* or (since I'm Italian) *"Wop"*, instead of *"faggot"*? Wouldn't the manager have asked her to leave immediately for insulting an employee? Would the crowd around her be more incensed at a racial slur than a homophobic one?

5. Would she have been that nasty to the salesclerk for belonging to any other group? Would she have been that nasty for any other reason than her religion?

6. That lady was a most likely a moderate. Living in America, we will give her the benefit of the doubt that she wouldn't want the *"faggot"* imprisoned, tortured, or killed. But denigrating him in public was A-OK. This is what religion does to people. Dehumanization, placing someone in an 'outgroup' is the first step to real discrimination. Just ask any black person. Or any Jew.

7. Ask yourself if you wouldn't be real tired as so many of my gay friends are, of being the subject of denigration by conservative Xians, as well as the incessant, but oh-so-sincere speculation by the "liberal" ones as to what the Bible really means about just what to do with those homosexuals?

"Should we ignore all the clobber passages like the secularists ask us, and just forget about thinking in terms of anyone's sexual preferences?"

"Should we hate the Sin but love the Sinner?"

"Should we commit them to reparative therapy, like my minister says?"

"Should they be imprisoned for the common good?"

"Do the Islamist states have it right, that death is the best option? After all, it's in our scriptures as much as theirs."

Wouldn't you be fucking sick of people discussing you and your behavior and what should be done with you? I would, I don't know how they put up with it. My buddy didn't. Most religions are dominant where they originated. The "Big 2" spread beyond their origin due to conquest; Islam spread to the left and right of the Arabian Peninsula. Xianity, with a 500 year head start, was the first to spread out of the Middle East. Riding on the coattails of the Roman Empire's prior subjugation, it spread to Europe, then it was transported without much competition to the New World. This shows us all how arbitrary our religious upbringing is, occurring solely by the accident of our birth.

Here's the numbers on the "Big 2" and the Reincarnation religions and the Unbelieving Scum based on an estimated 7.3 billion humans alive on the planet today:

Xians, over 2 billion.

Muslims, over 1.5 billion.

Buddhists and Hindus combined, 1.4 billion.

Non-Believers/Unaffiliated, nearly 2 billion.

So even if you are a member of one of the Big Two, please try to remember that 70-80% of the rest of us don't read your book. We will never pick one up to look for guidance in our lives, won't give it second thought, will never go to your church or attend one of your rituals, and won't convert on our deathbeds, ever. Get over your arrogance in thinking you got it all down and we will of course one day "see the light". The only light the rest of us see is the holes in your claim for having the one true religion. To you believers of course, your guy had the real revelations and everybody else's prophets just heard voices in their head...right. Us secular folks are now vociferously and stridently pointing out all religions are based on this same absurd and arrogant claim. It's only been a couple hundred years since the Enlightenment and barely ten since this New Enlightenment took off. We can put a real dent in the arrogant and unfounded idea that some guy's dream has any external validity at all. All prophets just heard voices in their head. Dreams don't reveal any ultimate reality. Despite the absurd pleadings of the holy: they are just dreams. It's time that the dreams of a select few charismatic males in history stop destroying the dreams of uncounted millions because they sanction the arrogant moralizing of the liberal, moderate, and pissed off conservative followers of religions worldwide. My gay buddy was pissed off too, he'd had enough. And to my liberal Xian friends, this moralizing is in your book. And it keeps the evangelizing types among you in business.

Moralizing to the Extreme

Barack Obama has made more than a few politically incorrect statements concerning religion now and again, throughout his candidacy, and time in office. A prime example was at the 2014 National Prayer Breakfast, where he had the unmitigated audacity to clearly observe *"Religions make all people do bad things."* In covering the huge flap over Obama's comment, the Washington Post did a nice job reviewing the details of the Crusades, Inquisition, US slavery and subsequent Jim Crow activities in the American South, and the resulting horrors perpetrated by Xians guided by their holy book. Their report was a great read, very factual and matter of fact, and a good sample of information about religion and the bad behavior it can initiate and sanction. The best part of Obama initiating the flap was that his observation was discussed, dissed, and cussed everywhere in the media immediately afterward. The first reactions of most of course, both from the journalists covering the story and from those commenting from the public at large, were predominantly conservative outrage: over-the-top emotional rants, full of "dissing my religion" reactionary rhetoric, or what I call "butthurt bitching" to use more modern vernacular. But the information got out there. The discussion was everywhere. The horrific pix of lynching's all over the South from the early 20th century were undeniable, and full of burned black male bodies, tortured, beaten, strangled, and filleted. And white folks, lotsa good Xian white folks, just standing around smiling, not worried in the least their god or anyone else might disapprove.

The comments to this particular Post article ranged from understanding the reality of Xiansanity's inglorious past, to outright denial and just more hatred of Obama. What was missing in the article and in the majority of the comments, was the admission that religion is and was to blame. As admirable a job of well-researched historical coverage which was published, the article let religion off the hook in the end, as most journalists, pundits, commentators, and those commenting from the public are apt to do. To many, it is extremism that is to blame, never the religion. Extremists can hijack any religion; Xianity or Islam are not to blame. The religions and their books are humanity's sources of moral guidance and behavior, so say the religionists. It is those damn extremists and their immoral behavior, that's where the blame lies. What's so bogus about that reasoning is, if one could eliminate the passages in the holy books that the extremists follow, try then to imagine what guidance and justification there would be for their very specific "extreme" acts.

The Charlie Hebdo killers couldn't have been clearer about avenging the Prophet for forbidden images made of him. Can you imagine them performing the same attack without those passages in their scriptures of Koran and hadith telling them to do so?

"Let's go kill some cartoonists in Paris today, just for fun, at random, something extreme to do because I'm feeling real extreme today."

Or on any given day in the American South of the all too recent past:

"Let's torture, lynch and set on fire a random man today, we did a Chinese guy last week. Let's do a black man today. We are extremists looking for something extreme to do and hey, let's get the whole neighborhood to watch, they really dig it"

Or the Crusades:

"On the way to the Holy Land lets rape, pillage, mutilate and murder an ethnic group in their enclaves in every big town we pass through, I know there aren't that many Gypsies left so let's get medieval on somebody else. We need something really extreme...hmmm. I know, those Jews!"

Without the specific scriptural verses or exhortations of theologians characterizing the Jews or blacks as subhuman "Christ Killers" or "Children of Ham, destined to be slaves" why would the Crusaders, off to reclaim the Holy Land from the Muslims, decimate Jewish communities along the way or centuries later, good Xian white folk lynch blacks? Why do Muslims get so incensed over cartoons? Just an "extreme" whim? No, it takes religion, religious thinking, absurd, religious ideas to make normal humans do extreme things to their fellow humans. Religions provide the sacred justification, the righteous feeling and the specific target. Religion has everything to do with it

Any ideology which puts its ideas, claims and behavioral proscriptions above individual rights and freedoms directly sanctions inhuman behavior. The ISIS Muslims of today and the white southern Xians of the recent US past, are and were just following what is written in their book. Few want to own up to that. Ideologies kill, both political and religious. Religion has everything to do with the "extremism" we see throughout history. Moralizing can go to extremes as Obama noted when religion is the driving force.

Evangelonepotism

Franklin Graham, Billy Graham's son, was featured in a 2014 Yahoo News report on ABC News' "This Week" panel discussion regarding gay behavior and marriage, which solicited over 6,000 comments in 2 days! Franklin, of course, toed the Evangelical party line and reiterated that gays are sinners for their behavior. Although the details of the concept and assignment of sin have been open to a wide range of interpretations for centuries, the verses are there in both the OT and NT, for pompous moralizers like Graham and his equally sanctimonious dad, to propound upon. They think they have the higher moral ground because they are hyper-religious and claim that gays are sinners and must stop their abominable behavior, repent it, or burn in hell. It's not a stretch of logic or an interpretation at all, the verses are all there in that nasty little book.

All the justification the keepers of Conservative Xiansanity like re-Graham and his ilk need is in any of the "clobber passages" of their "Good Book." OT passages in Leviticus and elsewhere, and NT passages primarily in that asshole Paul's writings (including the forged ones), characterize homosexual behavior as an abomination and deserving of death. Leviticus, chapters 18 and 20, and Romans 1 are prime examples. The Bible is a primitive, barbaric little book and women and gays have been paying for it for a couple of millennia now. Much to Franklin and Big Daddy Graham's chagrin, times are a-changing. More and more people, especially the educated and the "breaking-out-of-the-cocoon" younger Xians of today, don't buy the Grahams repressive Evangelical horseshit anymore. From the report:

"In the last decade, public opinion has swung dramatically on key issues pertaining to gay rights, including gay marriage and adoption. An ABC News/Washington Post poll from March found approval for same-sex marriage at an all-time high: 59 percent of total respondents said they approve, including 75 percent of respondents under 30 years old."

And why? Because most young folks today actually know some gay people. They interact with them on a daily basis. Normal human empathy and understanding, which all religions stifle for one cockamamie reason or another, takes over. The bullshit of this Bible verse or that, becomes readily apparent, and easily dismissed, as the unfounded, primitive, repressive old ideas that they truly are. Young people are better educated on the nastiness of the Bible, and refuse to repeat the bigotry of their parents and grandparents. Dinosaurs like re-Graham and his notoriously anti-Semitic dear old dad do not speak for people of today, who can see through the absurd moralistic claims of Evangelical Xiansanity. The 6,000 plus comments to the ABC News article ran the gamut of complete support for Graham and the Bible, to abject rejection. This was one of the better rebuttals:

"God, this thread is now over 6,000 posts and we're getting nowhere. So may I propose a solution? All of us who are in mainstream America need to stop giving a rat's butt what the fundamentalist evangelicaloonies want or demand. They will NEVER be happy, they thrive on having enemies to battle. That's their nature. If they don't have a political or social battle to fight, they have no purpose. They need a cause and they will always find something to hate. So let's just stop caring and ignore them. God, why give them any credence, as if what they say matters a rat's ass! Let's all get back to the process of evolution... without them!"

I couldn't agree more or said it any clearer. We do need to ignore the moralizing of the Bible waving buffoons like Franklin Graham, and continue to marginalize their influence on modern society. They should get no respect for their arrogance in telling us all how we must behave, to conform to their interpretations of Bible verses. We need to accelerate the dismissal of that shitty little book, and its sanctimonious interpreters. The trend is going that way. Let's make it exponential soon. We will move on quickly to a better, more tolerant, less delusional society without them. Evangelicals out of touch? Absolutely. They have been, for centuries. It's just become more apparent, and socially acceptable, to say so.

Stealth Moralizing II: Brainwashed by Xian Ideas on Sex

Darrel Ray, author and secular sex educator, often opens his talks with a rather direct and simple question: *"Do you masturbate?"* Having a rather hip crowd one night, the majority of us (your author included), raised our hands enthusiastically, and declared unequivocally: *"Fuck yeah we do!"*

But not everybody. Quite a few didn't raise their hands. He then reminded us all that surveys have shown for years now that roughly 93% of men and 70% of women, certainly do pleasure themselves, so there were more than a few of us out there that were lying! That sets the tone for many of the excellent points he relays throughout his presentations. We live in a culture dominated by religion, predominantly the Xian religion in its various forms here in the US, which shame us into denying our sexuality. Darrel relates an anecdote about a Baptist minister of whom he once asked that same "uncomfortable" question: *"Do you masturbate?"* The good reverend not surprisingly, pleaded the 5th and readily admitted should Dr. Ray ask his entire congregation of God-fearing Baptists that very same question, most assuredly no hands would be raised... and that yes, the vast majority would be lying. This illustrates a second major theme of his lectures: "Biology Happens." If you haven't read his book, *Sex & God: How Religion Distorts Sexuality* do so. Without giving any details away, this is the blurb from Amazon:

> *"Why are all the major religions consumed with sex? What makes sex so important, whether Buddhism or Islam, Christianity or Mormonism? What is the impact of religion on human sexuality? This book explores this and more. It ventures into territory that has never been examined. You will be surprised at how much religion has influenced your sexuality, who you marry, the pleasure you get or don't get from sex, and what you can do about it."*

Despite whatever religious upbringing we've experienced (or not), except for a select few, we all masturbate, have sex, watch porn, etc. Biology Happens. Sex is normal, yes, even self-sex. It is nothing to be ashamed of. We are sexual beings just like any other animal, but we humans are also very unique in our species specific sexual behaviors and physiology. Darrel spends a good portion of his speeches comparing the other primate's sexual behaviors and anatomy to ours. Just damn good, fascinating, no-nonsense, solid biological findings, and given Darrel's upfront and humorous style, very entertaining info that every American should know about our species' sexuality. By nature, despite what the churches tell you, despite the abject denial of our very normal sexuality by our Xian friends, like the Baptist minister and his all-too-typical congregation, ashamed of their own sexual practices, we are a very sexy species having thousands of sex acts for every live birth, way beyond the frequencies of any other species. We don't just have sex to procreate. We use it for bonding, stress release, fun, and it is all OK. That's the message. It is OK.

All the old virgin men in the Catholic Church (later joined by their similarly repressive Protestant counterparts), have been telling us differently for millennia and they are utterly, dead-nuts, straight out, fucktard wrong. Their negative influence however, in fact the utterly repressive influence of all religions on our psyche, is a theme Dr. Ray returns to again and again. Even us enlightened, liberated secularists who may have jettisoned the absurdities and cruelties of religious belief altogether, still suffer from Xiansanity inspired sexual shame and guilt. He points out one telling example of this in the reluctance, the shame, many of us "Christian Atheists" as he calls us, display when we have a hard time raising our hand when it is time to stand and be counted as masturbating humans, even when we know ourselves, and damn well most of us the rest of the audience, certainly are.

The first time I heard Darrel Ray speak years ago at SIU in Carbondale, Illinois, I just couldn't, wouldn't, didn't raise my hand either, I'll admit it. In a crowd of 100-200 strangers, 100 miles from home that was still way too personal, too revealing. Couldn't do it. And why did I feel that way, as many still do? Ray pulls no punches, in his book or his talks, in laying the blame for our shame squarely on the doorstep of religions, damn near all of them. Thanks to Uncle Darrel, I proudly raised my hand the next time around. Read the book, and/or next time Darrel Ray is in town, don't miss his informative, entertaining, and enlightening talk. His books and lectures are right on in exposing the absurd and cruel moralizing of religion, through just damn good education and compassionate acceptance of our very normal, healthy, and wonderful sexual abilities.

Sports Evangelizing

Max Lucado, pastor of Oak Hill Church, San Antonio Texas weighed in on the necessity and benefits of prayer on the football field in a 2014 USA Today article entitled *"Husain Abdullah needs our company in prayer."* Pastor Lucado assured all that the penalty given to the Kansas City Chiefs Abdullah during an NFL contest, brought to the forefront a more important issue than the 15 yards he got for prostrating himself in Muslim prayer posture. Pastor Lucado says prayer matters, especially to sports fans. His reasoning was that not only do many Americans pray, but 13% of those who do, go so far as to pray for their favorite sports team to win. Just as the openly Evangelical Xian quarterback, Tim Tebow, has prayed so regularly on the field to Yahweh and/or Jesus to help him win, Husain Abdullah thanked Allah for helping him intercept a pass for a touchdown.

No matter to Max that the ISIS fellas running amok across the Middle East are praying to the same Allah as Mr. Abdullah. They fervently intend for their team to win too, by ensuring Allah's caliphate is established worldwide, and forever. And those of us who won't convert to what they vehemently assert is the only true religion, their Islam, practiced only as they do, should be subject to the rule of the Islamic faithful, and pay the appropriate taxes to them, as it once was during the Golden Age of Islam. Check it out. It is in their Prophet's book and his sayings. The ISIS team is making it happen in the areas they have overrun, as we speak.

Never mind Max, that your Xian god to whom Tim consistently appealed, will send Abdullah and the other 1.5 billion Muslims on the planet straight to Hell for not accepting Jesus Christ as their personal savior as Mr. Tebow has, which he regularly demonstrates for our spiritual benefit. Max reminds us, we pray for all sorts of personal needs such as health, safety, parking spots, lotto wins, even safeties and touchdowns. Isn't it odd that the Creator of the Universe, whichever one you happen to appeal to, can't stop tsunamis or hurricanes, cure cancer, or Alzheimer's, can't regrow a finger or an earlobe back for ya, but he will gladly direct that spiraling pigskin into the hands of your teammate and not your opponent's... sometimes. Well maybe, one can never tell, but Max assures us that it is the prayer itself, the *"act of ultimate faith that counts."* Prayer, within two equally absurd and violently contradictory ultimate faiths, to be sure, but faiths to be respected nonetheless.

Max thinks we should join Abdullah in prayer. Cool. Let's have Tim, Max, Abdullah and one of the ISIS boys all get together to pray alongside each other, and discuss the wonders of prayer, who they are praying to, and exactly what they are all praying for, shall we? I'd like that. On national TV. Maybe halftime on Monday Night

Football. Tim got it all started, *"brought gridiron prayer to the forefront"* according to Max so let's let Mr. Tebow speak first about how Jesus, the Son of God, helped him win many a football game, and has guided him without question through his entire life, and will provide his eternal salvation because of his unwavering faith in the resurrection, just as Pastor Max's Oak Hill Church website proclaims:

"The death of Christ on the cross is the only sufficient payment for our sins. All have sinned, but all can be saved. This salvation is available for any who put their trust in Christ as Savior (Romans 3:23, 6:23; John 3:16). Those trusting Christ should repent of sin, confess their faith, and be baptized" (Romans 10:9; Acts 2:38).

Max would nod his head approvingly I'm sure, because he and Tim also know for certain that:

"Christ will one day return and judge all people (2 Thessalonians 1:8-10; 1 Thessalonians 4:13-18). Believers will be welcomed into God's presence in Heaven. Unbelievers will be in Hell, separated from God's presence."

However, Husain from the Chiefs and his Muslim brother from ISIS would probably just shake their heads in disbelief almost smugly, only somewhat bemused, because everyone knows Allah does not beget nor is begotten. So Jesus Christ can't possibly be the Son of God, nor God himself. There can be no Son, or two (or three), persons in god, or different manifestations of god, in some kind of Trinity. As the Islamic Shahada plainly states: *"there is but one god Allah, and Muhammad is his prophet."* Period. All else is utter blasphemy. It's on the ISIS flag, fellas, plain as day. And the Taliban's and Hamas' and Al Nusra's and the Saudi flag among others.

In addition, one can't help but notice there is a sword proudly displayed below the single most important tenet of the "Religion of Peace", on many of those flags. Be that as it may, as far as Tim and Max's equally important resurrection of their savior, well, it never happened. As all good Muslims know, Jesus never died in the first place, he wasn't really crucified, it just appeared like he was when, in actuality, he was whisked off to heaven in one of the greatest switcheroos of all time. Christ the non-divine prophet, was merely whisked back to heaven before he died, so sorry Tim and Max, no crucifixion, no resurrection, no salvation. Muslims know this to be absolutely true. Period.

But take heart folks, because Mr. Tebow and Pastor Lucado and the rest of us 5.5 billion non-Muslims on the planet have every chance to submit to the will of Allah, take an Arab name in recognition of the fact that we were born Muslim as every Muslim already knows, and obtain the only real salvation from a fiery eternity that otherwise awaits us all. Yeah, sure, let's all help Abdullah pray. Let us pray alongside of him as Max suggests. I wonder if Tim and Max, along with all the good Christian folks at Max's fundamentalist Oak Hill megachurch down there in Texas, really want Abdullah's god to carry the day and win the big game? As Max reminds us prayer can be: *"as simple as kneeling down in the end-zone of life in gratitude to God for a victory."* Team ISIS couldn't agree more.

6

CONSERVATISM

"It is the human being that is meant to be equal, not his or her beliefs. It is the human being who is worthy of the highest respect and who is sacred, not his or her beliefs or those imputed on them. The problem is that religion sees things the other way around and this is why religions must be relegated to a private matter. More importantly than the fact that it divides, excludes, denies, restricts and so on is the compelling fact that when it comes to religion it is not the equality, rights, freedoms, welfare of the child, man or woman that is paramount but religion itself."

-Maryam Namazie

"Old beliefs die hard even when demonstrably false"

-E. O. Wilson

Conservative Gloom and Doom

Cal Thomas is a conservative columnist who, with his counterpart and adversary Bob Beckel, a liberal Democratic strategist, has bantered for a few years now back and forth with Bob in the recurring USA Today *"Common Ground"* Op-ed installments. I usually skip reading what two old white guys might bitch about to each other, but Mr. Thomas had this to say in 2014, about his fear of the impending demise of the US, and it really put the hook in me:

"The world no longer respects us, terrorists don't fear us, the border with Mexico has been erased, major cities resemble war zones, a failure of US Middle East policy, $17 trillion debt, fewer fathers in the home, overflowing prisons, a sense of entitlement rather than personal responsibility ..."

There's a lot more, but I won't go much further with his laments. There's plenty enough to chew on already. Later in the same piece:

"When a nation loses its moral center... The modern media glorify promiscuous sex and everything else that would have shocked our grandparents, another cause of our decline..."

Then he quotes the Bible, and from Judges no less, which as we have seen is one of the most disgusting chapters written in any book, ever. Yahweh, when not smiting his own people for idolatry, is busy commanding them to slaughter men, women, and children, to burn them alive in their villages, gouge their eyes out, slit them from stem to stern, behead them, impale them through the forehead. Charming, right? Such a representative slice of moral centered-ness from the "Good Book" itself. There's more violence at god's command in those 17 pages of that particularly ugly chapter than in an ISIS training manual, and this is Mr. Thomas' source for moral guidance and perspective on modern problems? Holy Moly. He harkens back to a 2,000 year-old book from a rather un-advanced and barbaric culture, from the most primitive and repressive of times in human history, for guidance on how to reshape the future and tackle the problems of today that he sees as so depressing...and save America herself (hooray!!!). Oh my.

Where to begin? Looking backwards, instead of to the future for answers and looking back to what he sees as old "authorities", instead of looking forward and bringing modern knowledge to bear on modern problems. Really? That's the Conservatives idea of a fruitful approach? Fuck that old book, that's your first mistake. Cal is listed as an evangelical Xian in his wiki article, and referred to as both Catholic and Protestant elsewhere on the net. His own website and his Fox News bio don't say. His commentary leans toward evangelical; he is not happy about gays or birth control and he, of course, quotes the Bible. Whatever his affiliation, I'd like to address his pessimism for today's accelerating decline as he sees it. Let us turn the clock back 50 years to 1964-1969 for some comparisons:

"The world no longer respects us." How do you think the world felt about us in the midst of the Vietnam morass: the destruction and casualties, including the not-so-collateral damage of bombing Hanoi, Haiphong, and other sites as well as the Agent Orange and napalm decimation of civilians? Estimates of total dead on both sides, combatants and civilians ranges from 750,000 to a million, during roughly a decade of our involvement. Compare that to estimates for a decade of Iraq/Afghanistan conflicts, which left roughly 6,000 US, and maybe 100,000 civilian dead in "collateral damage." The carnage was worse by a factor of ten and not merely collateral, but much of it quite deliberate. What sort of respect are you looking for Cal? Did we really earn any respect then or deserve any now?

"Terrorists don't fear us?" Well, Cal, Obama as a Democratic sitting President, surely didn't hamper the military in taking out bin Laden, nor the Somali pirates, nor Gaddafi, and he's been under fire throughout his presidency from his own constituency and the rest of the civilized world for his sidestepping Gitmo, not to mention his hundreds of regular drone strikes on suspected Islamists all over the Muslim world. Just what else would you have him do? He was damn aggressive for any kind of President. I've said it before; if Obama was white and a Republican he'd have acquired sainthood faster than you can say Ronald Reagan.

As far as the Mexican border being erased. A common derogatory term one heard regularly in the 60's was *"wetback."* Illegal immigrants are not a new problem, and the economic reasons behind the border issues loom larger now more than ever. These workers are still a vital part of our economy. Speaking of Ronald Reagan, the patron saint of the Republican Right, Ronnie pardoned millions of immigrants with the stroke of a pen.

"Major cities resemble combat zones." Yes, Mr. Thomas, the gun violence in the poor neighborhoods of Chicago and LA, for example, is out of control. However, I remember as a kid during the 60's race riots when the West Side of Chicago and Watts in LA actually were burning for blocks, for miles. They literally were burned out war zones after the fires and mass looting. The gun problem in this country surely isn't the doing of the libtards. If we live in an obsessive gun culture compared to the rest of the world, blame it on your fellow conservatives clinging to gun ownership and accessibility, coupled with the equally insane drug war that creates the violent turf wars over one of the only sources of income in the economic wastelands of our inner city neighborhoods.

"A failure of US Middle East Policy." Should we go back to Bush's no exit, nation-building Iraq and Afghanistan fiascoes? The whole Middle East is a powder keg of Islamic sectarian violence, medieval political structures, repression, inter-denominational religious hatreds, underdevelopment, corruption, theocracy, and science denial. Like we are gonna fix all that somehow? Like the US is somehow responsible to fix all that? They may kill each other for decades. Do things still suck there as they have been seesawing back and forth since 1948? You bet. Our failure? Hardly. Our responsibility? Only partially, and no amount of military action will suddenly solve things. We armed the Taliban against the Soviets. The Taliban then performed atrocities on the defenseless Shi'a in Afghanistan, every bit as horrific and on the same scale as ISIS is doing today. The Taliban PR mogul just didn't post slickly produced YouTube videos back in the 80's. And we did nothing. The Conservatives now are screaming for boots on the ground against ISIS. Did we give a damn about similarly slaughtered and enslaved Afghanis of the wrong Muslim sect back then? The US's failure is in heavy-handed nation-building which is doomed to fail.

"$17 trillion in debt." 4 trillion on Bush's wars in Islamic countries, a 700 billion dollar defense budget bloated bigger than what the next 14 other countries spend? Can't blame that stuff on the liberal Democrats, gays, and welfare moms either, Cal. Oh, and I forgot all the subsidies and corporate tax shelters and breaks that leave many US corporations paying little to no taxes. Don't think that was part of the libtard agenda either.

"Fewer fathers in the home." The divorce rate among Evangelicals and Catholics (whatever denomination Mr. Thomas actually identifies with), isn't any better than the general population. Can't blame that on lack of religion, or the lack of a focus on the family, which Xians are so quick to claim they hold higher ground on. Hardly, Cal. Xians are no better than the rest of us as far as absentee fathers, and we all love our families regardless of religion or lack thereof. Times are changing, pal. Many of us do serial monogamy now. Even staunch conservative heroes like Rush Limbaugh and Newt Gingrich have hopped on the bandwoman, 'er bandwagon, so to speak (it was there, I had to take it), and have married and divorced how many times? Many

people worldwide opt not marry to have children, given their countries do not provide a US style tax break. So yes, our family structure is changing and Conservatives are as much a part of that trend as liberals. Get used to it.

"Overflowing prisons." We can hang that one directly on Conservatives as well. War on Drugs anyone? Billions pissed away and 2 million locked down in the US. That's more than China, a repressive regime with 5 times the population! Oops. Since Ronnie Reagan and George Herbert Bush led us down the path of righteousness to root out all those evil people making themselves feel better, or making a buck where there are no other jobs except drugs, we have loaded our prisons. And like every other nation in the world with 30+ years of utter failure to reduce demand or supply, we are finally legalizing benign drugs, and backing off on sentencing, no thanks to conservatives like Mr. Thomas.

"A sense of entitlement rather than personal responsibility." Don'tcha remember the 60's mantra, *"Tune in, turn on, drop out"*? Cal is as old as I am so surely he must remember those good old days. Damn hippies lying about getting stoned and tripping balls on Owlsley's Kool-Aid. Don't see as much of that as we used to but somehow with Conservatives, the present always sucks worse and is in decline. Yesterday was always better and a return to the "good old days" and "old time religion" is what's for dinner. And them ISIS fellas couldn't agree more. But my favorite whine of his just says it all:

"When a nation loses its moral center... promiscuous sex... another cause of our decline." You KNEW he'd get sex in there somehow. Whose moral center are we talking about? Demand personhood for zygotes and embryos, and cry murder over the abortion of a non-conscious, ball of cells or barely formed embryo, but a living adult human with relationships, dependents, loved ones... psshh, mere collateral damage or cannon fodder, or an injectable receptacle for righteous revenge under our remaining capital punishment laws. The death penalty, a Biblically inspired punishment, remains popular in heavy-duty Xian states like Georgia, Texas, Oklahoma and Florida, despite being jettisoned by the rest of the developed world. Gays and fornicators and atheists should all burn in Hell. Some higher moral ground ya got there, pal. Center this.

Promiscuous sex? Again, remember the late 60's when the pill was new, the AIDS epidemic hadn't appeared yet, and free love, hippie communes, the beginning of inter-racial and open homosexual sex were just taking off? That's when you lost the war between the sheets, Cal. Your whining is a bit late. Please try to remember whatever denomination you belong to, the vast majority of the rest of us don't go to your church. We may not buy into much of your belief system regarding abortion, birth control, homosexuality, or sexual practices either.

So, how much worse is it today really? What about the 5 decades of incredible progress in human rights: civil, woman's, gays, and now (horrors!) the secular movement! Charitable giving is at an all-time high. Even most poor people have air conditioning, damn few did in the 60's. Childhood deaths worldwide before age 5 have plummeted to a tenth of previous levels, despite more than a doubling of the population. All thanks to huge outpourings of aid to developing countries, in the form of vaccines and education on clean water, and municipal health practices. Can't Conservatives ever concentrate on what's been done, what progress we have made and can accelerate in the future? I'll take the less than 7,000 US service persons' deaths from Iraq/Afghanistan over the nearly 60,000 Vietnam deaths any day. I wonder if at times the Conservatives can't appreciate progress or even acknowledge it 'cuz progress is change, and they just don't like change. There is a lot of psychological data on personality types that tend to conservatism, and they tend to prefer less change.

Just what does Mr. Thomas want? What will save his vision of 'Murica? Well he longs for a *"revival,"* a *"concert of prayer"* like in the late 1800's. That will fix it all! Glory, Hallefuckinglujah! Fuck me. Didn't Michelle Bachmann and a host of other charismatic leaning evangelical politicos try prayer to stop Obamacare before it even started? Didn't Governor Rick Perry host that big August tent revival prayer fest in his home state before the 2012 election primary to fix our declining moral center, convert the gays, cure acne, and garner a few votes in the process? He even put out an official State proclamation to pray for rain to end the Texas drought not long before that. Revivals and prayer concerts with dorky Xian "rock" bands don't seem to work so good anyway, Cal. If there is a god, he knows that Xian Rock music suuuuuuckssss and shouldn't be called rock anyway. And if He exists, He ignores 99.99999% of prayers without doubt, and the other .00001% that people claim may have been answered are always sketchy with no real evidence ever forthcoming that god really did it.

Conservatives don't seem to like change, progress, *"social experimentation,"* sex in general, or drugs, it seems. Anything that might feel good, or change things must be bad somehow. Concentrating on the *"bad"* seems to be the preoccupation of the Conservatives, the religious. After all, they are taught we are all incorrigible, inveterate sinners that cannot function right without god's grace and will burn in hell for all our inevitable sins. With that bleak and absurd worldview as a starting point, it is no surprise you look for signs of the irreversible decay you are taught is the defining aspect of human nature. Yes, there are problems in the world, and in the US today. However, one could make what looks like a pretty strong case, as I did above, that the world has dramatically improved since the 60's when Cal and I were kids, and is comparatively a much, much better place, even for twice as many people to live in. The whole of human progress, since the Enlightenment and Age of Reason, and especially with the institutionalization of science, employing millions of full-time practicing scientists working on how the world really works and our real world problems, the exponential expansion of which we take for granted as normal in the 21st century, has been one of greater freedoms, less experience of violence, healthier living, and extended life expectancy even among the poorest of the poor.

Let's focus on that reality as a basis for our worldview, and perspective on human potential and a plan for the future, not on the phony bleak conceptions of human nature and ignorant perspectives we inherited from 2,000 year old hopelessly primitive and barbaric writings. One of these days I'll get a chance to research in depth the literature that must be out there on conservatism, because the more I observe, I really wonder, what have Conservatives ever done for us, ever, but preserve the status quo of repression, bitch and moan, and delay inevitable progress?

We went to the moon the first time 46 years ago. Haven't been back since '72. And we went on less computer power than all of us have on our smartphones in the palm of our hands. We now spend more and more on having things like 3-4 times as many aircraft carriers as anyone else, but gotta strangle the NASA budget down to the barest essentials and shitcan the Super Collider. That's what Conservatives have done for us, along with the War on Drugs, Wars in Muslim countries, and the Republican War on Women: their preoccupation with restricting woman's reproductive rights to whatever the Evangelicals think is what god really wants. A focus on our supposed "*innate depravity*" and the past does no good now, or ever. What if we had listened to the Conservatives like Cal Thomas, the "heavy-duty oh so certain they know what god wants us NOT to do and we'd better listen or else" Xians, the religionists, the people that cite chapter and verse? Black folks would be still riding in the back of the bus, maybe in chains, women wouldn't vote, and gays wouldn't be getting married anywhere. Yup, just what the world needs, more chapter and verse.

Don't Touch Yourself in the Middle East, in Fact Don't...Anything.

Consider the plight of an anonymous Iranian blogger, who has to deal with utterly invasive, persistent nonsense all day, every day, thanks to the smothering existence of the religion they call Islam. Between the corny, melodramatic comments about football and such in his 101 item list excerpted below, there are yet dozens of infractions against his stifling religion which his family, his peers, his neighbors, his teachers, his imam, his government, his entire ubiquitous and enveloping culture would be on his case about. It is maddening to read.

This is mainstream Islam, not fringe or extremist or fundamental. You would have to find some really hard-core Jehovah's, Baptists, or Church of Christ families, maybe Fred Phelp's Westboro Baptist clan or the Quiverfull Movement yahoos (think of the Duggar dumberrific dynasty) to find this level of suffocating ideology, that infuses damn near every waking moment of Muslim life. Oddly enough, only the Ultra-Orthodox Jews, the sworn enemies of the Muslims come as close to living in the complete mental cage, as Ayaan Hirsi Ali puts it, that so many, if not most, within Islam experience. It's like living under a fucking wet blanket which you can't throw off, and if you do somebody will see you. Xianity was once this invasive centuries ago, but for most Xians nowadays, they couldn't imagine living under such constant tension to behave properly.

Check out his list posted on the ex-hijabi fashion journal site:

101 Sins I Commit During the World Cup and Ramadan Just in One Day
1) *I eat.*
2) *I drink.*
3) *I smoke weed.*
4) *I masturbate.*
5) *I have sex (if I can get some).*
6) *I feel angry at a god who isn't there.*
7) *The spiritual speeches are revolting to me.*
8) *I continue being an atheist.*
9) *I drink alcohol.*
10) *I touch dogs.*
11) *I look at the hairs of women.*
12) *I watch porn.*
13) *I read the Koran again. The only catharsis is mocking the book.*
14) *I think of all the political prisoners. Are they fasting too?*
15) *I wish I could eat pork.*
16) *I actually feel proud – at least I thought for myself.*
17) *Against all odds I still hope. Isn't hope a sin?*
    See you all in Hell, my human friends.
I will have sinned at least 3,030 times by the time this month has ended.
See you all in Hell, my human friends.
haramadan

People aren't stupid. Anywhere. In any religion. When you get them thinking outside of religious thought, as with this young Iranian citizen, they can see they have to live different than 90% of the rest of the world. Especially nowadays with the Internet. It must be impossible for folks in Islamic countries (or any religious enclave within any country for that matter) not to plainly see how people in developed countries, mostly democracies, now both in the East and West, live in such comparative freedom than under the stifling theocracies of the Muslim world. They know deep down it is insipid and draining and worthless, but can't get out of it.

End Religion Now! That's my mantra. Let's free everyone who lives under its tyranny: gays, poor Catholic women having 6 kids, apostates in jail, women in veils (and psychological chains), kids living under fundamental Xiansanity, and a few hundred million or so young people like this Iranian brother hiding out as non-believers, who know better but are trapped in the cage of Islam.

Zygotes, Embryos, and Slaves

A short while back, one of the better-known conservative and outspoken professors where I taught likened zygotes, embryos, and slaves as equal in person-hood, in a rather lengthy editorial in our University newspaper. The longer editorial space was granted to longstanding respected academics, while us regular folks only got 800 words. I kinda took exception to his rather strained analogy in a reply to the editor. It probably didn't help my chances for tenure. Oh well.

A human fertilized egg (a zygote), a blastocyst (the hollow ball of undifferentiated embryonic cells), or the subsequent embryo are not persons, they have no functioning brain, no consciousness, and feel no pain. Many religious systems: Catholicism, Islam, and some Protestant Christian denominations make such a claim, denying our scientific knowledge of embryonic development. A slave was a living person, fully aware, with a full sense of self, who knew they were alive, felt pain, both the physical kind, and the mental anguish of a life in shackles. A slave was a feeling, thinking, being, fully cognizant of their short, brutal existence wasted in chains, anticipating in full sentience the next day of arduous labor, thirst, hunger, and despair.

The zygote, blastocyst, or embryo know none of this, having no more consciousness than the also very much alive precursor cells of egg and sperm. Most religious based anti-abortionists imbue the zygote with a soul and/or person-hood from the moment of conception, and then attempt to shame us into decrying abortion for killing an unborn human; for being baby killers. The lack of reality and ultimate irony in this sleazy sensational and emotional claim of the pro-life movement, is that their god (if it existed), whichever one they believe in, kills 50-70% of developing blastocysts and embryos in the first few weeks of development, making their god the biggest abortionist of them all by their own definition. Prenatal development, in any creature, human or animal, is an incredibly complex and delicate unfolding of the genetic recipe and thereby spontaneous abortion happens with regularity, primarily due to genetic defects in the first few days, and subsequent implantation difficulties within the first two weeks.

A blastocyst, or early embryo, doesn't even have any neurons yet, much less any sort of functioning brain that the slave or any sufficiently developed post-natal human possesses. Neuro-development: including new neurons, migration, axon and dendritic outgrowth, synapse formation, programmed cell death, and pruning of the nervous system, continues throughout the last 7 months of the prenatal period. It is absurd to think of the early stages of development as anything resembling a developed functioning thinking and conscious human being: a person.

In the 21st century a more reasoned approach to abortion is called for, based on current science and not old religious ideas based in millennia old speculations theologically developed during the Dark Ages. We don't want anyone's religion running our lives, and precisely for the reason that religious ideas are not based in evidence we can all share, but often in foolish antiquated ideas, or unfounded interpretations of some scripture thousands of years old.

Pro-lifers often counter that from the zygote stage and beyond, the fertilized egg has the potential to become a human being and that is what is important, differentiating it from mere sperm and egg. That "potential" idea is a problem. Every one of the at least 400,000 eggs a woman has inside her is also a potential human. By not having sex every time she ovulates one of the approximately 500 eggs she will release during her reproductive years, she denies the chance of another unique human to be born. Your parents could have allowed one of your unborn brothers or sisters to be conceived if they had sex without contraception just one more time. How selfish and cruel. And men produce 100 million genetically unique sperm per day. Untold kabillions (to use a technical term) of potential human beings are never fertilized, never born, reabsorbed back into the man's body or wind up cementing wads of Kleenex together. And remember more than half of the sperm and eggs that are fertilized, don't make it past the first 2 weeks. Some potential.

When we should grant person-hood to the developing embryo or fetus is the question and there is no one set moral answer. We have set a limit at 28 weeks based on viability. Should we use full neurological functioning, or consciousness, or apparent ability to experience pain? Many religions claim there is a full human person present with a god-given soul at the moment of conception. The science refutes both those very old ignorant suppositions. There is not one human cell yet, all cells are undifferentiated in the first days, and there is no evidence of a soul. If you believe a god plugs in a soul at conception, why does He kill 1/2 to 2/3 of them in the first few weeks? And what about twins? Does an angel come back down and quick plug in a second soul when the zygote splits in two? And what happens with twins that get reabsorbed? Does an angel swoop down to remove one soul from the twin whose brain never develops? Religious absurdities drive this whole discussion into silliness

If you leave the religious bullshit out of the issue, you can make an informed decision. We have chosen as a society not to kill persons, those with functioning nervous systems, the ability to feel pain, and other criteria based on a realistic evaluation of the facts of the matter and not on some medieval ideas of spirituality and vitalism, dictated by the irrational dogma of some church.

Progress Stifled for Ridiculous Reasons

"Culture keeps us in chains." I wrote that in my journal in junior college '73 or '74, over 40 years ago. Hard to believe at times. I feel every bit as strongly about the retarding effects of culture as I did then, if not more so. Whatever culture you were brought up in tells you what is acceptable in dress, speech, behavior, even thought. Some cultures are relatively open and accepting of variance; think Northern Europe for example. Others are incredibly repressive, and do not allow any variation in dress and behavior, especially for women, think the Middle East. And the cultural institution that enforces much of the stifling conformity is, of course, religion. We can change all that. That's much of what the New Enlightenment movement is all about:

diminishing religions grip on culture. We are steadily succeeding in loosening the repressive grip on our cultures. The main attack is, by necessity, on religious thought. It pervades every society to some degree. In some, you can get killed for not conforming to proscribed religious norms, with homosexuals and women being the main targets, in other societies it is much more subtle. Repression is not restricted to women and gays, there's plenty of rules for a man's behavior that diminish the enjoyment of our short time on earth or outright destroy it. A short example of what I call "cultural inertia" will illustrate what I mean.

I've been reading various sources on the Middle East and Islam sporadically over the years, but not nearly as much as I have read on Xianity and the West. I'm even less well read on Asian cultures and religions. I'm catching up a bit on Islam though, since, along with Xianity, it represents the "Big 2", the two largest religions, and thereby having the biggest retarding influence on progress worldwide. In reading a story about life in the Gaza strip, and the 1-2 million people trapped there, buffeted by the insane religious and political impasse of the Muslims and Jews in the Middle East, I learn of a man near 60 like me, in poor health (unlike me, I'm lucky enough to be in good health and have access to modern medicine to keep me there for some time longer) who lives in a pasted together shack next to a sewage plant. There's no air conditioning, and only sporadic electricity service to run the couple of fans he has to escape the desert heat. This is typical of the Middle East; the infrastructure is ill maintained and war-torn. He is most likely Sunni Muslim, as is the majority of the population.

The growth rate is 3.2% in Gaza, the 6th highest in the world according to Wikipedia. Nearly 2 million people are already crammed into a strip of beach essentially only 25 miles long and averaging about 5 miles wide (about 125 square miles). For comparison, a typical US city like Milwaukee, WI with a similar 100 square mile area has only a third of the people (600,000) with less than 30% of them below the poverty line, and even they have electricity 24/7 and A/C if they can afford it. Despite 70% of the population in the Gaza strip living below the poverty line, and the insanely crowded and economically isolated conditions for the man I read about and his fellow Gaza citizens, birth control is not an option. He has 3 wives and 20 children!

Perusing a number of websites on Islam and birth control, a few themes emerged. One needs to consult the cultural traditions in the Koran and hadith to see what is proper. One must see what the Prophet did, or what Muslims in the Golden Age did immediately after Muhammad's death, to see if some practice is acceptable today or not. Permanent birth control is forbidden, so sterilization is out. Vasectomy and hysterectomy are not an option. The pill is forbidden as well, unless there is a medical reason for the woman not to get pregnant, but the husband must agree. Good luck with that, as the imams will remind them it is virtuous to make more Muslims. Coitus interruptus is not forbidden, nor are condoms which effect the same thing. However, the hadith has verses which relate that these practices were used by Muhammad solely to avoid getting his slave women pregnant, so it is still best to have as many children with your wife as Allah allows:

"... some people have the foolish notion that the world is becoming overpopulated and the earth's resources are running out. But Allah has made His earth bountiful, and if we trust Him there is certainly enough food and water and air to go around."

-excerpted from the Muttaqi Ismail website.

Sunni Muslims appear to follow the above proscriptions, whereas the Shi'a are a bit more open to family planning. However, 90% or more of the world's Muslims are Sunni. So for my counterpart in the Gaza strip, his options were few. This is as extreme a case of cultural inertia as one may find, and driven mostly by religious thought, based in 1,500 year old writings and subsequent commentaries made by male imams through the ages. He did what he was supposed to. He married multiple times and had children as Allah provided, whether he had the resources to feed them or not. Again, this is not a concern as Allah provides a bountiful earth. He did what his culture, his traditions, taught him were proper and best. Any clear-headed analysis of the real-world modern situation is pre-empted by religious prescription. Progress is retarded by the religious thought pervasive in the culture. Culture keeps us in chains.

Now consider a woman living outside of a Muslim country, almost anywhere else in the developed world. Unless she is a member of a minority, extreme religious sect: Orthodox Jew, Xian Quiverfull, or maybe Mormon, she would most likely be free of such repressive and primitive thinking that my counterpart in Gaza sweats under for most of his life. Even if staunchly Catholic, she has most likely practiced birth control. Birth control nowadays in the US (unlike 50 years ago), and many other countries is available everywhere, even in Walmart, even on Sunday. Betcha my counterpart in Gaza can't stroll down to the local convenience store and grab himself a couple of Trojans and a six-pack. Even some of the more Conservative Protestants in the US, like the Southern Baptists and Mormons, who are as restrictive as Islam in their attitudes towards alcohol, (and homosexuals) allow use of birth control.

One reason birth control is available here, is that we are not dominated completely by cultural norms run on religious ideas. Despite the US being predominantly Christian in population, we have enough secular influence to keep the Xiansanity at bay in some areas. Our growth rate is only 0.7%. We can buy condoms and alcohol. We secularists certainly have much more work to accomplish in America, but be damn glad you don't live in an Islamic country. The influence of religious thought is still overly burdensome worldwide, although progress is definitely accelerating. We could be living in a society like Gaza or much of the Middle East and Africa, where religious thought controls nearly your every move and retards progress on nearly every front.

Faith and Reason

Two diametrically opposed approaches to the world. Worldviews completely orthogonal to one another. Agendas at cross purposes to one another. Two different highways that intersect briefly at common experience and continue on their separate paths down utterly different roads. The intersection is brief and ephemeral. Here's an observation. Reason has gone to shit in American politics. And maybe that's nothing new, plenty of other episodes in US history have seen partisan gridlock to the extent we have now. But we suck, in a lot of ways. We lost our edge in basic scientific research, and spend more than 14 other countries combined, to the tune of $700 billion, on our military, in the guise of defense.

Mitt Romney ran on not cutting a thing in the 2012 Presidential election. In 2015, the Republican primary candidates certainly haven't proposed any cuts in defense spending, and many are up front on spending more. While "defense" spending has grown and basic science and research spending has been reduced, we haven't been back to the moon since the 70's. The Super Collider project in Texas was scrapped years ago and subsequently the Higgs boson was discovered in Europe, at CERN. We got bridges and roads going to shit, with the majority of jobs being created at or near minimum wage, in the retail and food service industries, yet we're building another aircraft carrier worth $4-5 billion a pop, when we already have 3 times as many as the next country. The Republican Party has been hijacked by Conservative Xiansanity. Faith, and the thinking that goes with it, has spent this country into a hole.

Aren't you tired of Xian wars, on everything? I am. We got 2 million people in prisons, more than fucking China as noted before, thanks in good measure to the War on Drugs. Anything that feels good like sex or mood altering chemicals must be bad. Thanks a lot to JC and his idiot followers! The War on Poverty is another failure. Income disparity has never been this bad in the US, and is only getting worse by the minute. Onward Xian Soldiers? Go fuck yourselves. We don't want any more of your wars. The War on Women drags on with Republicans introducing bill after bill after bill to restrict women's rights. The War against the "Gay Agenda" is an example itself of classic Xian Propaganda, as promulgated by the War on Knowledge: Science Denial. Thankfully, we won the war on gay rights, with state after state approving gay marriage and then the momentous Supreme Court decision ending legal opposition to it. Get rid of Conservative Xiansanity and all misogyny, homophobia, science denial, the War on Drugs, the wars in Muslim countries, climate change denial, the overblown military budget, all of them go away without the underlying absurd assumptions of religion.

Don't Look Back

"Man is innately depraved. Life is all about suffering. Sin is inevitable. Humans need the threat of eternal fire to behave. Morality is exclusive to religion. Religion and its delusions are an irreplaceable part of human nature. Women are inferior. Gays and atheists are un-natural and should burn. Eternal truths and following them

are more important than human suffering"

All of the above are unquestioned tenets behind ALL religious thought (yes, even with the meek and mild meditative Buddhists) and they are all unnecessary, incorrect, arrogant, and hopelessly out of date. They focus overmuch on the negative aspects of our personalities (a hallmark of conservative religious thought worldwide) rather than emphasize our positive dispositions and behavior. Unquestioned religious thought is the bane of our existence, not its saving grace. We have to cure ourselves of the itch to look back to the supposed "wisdom of the ancients." Often, the ancients we revere so much, exhibited a level of behavior which prompted Lewis Black to describe them as *"just three hairs short of being baboons."*

In reality, they were just trying to get by, making it up as they went along, just as we are today, only without the benefit of another 2,000 years of progress and the incredible advances in knowledge won by the Scientific Revolution of the past century or two. The "ancients" had no special knowledge we need to refer to in order to control or improve our behavior in the 21st century. The ancients of 1,500-3,000 years ago, the time frame from which most of our religious "truths" originate, were living in a most barbaric, primitive, and ignorant time, during which for many, life was nasty, brutal, and short. They operated with a dearth of real knowledge about how the world actually works, most of which our species has painstakingly assembled since. We don't need Buddhism, Hinduism, Shintoism, or Jainism, any more than we need the repressive and utterly failed political ideologies of Marxism, Stalinism, or Maoism. We certainly don't need the absurd ideas of the dastardly Abrahamic religions of Christianity, Islam, or Judaism either.

All of these ideologies claim to have knowledge exclusive to them, based on their equally exclusive authoritative writings, which reject any correction by new information. That is why they all reject science to some degree, should it conflict with their preconceived explanations of the natural order or factual claims about the world. Ask yourself what other institutions, other than those that run on religious thought, uphold and promulgate the misogyny, homophobia, divisiveness, and science denial that religions do?

The average religionist, be they Xian, Muslim, Buddhist, what have you, isn't stupid. Like all the rest of us, they are just trying to get by and maintain some security, comfort, and time with their loved ones. Most of us on the planet are merely trying to keep the kids fed, pay the mortgage, get some vacation time, earn further control over our lives, enjoy our favorite past times, and get laid on a regular basis. Any person on earth is capable of learning. Some, who may not be bright enough to earn a college degree, or the many who may never even attempt college instruction, none of them are stupid. Not in the least. I do not subscribe to either the innate depravity, barbarism, or ultimate stupidity of the average human that they need to be led around by the nose.

I asked a Xian apologist I knew once, if he would let his charges read the other side, works from the dark side: Dawkins, Hitchens, and Harris, for example, or Bart Ehrman or Dan Barker, along with the Xian apologetics he so enthusiastically recommended to them. Pausing for a moment to reflect, he gave a very thoughtful "No" for an answer. At first I assumed it was because he thought the kids under his spiritual guidance were stupid, not bright enough to handle the dialogue between faith and reason and to figure it out on their own, that he needed to spoon feed them and not overwhelm them.

Then I realized I might be wrong, that in all actuality, he's afraid. He knows they're not stupid. Like me, he just might know how even the least of the academically inclined among them are plenty bright enough to figure it out, and he runs the risk of them seriously questioning, or even rejecting religious "truths" outright, if he lets them read the secular literature critiquing religion and religious claims. Ya gotta keep 'em in the cocoon, or you won't be able to keep them in the fold. His upfront denying his spiritual charges access to secular writings, knowledge that directly contradicts the teachings of the faith he enthusiastically defends, belied his understanding that they weren't stupid at all. In fact, they are smart enough to figure it out, see the obvious bullshit of their faith, and leave it behind. So I think rather he knows it too, as does Comfort, and Ham and the whole host of "authorities" like them. They know their flock is smart, smart enough to look behind the veil, so they gotta keep 'em buffaloed... and they do a bang-up job of it.

The New Enlightenment books and blogs, podcasts, videos, articles, meetups, talks, and conferences are all dedicated to dispelling the unquestioned assumptions of religion. Such as, we are naturally, hopelessly, and predominantly evil, and other such fantasies dreamed up 2,000 and more years ago. The ancients did not know more about human nature than we do now. We know more. We don't know it all, but we will learn more. Throw those old books away, stop going to church and stop being hosed, by the priests, ministers, apologists, science deniers, and moralists who have no special knowledge distilled from ancient texts. There is little wisdom from the ancients. There's some, it is true, but doing the best they could for the time to figure it all out, they had no special gifts, insights, and especially no revelations from any god. Conservatives want us to go back to a wisdom that was never there.

Normal Human Empathy

TED videos have become regular additions to my classroom presentations for the past few years now. The format is great, 20 minutes tops, no professors droning on for an hour or more. No bullshit, and no wasted words. You gotta get your point out quick and concise. One can find info on any subject imaginable: the arts, current topics, and a great deal of science. There's a bit of New Age bullshit of course, but for the most part, mostly a lot of good science accessible to the average citizen. In perusing dozens of these innovative and informative videos over the years, I noticed an unexpected similarity. Despite the incredibly broad range of topics covered, a consistent theme appears; making the world a better place for our fellow humans.

Normal human empathy abounds. The second theme you will notice, the efforts are overwhelmingly secular.

For but one example, there's a heartfelt and optimistic perspective delivered by Peter Diamandis, in a presentation which summarizes his book, *Abundance*. He paints a picture of accomplishment and optimism, emphasizing the better angels of our nature, our curiosity, creativity, and drive for knowledge. Most importantly, to what purpose...more money, faster automobiles, owning another football team? No. The goal is to make the world a better place, to increase access to clean water, feed everybody, produce cheap and accessible fuels, provide cleaner air, and give everyone the chance to live a secure, self-fulfilled life, free of disease and violence. Sure, innovators and manufacturers hope to make money on any venture. But you see much more than just the drive for profit in these presentations. Most of the videos you might view, display this underlying theme: empathy for others. Concern, and a real desire to help the untold millions of fellow humans who don't have it as good as we do, folks we will never see, never know, never meet in our lifetimes. Yet, we still want to help them. TED speakers talk of all the good humans have done, can do and should do for each other... and there are no barriers.

This is quite the opposite of what religions emphasize. Despite their formidable involvement in charitable activities worldwide, religions emphasize the negative aspects of the human psyche and they promote divisiveness over absurd old myths and rituals. *"Life is all about suffering"* is the first of the eight-fold truths of Buddhism. Mankind is assuredly innately depraved, doomed to sin, evil, even disgusting in the eyes of god, incapable of moral living without the threat of eternal fire in the Xian scheme of things, repeated ad nausem throughout our culture. A rather dismal set of views, East and West.

In contrast, the secular content of the vast majority of TED videos speak of how far we have come in the modern era to alleviate hunger and suffering, or in advancing medicine and technology. Again, all this done to make a better world. Most importantly, we're not done yet. The emphasis is on building on our accomplishments and developing more of the natural human innovation and empathy we have evolved to an unprecedented level, almost obscenely so compared to the precursors seen in our animal cousins. On the empathy scale we have left the realm of the other animals, even our closest genetic relatives, far behind. A small vignette drawn from a discussion on morality entitled, *The New Science of Morality* from the edge.org website should suffice to illustrate the point.

Any day, every day, all over the globe, at any moment in dozens of places an airplane sits waiting on the tarmac, delayed minutes, hours, all too often, many hours. Given the over 93,000 airline flights worldwide per day there's dozens, maybe hundreds of delayed flights at any given moment. They're mostly full of total strangers, 100 or more unrelated humans on the average flight, a bit dismayed, impatient, even perturbed. But despite the occasional boor who exhibits some bad behavior, these unrelated bipedal primates behave themselves admirably for the most part, respecting each other's personal space, sympathizing with each other's plight, even assisting someone with an infirmity or a small child until they finally depart for their connections or, disappointingly, to the last minute accommodations resulting from canceled flights. Very rarely, is there a report of an argument or altercation, much less a mugging or a murder.

Now put 100 unrelated chimps, in that plane, on the tarmac. Strap them in first, in that long aluminum tube and slam the door, tight. You'll have body parts in minutes. They will tear each other apart in fearful frenzy. We are not over-evolved chimps. Chimps are not undeveloped humans. Despite sharing 95-98% of our genetic material (depending how you measure it), we are separated by 5-6 million years of divergent evolution. We have similar body plans, plus a host of other features common to all primates, but in spite of sharing a disturbing propensity for male coalitional violence, we possess a level of empathy, a capability for respect of the rights and well-being of others, even total strangers of our species, which is utterly unprecedented in the entire animal kingdom and wholly unrealizable by our closest genetic cousins.

We give billions in aid to total strangers on the other side of the world every time there is another natural disaster, another humanitarian crisis. We could do more to be sure, but what the human animal does for non-kin is off the scale of even the most altruistic of animal behaviors. There is no precedent for it. While the world's religions are tripping over themselves, in promulgating their depraved medieval interpretations of already dismal Bronze Age perspectives on the human psyche, all the good folks pleading their case for an even better world at TED, are exercising the better angels of our nature. What do you do when you have enough money to live, eat, drink, stay clothed, housed, enjoy some leisure time and have a bit of vacation money? Maybe you have a satisfying family life, spouse, and children, a good job and recognition for your talents and hard work, maybe enough money and time to engage in your hobbies and enjoy a little art, music, or other things you find beautiful. Maybe you "got it made". You may not have as much extra cash, to put it mildly, as Bill Gates and the other nearly 1,700 billionaires around the world, or even the *12 million* millionaires around the globe. When you do obtain whatever level of cash and financial stability and freedom you are happy with...what next?

You give stuff to total strangers. And you don't have to have $76 billion like Bill Gates to help others you don't know or will never meet. In an informative and heartening TED interview, Gates and his wife Melinda describe the charitable foundation they set up that will eventually distribute 95% of his wealth *(over $70 billion)*, through support to programs to eradicate disease, increase access to birth control, improve and provide education worldwide and a host of other projects. Others among the worlds' wealthiest are joining in the philanthropy to an unprecedented degree. In case you are worried about Bill and Melinda now that he's retired and giving away 95% of his assets, he will still have $3-4 billion left down the road. Trust me, we don't need to worry about his retirement ever being in jeopardy.

Melinda discusses the desire of women worldwide to have their reproductive rights. What she's heard from the women of the world, all over the world is: *"I need that tool (birth control) to space the births of my children, and then I can feed them and have the chance to educate them."* Over 210 million women in the world want contraception, but the political (read religious) controversy in the US over birth control often prevented them from getting it. Insanity. Good things happen when religion is ignored. The secular world then bypassed the roadblocks of religion and politics and pressed on regardless. The Gates foundation commitment to providing contraception is a classic example of transcending religious obstruction, as Melinda is Catholic and adamant about the need for contraception across the developing world.

Bill chimed in with his explication of a rather dramatic graph, displayed above him, that shows the incredible results that vaccination and sanitation (mostly vaccination) has had on reducing the number of children dying before age 5 worldwide, over the past 50 years. It is incredible. Despite world population more than doubling in the last 50 years, from 3 billion to over 7 billion, children who die before age 5 dropped from 50 million a year in 1960 to only 6 million in 2012. It should have gone up to well over 100 million. Imagine that.

Without this largely unknown effort and incomparable success, by 2015, over 100 million children would be dying of disease before age 5 every year. That's a third of the entire US population. Try this illustration on for size to get your head around the magnitude of that number. 100 million is more than the entire population of Iran, or Germany. Imagine if we moved all the kids under 5 who would die in one year to one of those countries. Replaced all the citizens of a whole country with these kids. Come back a year later and the country is empty. Empty of living souls. 100 million little corpses dotting the landscape, filling the cities. An entire country. Instead, we got it under 6 million, and Gates and his fellow philanthropists are shooting for extending that decline to as near zero as they can get it, in the next decade. All for strangers. The numbers are a testament to human invention, and unfettered empathy.

Yes, when driven by ideologies; political or religious that divide and dehumanize us, we are capable of killing 10's of millions at a time directly, or condemning 100's of millions to a life of oppression or poverty. Genocides based in racism, religious wars based on competing myths, political upheavals based in untested and inhumane ideologies, Islamic rules for women, or Catholic birth control prohibitions, diminish, even destroy, the lives of 100's of millions all over the world. Conversely, the secular world, driven by reason and tolerance and enabled by science, unites us all as one species, and attempts to alleviate suffering, while increasing education and personal freedoms. That effort transcends all unfounded and archaic religious ideas. This is what we can emphasize, what we can exercise, when we have our own needs covered: normal human empathy and self-actualization. Giving back. Gates speaks for all of us towards the end of the talk when he says: *"It's the most fulfilling thing we've ever done."*

This is what we can concentrate on, the future and improving it, versus looking back to the past to recreate it. No more "old time religion", in fact no more "old time" at all. Instead of telling people to look back to discover how they must behave to please some god, let's look forward and focus on how we can improve the lives of everyone on the planet, even those not yet born.

7

CHILD INDOCTRINATION

"Religions would collapse under the weight of their own absurdity without child indoctrination"

Anonymous

"My best advice to anyone who wants to raise a happy, mentally healthy child is: Keep him or her as far away from a church as you can."

Frank Zappa

Save the Children

Somebody has to tell them. We can't keep quiet. Stridency is in order here. Tell the believers they have been hosed. They were sold a bill of goods as defenseless kids, and that's the only reason they uphold religious myths and negative judgments of out-groups. Why for example, is condemning others to eternal gruesome pain in some Omnipotent Prick's never-ending medieval torture chamber politically correct? Why is it considered a normal facet of religion? Why is it allowed, unchecked, unchallenged? Why do we fill kid's heads with these medieval fantasies? No more. All this from the religion of love: *"God loves you, but if you don't believe what I believe, what we believe, or believe it in just the same way we do at our church... you will burn forever and deservedly so!"* Religions convince kids this is real, normal and accepted. You wouldn't buy it for a minute as an adult. That's why religions go for kids. It is reprehensible. What a crock. Nobody in a believer's immediate circle, even if they might think for a moment that condemning others is reprehensible as hell, (pun intended) dares to tell them, or even dares to think it for more than a moment.

But we non-believers can tell them, should tell them. Daily. Refute it. Constantly. Stridently. It is up to us. And we are telling everyone, and at unprecedented levels in the past decade since the beginning of the New Enlightenment. Never before has the skeptical freethinking non-believer community come out so strong, so vocal, so visible as in the past decade. But a generation ago, folks like Madalyn Murray O'Hair were doing it all on their own and were ostracized, hated, and on the fringe. The vast majority of atheists were in the closet. You wouldn't dare bring up atheism in mixed company, and if you did you were immediately associated with those dastardly commies: Chairman Mao, Khrushchev, Stalin and Lenin. Atheists were monsters that persecuted Xians and took away prayer and Bible reading in our schools. Now, nonbelief and the critique of religion is mainstream and everywhere. We can now do so much more to reverse the damaging effects of child indoctrination on eternal damnation, and all the other arrogant thoughts, kids have been conned into.

Once, while in downtown Chicago, I got up close to a young man in a street corner demonstration, who was holding up a sign typical of Xian evangelists street preacher groups, that said "Fornicators and Faggots Burn in Hell", or words to that effect, and patted him on the shoulder and nicely said "It's all bullshit, pal." I said it kindly. I was as nice to this late adolescent, as I would be to any other human, as we all deserve respect. But, I was not in the least bit respectful of the religious ideas he was displaying, which deserve none. Somebody has to tell them. Every seed you plant can be another nagging twinge of cognitive dissonance. The religious aren't stupid, merely hosed and the hosing started when they were young: captive, vulnerable, trusting and unsuspecting.

Religion just gets in the way. At best, it is a harmless diversion if kept to one's self, but most often it is the prime if not only source of misogyny, homophobia, science denial, and division left in the modern world. At worst, it remains the world's main source of xenophobia, dehumanization, and horrific violence toward women and non-believers. We don't need this shit. Tell believers, at the risk of not being PC, tell them. They were coerced into it as unquestioning children or vulnerable adolescents. It is not their fault. Tell them not to live a life deluded by blind adherence to whatever brand of bullshit they were taught as children. You wouldn't let your friends drive drunk, don't let your friends drive Xian or Muslim either.

Buddhist B. S.

Consider Buddhist ideals, conveyed to us over nearly 3 millennia. The Buddha was said to have lived sometime around 400-500 B.C.E. The first writings about him (he, like JC evidently wrote nothing of his own) don't appear until 500 years after his death, in the first century C.E. Be that as it may, the first claim of the 8 fold path of Buddhism is: "Life is all about suffering." Really, do you teach your kid that? Like the Conservative Xians teaching about this diseased world, our innate depravity, our propensity to sin, and our inevitable susceptibility to evil, the net effect of both approaches is to set up a reason why you need a religion to get through the suffering and depravity of existence. In the case of the re-incarnation religions, Buddhism for one, only by breaking the cycle of rebirth (another wholly fanciful idea taught to millions of children as the truth) can we end the suffering of life.

This bleak outlook may have been completely understandable in the 5th century B.C., when life expectancy was but 32 years or so and childhood disease took 3 or 4 out of the 7 babies a mother might bear, until she died herself from childbirth in her early 30's, from having child # 8, for example. But is it relevant today? Do we teach life is all about suffering in pre-school and grade school, or how we must break this endless cycle of pain? No, we teach our kids all over the world how they can be good to their neighbors, love their family and their own children someday, and how they can learn, and grow up to be whatever they want and live a good productive life. Buddhism is just more old bullshit. It attempts to avoid this life altogether, with its desires, despairs, accomplishments and failures, attempting to break the endless cycle of suffering through meditation. The idea is to attain some supposed mystical state of nirvana, for which there is no proof at all that anyone, including the Buddha himself, ever achieved. It seems to be an ephemeral diversion at best. What the fuck good for humanity, for one's neighbor or family, or one's children is withdrawal into monastic self-absorption, full or part-time, endlessly repeating meaningless rituals and prayer, or occupying oneself in some subjective mind exercise where all one hopes to achieve is true nothingness?

A Buddhist monk, looking to be in his early thirties at the time, spoke at the university where I taught some years ago. Besides explaining Buddhist ideals, practice and beliefs, he did open up a bit about the life of a monk and gave the audience a glimpse into his personal feelings on his life in the monastery. *"The life of a monk is hard,"* he said. No doubt.

No sex, little to no entertainment. Study, prayer, menial tasks, prayer, meager meals, study, chanting, ritual, more prayer, rinse, repeat. Days, months, years on end. He said he entered the monastery when he was 13. Thirteen? He made a decision about what he would do for the rest of his life while still a clueless early adolescent? You know he did not one day wake up and think to himself, in between learning to jerk-off and going fishing down at the creek... *"I know, I'll sign up to a life of dull drudgery, ignoring all pleasures and responsibility, wearing the same robe forever, and living on handouts of rice and vegetables. Gosh, golly gee that will be swell, glad I thought of it!"*

No, somebody talked him into it. Somebody convinced him, through persuasion for some higher purpose, enabled by the complete diffusion throughout his culture of the legitimacy of the dogma of his religion, that this was the noblest and best way to spend one's life. What a crock of shit. Try talking an adult into that one. Sure, a few might buy into it and go, but the vast majority of mature folks with fully formed frontal lobes, a modicum of post-teen self-esteem and awareness, and just a teeny bit of real-world experience, would tell you to get fucked. In a heartbeat. But you can bullshit a pimply vulnerable adolescent who hasn't had his first blow-job, that the monastic life is a real keen idea. Whatever the religion, youth ministry is the scum of the earth.

Oh sure, I could do that gig. Couldn't you just see me in flowing robes begging for Cheetos at the airport? Oh yeah. I'm gonna blow on the sacred goat scapula horn and ring little bells for the rest of my fucking life. Then I'd be a true holy man, right? Revered and respected for my ascetic denial of base human passions, especially the defilement by relations with a female that seems to be the ultimate purity, the height of spiritual attainment of all patriarchal religions. The true holy man doesn't touch a woman. This is what Buddhist kids are told. As nonsensical as anything any Xian youth minister would tell his adolescent charges.

Youth ministry is disgustingly dishonest and coercive, be it to tell a kid that all the answers to everything and ultimate salvation await him in the Koran and the madrassa, or the Bible and Xian camp, or the Pali canon and Buddhist monastery. Hare Krishna's or Hitler youth, it is all the same. Selling a prepackaged, narrow minded, thoughtless, identity to the cognitively immature, and emotionally vulnerable adolescent is reprehensible and needs to stop. It is probably the sleaziest practice of all religions. We have to stop teaching children the absurd lie that everything we need to know is in some ancient book if we just decipher it right, and then to follow it just right, whether it is the Koran, Bible or Bhagavad Gita. There is something obviously wrong here, yet the whole world accepts child indoctrination, the recruitment of underage minors into a faith for their entire lives as a normal and unquestioned behavior. Let's end it now.

"And Then They are All Mine."

I wrote many a secular editorial and eventually a regular column while teaching at a state university in Kentucky some years back. The following piece was one of them. It is a rebuttal to a web-log article penned by one of the top dogs among US Baptists:

> "The start of the school year is a time to reflect on the purpose of higher education. The transfer of information is the best of man's endeavors, responsible for taking us beyond a barbaric and short existence to relative ease and longevity, improving the lot of billions. However, some see an inherent danger in college education. Dr. Albert Mohler, president of the Southern Baptist Theological Seminary expressed his concern on his website over the alleged excesses of some higher educators. Of college instruction he warned "… most new professors find the experience to be nearly intoxicating" and "… the power of the professor in a classroom is immense".
>
> Although myself and my colleagues thoroughly enjoy the teaching profession we're hardly drunk with it, nor do we wield immense power over our students. Very little in fact. He then related the statements of two professors he claims engage in 'ideological indoctrination," a "matter of deep concern" to Christian parents and students since there may be a lot more college instructors having just such an unspoken plan. This agenda includes secular ideas which may be antagonistic to Christian truth claims: exposing students "to the world outside of their town and to moral ideas not exclusively derived from their parent's religion." Sounds like Dr. Mohler would prefer students to remain inside the Xian cocoon shielded from any "outside knowledge."
>
> I'd wager that the vast majority of college instructors do feel that

exposure to ideas different from the culture one was brought up in, including religious ones be they Christian, Muslim, Buddhist, Hindu, etc., is an enlightening experience: one good for any student. However, I suspect the vast majority of college instructors could care less about and remain unaware of their students' religious affiliation out of respect for the student's personal business and given that the students' beliefs are wholly orthogonal to the course subject. In addition, the teaching of critical thinking, inviting students to disagree, question and argue is standard in every classroom. Dr. Mohler incorrectly surmises that college instructors teach in the same manner as religious instructors do worldwide where the student is expected to fully accept everything, without question and under threat of strict penalties now and forever. And even the two instructors he quotes who may well have overstepped their bounds in attempting to ram their views uncritically down the throats of their students, share a crucial difference with all college instructors from religious teachers: we wait until our students are adults. Our students are not underage children. Our students are all 18 years of age and older, who freely choose their courses and can seek redress should we overstep our bounds. If we become boorish and stifling, "preachy" they can drop our class, give us appropriately low evaluations as is their right, they can tell all their friends to avoid our sections and nowadays with the ubiquity of Internet use, really rip us a new one on "Rate my Professor". They are not children who have no option to drop Sunday school, Catechism, Bible study, leave the madrassa or monastery or dare walk out on a Sunday sermon in front of pastor, family and community. Imagine if religion students did semi-annual evaluations of their preachers, and had access to "Rate my Minister." The noted Christian apologist, Josh McDowell, recently decried the hemorrhaging of the ranks of American evangelical churches, as the young are staying away in droves. One factor he blamed was college instruction. But consider that any professor has but one or two semesters to influence an adult student's (not a child's, nor an adolescent's) perspectives in a free open forum, while religious instructors have a decade or more of exclusive preaching to a captive audience of underage children, who are not allowed to question, lest they incur the disdain of their parents, preachers, family and community. Consider also that youth ministers are charged with recruiting new converts from the emotionally vulnerable and cognitively immature early adolescent. Who really wields "immense power"?

The real power is in the information and its free exchange, which is the purpose of higher education. It's difficult to hang onto outmoded cultural ideas which have lost their relevance in modern times, or may be cruel, repressive or just plain wrong in light of new information. And however intimidating a professor attempts to be, he can't threaten his students with eternal damnation either. It seems Dr. Mohler and Mr.McDowell just don't like competition, even when we play fair, as even the worst among us wait until their students are old enough to tell us to "go to hell".

Snake Handling and Reincarnation

Back in 2014, Kentucky pastor Jamie Coots died of a venomous snakebite, thinking he would be protected by God. Such an idea is clearly stated in the passages at the end of the Gospel ascribed to Mark. These passages appearing after Mark 16:8, were added to the Gospel decades, maybe centuries later, by an unknown scribe(s) (there's half a dozen different endings to Mark), to an already anonymous manuscript dating to sometime near 70 AD. Also, the Gospel of Mark was penned four decades after JC's alleged death and resurrection by someone who never met Jesus. It is not an account of anyone that knew him. The earliest fragments we have of this anonymous work are from the 3rd century, with complete manuscripts only available dating from the 4th century. Yes, you got that right, 400 years later. So why would an otherwise seemingly normal educated 21st century man, who operates a motor vehicle, a computer, a cellphone, who probably takes antibiotics and such, and who quite likely appreciates modern medicine, trusts science, logic, and material causality in 99% of his waking life… why would he believe the outlandish claims in an anonymous interpolation into a larger and also anonymous work. One nearly 2,000 years old, for which we have no originals, only copies of copies of copies, from centuries later, which have multiple endings and multiple other interpolations? Why would he believe these ancient words that tell him he can be bitten by snakes (and drink poisons) but won't die?

The vast majority of Xians on the planet (in the neighborhood of 2 billion of them) don't believe those verses one bit, but of course, believe much of the rest of this Gospel to relate true information about the life, death, and resurrection of Jesus. Some folks say, even many other Xians, Pastor Coots was an idiot and got what he deserved for being so foolish. Yet, they fervently believe the rest of the Gospel. I don't think he was an idiot. Nor do I think any Xian, any believer is. So just how did Jamie Coots and other snake handlers come to believe? Seems crazy to most of us, even to most Xians, but is it any crazier to believe any other religious claim that also has no evidence for it, having only scriptural verses that say such claims are true, despite mountains of evidence against them being true?

Take reincarnation for example. In the US, and most of the West, unless one is a New Age spiritualist, you won't take the idea of your soul somehow re-appearing in another human (or animal) after your death too seriously. The predominant belief about souls in the Xian tradition is that they go either to heaven or hell when you die, and that's it. One shot, no recycling. But in much, if not most of Asia, it is claimed in the "Karma 2" (the reincarnation religions of Buddhism and Hinduism) that without question the reintroduction of the soul into another human body is an eternal truth, one which is integral to their teachings. And it is taught unquestionably as such. So many, if not most, Buddhists and Hindu's believe it. Again, this is regardless of there being absolutely no evidence for such a claim, and mountains of evidence against it. After nearly 3,000 years of wishful thinking by these religions, and now 150 years of neuroscience, there is absolutely neither any evidence that some portion of the intellect, essence, mind, personality, "*soul*" if you will, survives the death of the body, nor that said soul is somehow reinstated into another living thing. It is pure fantasy, but nonetheless, an accepted understanding of a billion or more people on earth. Without child indoctrination who would even think of it nowadays? How is it any more or less crazy than snake handling? Or believing any other of the unfounded claims of anonymous 2,000 year old writings that have no evidence of their factuality? This is a prime example of the arrogance of religious thought. It is OK to promote and defend ideas with absolutely no proof and pass them on through the generations by child indoctrination, supported solely by the unquestionable authority of scripture and religious leaders. Reincarnation may be considered to be a harmless delusion, certainly incomparably less deadly than snake-handling, but is that a good excuse for lying to children and perpetuating really old ideas that have no merit, no proof? In addition, accepting one delusion legitimizes others, and often facilitates much more dangerous nonsense. Moderate Xians legitimize belief in deadly snake handling because, after all, it is part of their holy gospel, to them it is the word of god.

The oldest manuscripts of the Gospel attributed to Mark end at 16:8, and do not include the snake handling verses which were the good pastor's main reason for mucking about with snakes in his bare hands, and thinking he could get away with it. The endings of Mark (yup, there's 6 of 'em, some inerrant scripture, huh?) were added later, to be in agreement with passages in the other Gospels written after Mark. Just think, some scribe or church father, 1,500 years ago or so, added these "Gospel Truth" verses which gave this poor guy the justification to kill himself with a poisonous snake centuries later. Insanity. You could call him an idiot, but he truly believed this crap. Jamie Coots wasn't born that way. He learned it. He was taught it and told he could not question it. Left alone, he would have had a normal informed fear of snakes and their venom. He got fucked. By a religion. By religious indoctrination. Maybe his parents, his pastor, or somebody in his spiritual past, all blinded by their faith, and probably loaded with the same delusional *"good intentions"*, convinced this poor schmuck somewhere down the line, that the Bible is the inerrant word of god, and you ain't a good KY Xian (most snake handlers reside in eastern KY) unless you prove you believe the insane verses 99.9% of other Xians ignore. Left to his own devices, he might have been a normal clear-thinking adult human, as he most likely was in the majority of the rest of his all too short life. Child indoctrination killed this poor bastard. Hitch was right... *"Religion poisons everything."*

Dying for an Addendum

Cody Coots, Pastor Jamie's son, has been bitten nearly 1/2 dozen times as well, just like his dad, but unlike his dad, he has recovered to preach and handle snakes again. Many non-believers, but damn few Xians, are aware those passages at the end of the Gospel attributed to Mark that encourage snake handling are not in the earliest manuscripts and were added later. Those admonitions to handle snakes that Cody and his dad, Jamie take/took completely seriously, and were compelled to follow to the letter to prove their faith, were added as we said, centuries later and completely anonymously to an already anonymously penned Gospel. That Gospel, in turn, was written down decades after the time of Christ, by a highly literate Greek writer (not an illiterate Aramaic speaking apostle) who never met Jesus. When you have been taught that your Bible is, in every word, the Word of God, you may be persuaded that risking dying for it is a good thing. Cody and his dad weren't born this way. Somebody taught them to revere these words as undoubted words of god... a complete fantasy. There's only a half a dozen churches, all in the Appalachian region of the US, where snake-handling (which originated there in the early 20th century) is still practiced. We need to stop lying to our children, to all children all over the world, about any and all supposed "*Scriptures*" revealed to someone by somebody's god. It is a complete and often dangerous fantasy. It's time we outgrow it. It killed this kid's dad and dozens before him. It may kill the son as well. We witness this completely needless loss of life, all because we respect religion and the teaching of it to children.

Overcoming Child Indoctrination

Rachel Held Evans. She doesn't know me, but I owe her a great deal of thanks. Although we share a compassion for other humans above mere ideas, she is after all a committed Xian and I am unrepentant Unbelieving Scum. So we are kinda diametrically opposed on this whole belief thing. I have applauded her daring honesty in my writings many times before, in grappling with the questions that are paramount in young Evangelicals and many Xian's minds of every stripe as well: the homophobia, moralizing, science denial, and the misogyny inherent in the Bible, and modern Xian practice to varying degrees. She embraces evolution and rejects homophobia, and is working on how to reconcile the findings of modern science, such as our expanding knowledge of prenatal development and embryology, with long held ideas about souls and person-hood in the womb, in the abortion debate.

But she certainly hasn't let go. Not that I would chastise her or any other Xian raised in a very Conservative Xian setting, the "Xian cocoon" as I call it, for not letting go. It has got to be tougher than quitting smoking. You really can't expect anyone to just chuck it all one day. Some few are able to do that, but for most who underwent the heavy duty brainwashing of Evangelical Xiansanity, the dropping of religion takes years. Sometimes it is a decades-long process. Read Seth Andrews, Mike Aus, Jerry DeWitt, Dan Barker, John Loftus, or any of the thousands of de-conversion experiences related in books and blogs, for excellent examples of what it is like going from hard core Xian to unabashed atheist. It ain't gonna happen overnight. Letting go ain't easy.

One of Rachel's blog posts covered that very subject: *Post Evangelicals and Why We Just Can't Get Over It*. Once again Rachel's heartfelt no-nonsense yet endearing way of letting you into her head and her heart explains why she, and I suspect, many questioning religionists, just can't let go. Rachel always manages to be genuine without trying. A gift, really. Rachel:

"I've been reading articles lately about how people like me need to just get over it already, either suck it up and embrace evangelicalism or pack up and move on.... But when you grow up believing everyone outside evangelical Christianity is going to get spewed from God's mouth at best or cooked for eternity in hell at worst, when the people you love most in the world belong to the evangelical community and want you to belong to it too, making a deliberate step out of that tradition is a big deal. When you grow up believing that your religious worldview contains the key to absolute truth and provides an answer to every question, you never really get over the disappointment of learning that it doesn't."

Bravo. Ain't that more than just a little disgusting? Teaching little kids the "others" will be *"cooked for eternity in hell...."*

She continues:

"... And it was evangelicalism that first told me that being a woman limited my potential that science was not to be trusted, that democrats and gay people and Episcopalians were my enemies, that asking questions about these things was wrong. It was evangelicalism that told me who I was and it was evangelicalism that told me who I wasn't. You don't just get over that. You don't just trash it all and walk away." "And yet I glommed on to the label, to any label really, because a label means you're not alone. A label means you can be classified along with species of a similar nature. A label gives you a family, an order, a name....Seems like we're all a little post-something....Like it or not, our religious traditions help forge our identities"

This is what religions teach children. Misogyny, science denial, divisiveness. WTF? Just slip "Islam" in there wherever she says "evangelicalism" and it will read seamlessly; the parallels are scary. What is it about the ancient Middle East that spawned this repressive insanity anyway? I proudly identify with being Unbelieving Scum, using that term affectionately, as signifying living by reason and tolerance versus religious superstition and imaginary division. I use it snidely at the arrogance of all religions that paint non-believers as less than moral, as less than human, and worthy of frying in some Omnipotent Prick's hell. Me, and the rest of the heretics and infidels, will be "spewed from God's mouth?" Oh, fuck you. How arrogant can it get? Fuck a bunch of Islam and Xiansanity. We teach this to children like Rachel and millions of other children all over the world? Insanity. Reprehensible insanity.

The crux of the biscuit for Evans and so many others is community. One can't just up and leave the family, the nest, the hometown of fellow evangelicals, the connection. Understandably tough. Jerry DeWitt, Neil Carter and many others lost a great deal when they walked away.

Religion's other grip, the one that really galls me, and exemplifies the arrogance of religious thought is: *"you grow up believing that your religious worldview contains the key to absolute truth."* What a scam, what a lie, what arrogance to smother a kid with. All religions live on that lie: *"Our worldview has the inside track to ultimate truth. At worst, the rest are just made up, at best they are merely inferior versions of our righteous path to the real truth. Ha, ha aren't we just special?"*

More and more people, some even in the worst of smothering religious communities, are figuring out a way to let go. Good luck to anyone on that journey. You have a new label. Questioning Scum. We're already proud of ya, whether you make it to Unbelieving or not. Bravo. It ain't easy. We are rooting for you.

Somebody once said: *"Religions would collapse under the weight of their own absurdity if not for child indoctrination."*

'Nuff said! I love that line so much, I just had to repeat it! Only the disgusting practice of child indoctrination keeps them afloat. Changing cultural inertia requires a lot of constant consciousness-raising over decades. Look at the success of the gay rights movement. It took over 3 decades of consciousness raising, since the 70's, to eventually watch the gay marriage issue roll over in state after state here in the good ole U S of A, with the 2015 Supreme Court decision closing the door on religious opposition in our secular society once and for all. The tide did not turn overnight. But it was at the same time, phenomenally quick. Who in the 70's would have said it would be a done deal in less than a generation? Nobody. Given the centuries of religious entrenchment in our society, and the strength of religious belief and propaganda against homosexuality, whoda thunk it wouldn't take decades more, maybe at least a century? And yet it is a done deal. Why not consider we might raise consciousness on what a heinous practice child indoctrination into religion truly is, and accordingly, put a real dent in it, as just another unquestioned cultural norm that needs to go as well. We could eliminate child indoctrination and religion with it. Dare to think it. That's the first step.

Consider that it was barely ten years ago, that Richard Dawkins first brought this perspective to light in his landmark 2006 *God Delusion*. I remember reading him describing religious indoctrination as a form of child abuse and thinking, *"Whoa, now that's really hardcore! Boy, I don't know maybe he's gone too far with that one."* I got really defensive reading his no holds barred words. Though I had been a secularist for years, it offended my sensibilities. I had been raised Catholic, in a very liberal setting so to me, what's the big deal? People just teach their kids religion. I knew religion was all bullshit, but what's the harm, it's what people do, and we have done so for millennia. Cultural inertia gripped me as well. It didn't take very long to realize I reacted negatively, even a bit angrily initially, because teaching young children their one and only religion was such a longstanding cultural norm, that of course even to me it was normal and respectable. It was difficult for me, even as a long-term non-believer, to hear. Challenging cultural norms, overcoming cultural inertia as I call it, is not easy for anyone. Our first response is to get defensive.

Within a few months it didn't bother me in the least, and I could easily see child indoctrination for the child abuse that it is. That little step was a challenge for me. Despite being raised nominally religious with little coercion by my parents beyond having to go to Mass on Sundays, it was hard for me to hear a religious truism challenged. I can only imagine what those raised in that hard-core Xian cocoon go through. Islam looks to be even worse to walk away from.

The kickoff of the New Enlightenment is over a decade old now, since the 2004 publication of Sam Harris' *End of Faith*, and Dawkins' *God Delusion* shortly thereafter. Now, we have a number of secular activist organizations openly calling for the end of child indoctrination. We can break the underlying assumption that says we should allow, even respect religion's brainwashing of cognitively and emotionally defenseless children, as a normal, even a holy practice of culture. We can expose it for the sleazy custom that it is. We can change the culture. We can win.

People of the Book: The Abrahamic Delusion

If, your neighbor was out back preparing the barbecue and instead of brats and burgers, he had his first born son all set up on the grill about to be impaled and roasted, would you drop to your knees and praise the lord for his loving ways? I didn't think so. The 3 Abrahamic religions are based on this story, this heinous act, this barbaric myth. The two largest religions, the "Big 2" encompass nearly ½ of the world's population and its members are taught to revere the patriarch of them both, and his blind devotion to some imaginary, and very ugly god. This is what we teach our children to respect?

USA Today reported in 2014, in one of their little factoid graphics in the lower left corner of the front page, in southern cities like Chattanooga TN, and Birmingham AL, 50% of the populace *"read the Bible in the past week and believe strongly in its accuracy."* In stark contrast, comparable cities in the north, Albany NY, and Providence RI, both clock in with only 10% or less of their populations reading or buying the myths in that nasty little book. The situation in the US as depicted by this data is a microcosm of the situation with every religion all over the world. It is purely a geographic accident, a consequence of your birth location, what religion you are indoctrinated into and what religion you take seriously. It takes indoctrination to accept the lunacy of stories like Abraham, all set to skewer and barbecue his son, is the act of a loving god, an uplifting episode from a "Good Book," a story to live your life by. We can do just fine without this shit.

Those figures also demonstrate that the other 50% of the folks in those hyper-religious Southern cities, don't buy into, or need the damn Bible at all. The figures from every recent poll, show non-belief as growing among American youth, both North and South, and lastly, a full 90% of the folks in some areas "Up North" don't read nor need the damn thing at all. Neither do 5 billion of the over 7 billion of our fellow humans on the planet. Most humans are not Xians, never have been, never will be. That's the key point. Without child indoctrination, Xianity nor any other religion, wouldn't last very long.

Lawrence Krauss and Child Abuse

A few of the atheist folks out there don't like that Lawrence Krauss has come out and plainly said teaching Creationism to children is child abuse. They think it is going too far, not being respectful of the parent's sincere belief. But I must disagree completely with the assessment that Lawrence Krauss is wrong and not being helpful in calling the teaching of Creationism to kid's child abuse. In fact, Krauss is spot on. Telling your kids things you don't know, can't possibly know, and that it is the total and unquestionable truth, is abuse. All religious child indoctrination is abuse. Mental abuse. It does not have to be physical or of a certain severity to be labeled abuse. If a parent did that in any other domain, like telling their kids that folks of other ethnic groups were inferior, the earth were flat or people had babies that came out of their ears at age 100, and demanding they believe it, that is lying to them as deeply as selling them the absurd fantasy of Creationism.

Blocking their access to contradictory and true information, or telling them they dare not believe anything to the contrary…yeah, that's abuse. Home schooling them for the distinct purpose of keeping them from learning the truth, and worse still under the threat of hellfire and being ostracized by family and friends? Yup, qualifies as abuse. I was lucky. While exposed to religion and sent to Catholic schools, there was no compulsion, no demand ever by my parents to believe. They just thought providing religious instruction was a good idea, something everyone did like saying grace at Thanksgiving, Christmas and Easter meals. We never prayed otherwise, we weren't all that religious. I was left to my own thoughts, and felt very free to come to my own conclusion that religion was all nonsense and wholly unnecessary, by the time I got to high school. Everything I learned subsequently, only confirmed that conclusion.

The *"It's not helping"* claim one hears regularly from those who want us to be nicer is nonsense. Secularism is growing like a weed because the gloves are off, and religious claims and practices are being properly labeled as arrogant and abusive as they are. Religions set kids up for a lifetime of guilt, and conflict with reality. That's abuse. It needs to be said more often, and louder. Sure, true believers often do recoil at the sound of being called out for what they are doing, and will bluff and bluster when challenged. Look at my first reaction to Dawkins calling child indoctrination abuse. I was already a non-believer! I was entrenched at first as well. But having my assumptions challenged straight up and not sugar-coated did the trick. It is how we learn. Many of us non-believers despair when the hard-core Xians are repulsed by attacks on their cherished beliefs and draw the wagons. We assume incorrectly that no-one, or damn few, will ever de-convert, all because we have been too harsh. Many claim that the direct and strident approach only backfires, so we should just be nicer.

Nothing could be further from the truth.

The number of de-conversion stories, like those of Neil Carter, Jerry DeWitt, Dan Barker or Seth Andrews, John Loftus or Matt Dillahunty, etc., etc., or the thousands on Dawkins' website Convert's Corner and the tens of thousands that didn't write a book or blog about it say otherwise. It is helping the secular cause by calling a spade a spade, and it is helping immensely. A gaggle of momentarily butt hurt, hard-core Xians doesn't make the case against telling it like it is. The overwhelming number of people who eventually respond to the honest assessment of religion do make the case, for Dawkins' and Krauss's level of truthfulness, politically correct to some or not.

It usually takes years for anyone to hear enough reality about their own religion to walk away from it. It is not easy to hear you have been hosed, or that things you thought were true are nonsense. And anyone's first reaction to their ideas being challenged is refusal, anger, consternation, and complete denial. But with the repeated exposure to the absurdities and cruelties of religion that is so prevalent today, many come to understand, accept the new knowledge, and eventually turn away from their faith. Pew Research, and other polls, keep showing the "Nones" rising year after year, especially among the young. They are figuring out the truth quicker than ever before, that they have been hosed by their religion on a whole host of subjects: homosexuality, birth control, sex, the afterlife, the existence of a soul and yes, the absurd fantasy of Creationism that deserves all the ridicule one can heap upon it. A good many of those who have de-converted, were once every bit as hard-core and as "unmovable" as any of the most vehemently fundamentalist Xians kicking today.

The truth works. People aren't stupid. Xians are not dumb, merely hosed. It may take a while, and believers may be offended and go uber-defensive at first, and maybe kick and scream and rail and argue against the obvious for many years. It is true that some will just never change. But so many do. Many are pulling away as we speak. The numbers don't lie. In 2014 22% of Americans identified as "Nones" in the overall US population and 36% did so in the 18-24 age group. These numbers are up from single digits a generation ago. Now that's progress! Sugar-coating the critique of religion does no good. Being up front and clear without pulling punches does. Krauss isn't being illogical, nor exaggerating when he says teaching Creationism is also withholding info. Whether the parents sincerely believe it or not, they purposely don't let their kids access other info to the contrary, which is all around them. That's why they attempt to keep their kids in the Xian cocoon, by home schooling and the like, giving them phony Xian textbooks, or telling their kids not to listen to their biology teachers when they do go to school. It happens, even at the university level, I've experienced it. All of which, are blatant examples designed to withhold the real information from their children. Despicable, and abusive. Krauss' words are controversial and get attention, but they are not contrived, nor done solely for effect. They are an accurate assessment which challenges the stranglehold that conservative Xian thinking has on our culture. It is time we called a spade a spade. Being honestly blunt does command attention, but that doesn't make it untrue.

Richard Dawkins has been accused since the beginning of being strident, too direct, and offensive. And plenty of commentators have derided secularists like him of being too harsh and thereby counterproductive, like the silly pleadings of many to be "nice." There are a few million copies of *God Delusion* in print, and just the title is provocative enough to offend a great many religionists. Dawkins is credited with how many thousands of conversions, despite being as strident and blatantly honest as it gets? I don't believe for a minute that if Dawkins had toned it down, been "nicer" that the impact of that book would have been enhanced in the least, in fact it would have been much less powerful. Much of the *God Delusion's* appeal is Dawkins' unbridled honesty. Lying to your kids, that your 2,000 year old book of primitive writings is the unquestionable word of some god is child abuse in itself, whether it includes the absurd fantasy of Creationism or not.

We used to be nice. While the other rights revolutions were taking off in the 60's and 70's we stayed "nice." Religion got a free pass while the "uppity niggers" demanded to vote and be treated like human beings. They stopped being nice, and directly challenged the status quo of racism. The feminists were branded "men-hating bitches" because they stopped being nice, and dared call out for equality and the end of patriarchal rule in our society. The gays came out of the closet, and protested their long persecution at the hands of absurd religious ideas. They stopped being nice. Madalyn Murray O'Hair wasn't nice, and was hated for it, especially for being 50 years ahead of her time, but she helped get mandatory Bible reading out of our schools. Removal of school sponsored prayer had happened the year before her suit was settled. Now with the New Enlightenment's direct attack on religious absurdities and cruelties, on religion's built in misogyny, homophobia and science denial, we have made huge strides, precisely by giving up being nice or respectful of religion's ideas. We may be called strident, even hated, for daring to call out religious indoctrination of children into any or all religion's for the abject child abuse that it is. Child indoctrination is not nice, either. It is heinous and needs to end.

8

DENIAL OF KNOWLEDGE

"I am against religion because it teaches us to be satisfied with not understanding the world."

Richard Dawkins

"Forget Jesus. The stars died so that you could be here today."

Lawrence Krauss

Embryology and Abortion

Rachel Held Evans, the former-Evangelical, but still Xian blogger, has often demonstrated the indefatigable truth-seeking about sex and gender, which appears to characterize her entire generation (30 somethings). In one of her 2014 blog entries, she once again did a great job getting her fellow Xians thinking and talking about real issues that challenge the conservative Xian claims, they grew up believing. In but 2 days, she garnered over 800 comments to this particular entry, which related Rachel's own discovery of modern scientific knowledge about conception:

"The fact that a woman's body naturally rejects hundreds of fertilized eggs in her lifetime raises some questions in my mind about where we draw the line regarding the person-hood of a zygote (fertilized egg). Do we count all those "natural abortions" as deaths? Did those zygotes have souls? Will I meet them in heaven? Honestly the more I learn about the reproductive system, the harder it becomes for me to adamantly insist that I know for sure the exact moment when life begins. And its' even harder for me to insist that everyone else agree."

You could not have more elegantly, eloquently, or clearly demonstrated my favorite byline: "Information Kills Religion." Religious assumptions, claims, and propaganda can't survive real, live, data.

Her key words above... *"the more I learn."* Bravo, girl! Youbetcha! The more you learn, the more 2,000 year old assumptions from primitive cultures that we teach our kids as truth, start looking pretty untenable. In light of modern knowledge, they just don't wash. As explained, back in Chapter 6, the fertilized egg divides and becomes a blastocyst, a hollow ball of undifferentiated cells. There are no specific cell types yet. There are no lung cells, brain cells, heart cells or skin cells. This is not a human being, not a person. It doesn't walk, talk, think, feel, experience consciousness, contemplate its own mortality, or google. There is no evidence it has a soul. I purposely teach the facts of natural abortions, as Rachel discovered, in my Introductory Psychology course, when we cover prenatal development. My students are just as surprised as Rachel to learn that estimates range from 50% to as high as 70% of fertilized eggs (zygotes) don't make it past the first week or two. Prenatal development is such an incredibly delicate, rapid, and complex process that so much can go wrong prior to, and after implantation, which usually occurs by the end of the second week.

Every Xian, every person in America, should know these facts which Rachel and some of her readers were just discovering. I hope Rachel continues to read up on embryology. The details of how and when identical twins form, kinda messes up the ideas about "souls" every bit as much as do spontaneous abortions. Does god quick send an angel down with another soul, when an egg splits in two after a few days producing an identical twin? Does he send the angel back down to retrieve it when that twin gets reabsorbed into the other and a chimera (google it) is formed? Does he wait to see if conjoined twins develop two separate functioning brains before he decides to dispatch that angel back for the extra soul if they don't?

Rep. Paul Broun (R) Georgia, a good Baptist, not only declared that evolution and the Big Bang were *"lies from the pit of hell"* a while back, he tellingly included embryology in that list. Rachel showed us why. Studying embryonic development makes it really, really, hard to reconcile old religious claims about the beginning of life, and the soul and such. Maybe these old ideas are just that: old ideas. Thanks again to Rachel and her readers, who despite remaining incredibly entangled in the nonsense they've been taught, exhibit the courage and tenacity to educate themselves and deflate the idiot claims of their own Xian brethren like Broun and the other Republican "*experts*" promoting absurd and painfully wrong views, and for questioning their beliefs in light of real data, real knowledge.

There is only one source of all this ludicrous misinformation about souls and person hood in embryos that conservative Xians are bullshitted with. It is what they were taught as unquestionable truth by their religion. They believe the crazy and often cruel (think homophobia) things they say because they are supposed to, they were taught to, and most of them probably didn't have much choice in the matter, being raised Evangelical. All too often, the primary if not the sole source of utterly unscientific nonsense about the world we live in (Creationism, homophobia, inferiority of women, souls, abortion, end-of-life issues, anti-vaccination etc.) is Conservative Xianity. Being a good Baptist like Mike Huckabee, Sarah Palin, Michelle Bachman, and other Republican figures who made incredibly ignorant claims during the 2012 presidential election, Rep. Broun just can't accept the real data, the real facts of embryology that directly muck up the ancient ideas his religion teaches him. Best part is, Broun is an MD as well, and he's not the only MD who can't handle the science he learned in medical school, which makes the religious claims he grew up on, appear as the primitive and absurd ideas they are.

Ben Carson

Ben Carson. Conservative Xian, repeat Republican Presidential hopeful. Dr. Carson has been the source of a number of absurd claims during both his presidential primary runs. One in particular stands out. His reasoning on how homosexuality occurs and must be a choice, and for which he subsequently apologized. His evidence was, that since some guys evidently turn gay in prison, this was enough to affirm to the good doctor that homosexuality is obviously a choice.

"A lot of people who go into prison go into prison straight, and when they come out, they're gay,"

Done. See how simple? It's not the cause of homosexuality that is simple here, it is the good doctor being simple. But this man can't be simple minded. He has an MD. He was a respected pediatric neurosurgeon. How can he be simple? He must, on the contrary, be very bright. He made it thru medical school, no mean feat. And he wound up at one the most prestigious medical centers in the world. He truly had an impressive career. This is not a stupid man, so how can he make such a stupid judgment, and act so simple-minded basing his conclusion on a dubious assumption and ignoring mountains of real evidence on the subject? From Wikipedia:

"Carson was a professor of neurosurgery, oncology, plastic surgery, and pediatrics, and he was the director of pediatric neurosurgery at Johns Hopkins Hospital. At age 33, he became the youngest major division director in the hospital's history as director of pediatric neurosurgery. In 1987 Carson successfully separated conjoined twins, the Binder twins, who had been joined at the back of the head (craniopagus twins). The 70-member surgical team, led by Carson, worked for 22 hours. At the end, the twins were separated; both survived"

So how can a neurosurgeon, at Johns Hopkins no less, demonstrate such simple and wrong reasoning? All through his training, practice, and the hundreds of surgeries he must have performed, especially in preparing his use of pioneering techniques to separate and save those conjoined twins, he had to use quite sophisticated reasoning dependent on multiple sources of information, to make deeply considered decisions employing multiple types of detailed data to arrive at correct, insightful answers. When he worked in his role as a surgeon, he thought like an evidence demanding, cautious, reasoned scientist. But when he shot his mouth off about the cause of homosexuality, he reasoned like a religionist.

He used one data point, (which wasn't even correct) didn't bother to check out if it was true or not, didn't bother to check or consider the wealth of other information such as the facts or frequency of consensual homosexual acts or rapes in prison, nor how many men actually identify as newly homosexual after experiencing prison sex (or go back to being heterosexual when they are out and have access to females again), nor the massive amount of knowledge we currently have on the biology and psychology of sexual orientation. All of which, as an MD, he could source and understand in a heartbeat. But he didn't. He made an asshole statement completely belying his obvious intelligence, scientific training and acumen. Carson is a Seventh Day Adventist. When you think religiously you ignore the standards of evidence one uses in science, and often decide beliefs with minimum of data points, or none at all, with Scripture and its current interpretation as your replacement for evidence. All with a level of credulity and certainty strenuously avoided by science. From Wikipedia on Seventh Day Adventism:

"The first fundamental belief of the church states that "The Holy Scriptures are the infallible revelation of [God's] will." Adventist theologians generally reject the "verbal inspiration" position on Scripture held by many conservative evangelical Christians"

Dr. Carson belongs to a church of the ultra-Conservative wing of Conservative Xiansanity. Seventh Day Adventists believe in Creationism, the immanent Second Coming of Jesus Christ, Satan, that Jesus is really Michael the Archangel and vice versa (no shit) and homosexuality is not accepted in any way. Done. He doesn't need to research homosexuality like he would a new surgical procedure or medical finding, he doesn't need evidence and he doesn't need to reason about it. His Church, his faith already told him the exact truth of it, because it is in his Book. Science, medicine, research, data, evidence and reason mean nothing when you already know you have eternal, absolute truth.

All religions teach this to varying degrees. All rely on jettisoning reason and evidence for faith. Ben Carson is not a simple minded man by any means. But he speaks like one when he thinks in religion mode. Religious people often slip seamlessly from one mode of thinking to the other. On any other medical question, Dr. Carson would use his training and skills, check out all the evidence, verify the data, but not this one. No need. His Bible has the final word.

When Dr. Carson was prepping up for that eventual 22 hour conjoined twin surgery, wanna bet he did his homework well? He most likely didn't just get lucky. He boned up on the latest techniques and procedures, and read all the available data on the subject of conjoined twins, their complicated anatomy, circulation, entwined nervous systems, etc., etc. You can bet he left no stone unturned, considered all the previous empirical findings, and he pulled it off. But when he made his statement that prison sex makes men gay, he considered no evidence at all, didn't do any homework, didn't consider any available data, and just made it up ignoring at least three significant lines of evidence:

1. Male prison sex. Most of it is rape. Estimates vary that 1/20 to 1/10 of male inmates experience coerced sex. That's 90-95% of inmates that don't get raped or forced into some sort of same-sex activities. Carson's claim *"A lot of people who go into prison go into prison straight, and when they come out, they're gay,"* ain't

so. If any do, it ain't *"a lot."* Does the good doctor have any data on how many, if any, of the minority of men that do get raped in prison subsequently prefer sex with males and avoid women for the rest of their lives? Or do they retain their heterosexuality both in prison and when they get out? *"Yeah, I'm one of the 5% that got forced into passive anal sex while in prison and now I don't find women attractive anymore and find some men to be very attractive and only engage in homosexual acts now. I'm gay."* Right. Got any evidence anyone ever says that, Doc?

2. The biology of sexual orientation. Any MD, or anyone really, is able to scan the literature and see the variation in chromosomal sex, gonadal sex, genital sex and the now well documented sex differences in the brain. Sexual development is under the influence of different hormones at different stages of prenatal development. The behavioral genetics data from identical, fraternal twin, and sibling studies, along with the psychological and sociological data…all point to a biological origin of sexual orientation, none of which supports the hypothesis of it being a "choice." But his ultra-Conservative Xian church cannot accept any biological cause for sexual orientation, it must be, as most other Conservative Xians unfoundedly affirm, a choice.

3. In 2013, over 2 million men were in prison. Of the 320 million people in the US population, 49% are males, that's 128 million US males, 75% of which are over 18, which gives a figure of 96 million adult males. Two million of them are in prison which gives us an incarceration rate of 2%. So assuming homosexuals are incarcerated at the same rate as heteros, then 2% or less of the gay population ever experience prison life. So 98% of gay guys don't get gay from a prison en counter. So even if Dr. Carson's claim were true, that prison sex makes guys gay (it most likely isn't) it wouldn't account for the vast majority of gayness. Homo sexuals don't become gay from experiencing same sex encounters in prison. This is your brain on religion. It make us stupid, even when we are not.

Dr. Carson apologized the next day and offered no support for his position. There is no evidence that homosexual encounters, coerced or consensual in prison change anyone's sexual orientation. Maybe that's why he was silent on the issue. Again, here's a man who spent his entire adult life, over 40 years, from age 18 to age 60 when he retired, immersed in learning, researching and considering mountains of factual data on the human medical condition, from his pre-med undergraduate days through medical school, internships and residency and throughout his impressive career. This is a man more familiar than most with the rigors of discovering and assimilating cutting edge human knowledge. One would think he would have defended his statement like a champ, supporting his reasoning with study after study, as he would defend any diagnosis he ever made, or any surgical procedure he meticulously planned and executed. Instead he gave no support for his statement, withdrew it and apologized. Done.

Carson certainly appears more than capable of making an informed statement on sexual orientation. He must be a very bright man. But it also appears that he ignores his own intellect, training and skill and allows his faith to dictate his decision making when the reality may conflict with what his Church demands as a matter of faith. Reason and evidence are rejected, for acceptance of scriptural authority and an attendant denial of actual knowledge. This is not a good candidate for a President. This is a very bright man, losing whatever credibility he had, which he may have rightly earned through his efforts and success as a prominent physician. This wasn't the first time his Conservative Xian claims have not helped his candidacy. This is your brain on religion.

Carbon 14 Can't Work

Todd Friel, Xian commentator extraordinaire, couldn't be more dishonest. In his video review of the famous Ken Ham/ Bill Nye Creationism/Evolution debate, it only took him a bit over 2 minutes to straight out lie to his viewing audience about the science of tree-ring dating (dendrochronology), and Carbon 14 dating. He actually says this at 2:15 into his video:

"How do we date trees that are hundreds of years old? It is not by tree rings, we need to use dating mechanisms like Carbon 14 dating which have been demonstrated and proven to be unreliable. That is proven.... We don't have an accurate way to date those trees."

I almost fell out of my chair. It takes just 12 seconds for him to tell those two completely horrendous lies about the reality of the science, so here's the facts of the matter. We don't use C14 dating on anything that is still alive, much less living trees. Carbon 14 is used routinely all over the world and has never been *"proven unreliable."* We do use tree rings and quite accurately to date trees hundreds and thousands of years old, alive and dead.

Then he had the 24 karat audacity to say Bill Nye was lying! You can check out the science of tree ring dating and the worldwide use of C14 for yourself at dozens of websites, starting with the comprehensive and well-referenced Wikipedia. Friel then goes on to say his viewers can look it all up and see that it was Bill Nye who was lying. What balls! He is, of course, banking on what he really knows about his audience. The vast majority of his followers will never bother to look up a Wikipedia article or anything else on the science of dendrochronology or C14 dating, they will just take his word for it. Furthermore, if they do make an effort to look it up for themselves, it might well be on Ken Ham's Answers In Genesis website or Ham's YouTube video dissing C14 dating, or similar dishonest Conservative Xian propaganda, which is also completely wrong. His audience will most likely never see the science and he knows it.

There are over 130 C14 labs worldwide cranking out dates as routinely as you get a blood or urine test from your doctor. And there are trees, lots of them, older than

6,000 years. Dating science is solid, and corroborated by dozens of methods that all hang together. Friel has only one way out. He looks straight in the camera and lies about it. We must keep attacking this kind of pseudoscience promoted by Conservative Xiansanity. It doesn't get a free pass anymore. We should be strident.

C14 Redux: The Shroud of Turin

So we know Ken Ham, Todd Friel, Ray Comfort, and lot of other Xians don't like Carbon 14 dating, or the 40 other radiometric dating methods that also employ naturally occurring radioactive elements, nor the dozen other non-radioactive methods like tree ring counting, because they expose the absurd lie that the earth is only 6,000 years old. The Shroud of Turin controversy has been raging on for a few years now, with the pious desperately in search of some artifactual evidence of JC and his resurrection. Nobody trades much in pieces of the cross or bones of the saints anymore, although one can find little churches all over Europe and Asia Minor that claim to have some chunk of wood from Christ's cross or the tears or blood of a Saint, but most of that stays pretty local nowadays. The Shroud is a whole other matter.

In 2014, an article was published in what looks to be a standard science journal, which proposed some rather speculative and far-fetched theories about the dating and origin of the image on the Shroud. The religious types have not been happy that the Shroud was dated by 3 different C14 labs independently to 1,000-1,260 C.E., which is around the time that the Shroud first shows up in the historical record. The journal article by Carpentieri, et al., claims that an earthquake around the time of the crucifixion, may have caused neutron radiation to be released which not only made the image, but re-calibrated the C14 in the cloth to make it come out with the "*false*" late dating, of after 1000 C.E. instead of around 30 C.E., the alleged time of Christ. Now that's quite a stretch. The journal this rather far-fetched piece was published in is called *Meccanica*, an Italian science journal that looks reasonably respectable. From the Meccanica web page:

"*Focuses on the methodological framework shared by mechanical scientists when addressing theoretical or applied problems. Includes contemporary research on general mechanics, solid and structural mechanics, fluid mechanics, and mechanics of machines. Includes full length papers; topical overviews; brief notes; discussions and comments on published papers; book reviews; and an international calendar of conferences.*"

Pretty normal stuff for a highly specific journal within a sub-field of physics/engineering. So how did a highly speculative paper on the Shroud of Turin's C14 content being somehow altered by hypothesized neutron emission, from an undocumented earthquake, that also by some other unknown process of said neutrons, then produced the image of Christ, wind up in a journal on structural and fluid mechanics? How the fuck does something like this get through the peer-review critique and analysis to even be considered, much less published in a seemingly respectable physics/engineering journal? It didn't.

The first author is the editor of the journal. He published his own bullshit in his own journal. Unbelievable balls. An engineer, who may be a whiz at structural or fluid mechanics, probably doesn't do earthquake research, and may not know shit about them. Also, someone with expertise in the mechanics branch of physics, may not have relevant background in particle physics or atomic chemistry, or know much about neutron emission, much less understand specific research on neutrons affecting other elements and their isotopes, nor the even more speculative suggestion of some sort of neutron imaging that is suggested to have occurred. One of the comments on Jerry Coyne's *New Republic* piece on the *Meccanica* mess said it all:

*"Scientists who use stable isotopes like 13C and 15N for well-accepted purposes like inferring carbon sources (C3 vs C4 plants) or trophic position know that C and N are incorporated into plants and plant products like cotton and linen as the plants grow. C is fixed from atmospheric CO2. I can't think of a plausible mechanism where the 14C signature could be altered after the plants are harvested, spun and woven into cloth. This is testable, but I doubt if the people who did this work thought this through...***The paper in question would never have made it through even a cursory peer review in a real scientific journal.*** (emphasis, mine). And peer review is the standard – if you claim something extraordinary, be prepared to answer a lot of questions and criticisms about how you are probably wrong."*

Peer-review? Scientific vetting of ideas and information? *"Fuck that. I'll just publish in my own journal. Hey, I'm the editor, what are they gonna do?"* So Ken Ham hates C14 dating without reservation, and Dr. Carpentieri knows too much science (maybe not so much about research, eh?), that he can't just dismiss it like Ham. But he desperately wants C14 to work in support of his preconceived religious convictions, and thereby will propose absolutely absurd ideas, and sneak them around the normal vetting process, in an attempt to give them credibility they don't deserve. He ignores not only the publication process to promote provable science, but denies most of his science training and the mountains of real knowledge on the subject. Such is the arrogance of religious thought.

Ex Nihilo

In 1215 The Lateran IV Council of the Catholic Church proclaimed that:

"God... creator of all visible and invisible things, of the spiritual and of the corporal; who by His own omnipotent power at once from the beginning of time created each creature (from nothing), spiritual and corporal, namely, angelic and mundane, and finally the human, constituted as it were, alike of the spirit and the body (D.428). Deus... de nihilo condidit."

God, out of nothing created all things (even the angels). Angels, huh? Really? Lions and tigers and bears, oh my. *'Ex nihilo nihil fit,'* "Out of nothing, nothing comes." Unless God decides to create something from nothing, nothing can come from nothing. Only He can do so and did so. That's the crux of the theological and philosophical biscuit. This idea has been around for millennia. And thus it came to pass, the existence of "nothing" became a religious truism and a dogma of the Church for the last 1,000 years or so. More importantly, it has crept along silently, deep into our culture ever since as sort of an unquestioned cosmic given:

"Once upon a time there was absolutely nothing, and God made everything out of it."

It seems to have permeated philosophy as well as theology, although not modern science. Scientists are always willing to adjust their metaphysical assumptions to whatever they actually find in the world, while our theological and philosophical friends appear a bit more recalcitrant. What if, despite the Lateran Council's authoritative proclamation, there is no true absence of matter or energy (which we know from Einstein's $E = mc^2$ are manifestations of the same thing)? What if we discover, as is the case with otherwise empty space devoid of matter, there is an energy there, and space isn't really, completely empty? What if we find there is always something there, matter or energy. Suppose we find the true nothing, the "nihilo" we have assumed must precede everything doesn't really exist?

Could it be this nothing, this nihilo, is merely an idea, an old idea, a very old idea, existing only in philosopher's and theologian's heads? What if true absence of anything is merely a metaphysical construct, an imaginary idea like the firmament, caloric, heaven, phlogiston, ectoplasm, monads, hell, soul, or the luminiferous aether. These are all entities once proposed to explain how reality truly is, that turned out not to exist in the world we find ourselves in. Like unicorns. Those are in the Bible, after all, but like Bigfoot and fairies, they don't exist either, never did. What if our standard conception of nothing, enshrined in Church dogma and foundational in our culture never existed either?

Lawrence Krauss's 2012 book, *A Universe from Nothing* is a fascinating and dense wind through modern cosmology, which redefines nothing and shows that from the kind of nothing the physicists find something (our universe and everything in it) can, and most likely did, come "ex nihilo" without need, without evidence of any god. Some philosophers, and most likely all the theologians, aren't satisfied with the cosmologist's claim. They want theoretical physics to describe and experimental physics to discover the theologians' *"true and absolute nothing"*, *the "nihilo"*, the kind out of which nothing comes, unless God decides to create it. Some also want evidence of god. So far none is forthcoming on either desire. Krauss explains, that the nothing discerned by modern cosmology isn't really nothing; empty space has energy out of which virtual particles appear all the time, and out of which our universe came. Furthermore, the physicists and cosmologists are also led to the construct that our universe just may be one of an infinite number of universes (the *"multiverse"* conclusion). There may not be the kind of nothing the philosophers and theologians have traditionally assumed to exist for their god to pop all of existence out of, and our universe may not be the only one.

For Krauss and the modern-day cosmologists, the multiverse is a *"well motivat-*

ed" conclusion, while many theologians and philosophers decry that Krauss and his colleagues are merely engaging in their own speculative metaphysics (like philosophers and theologians do - it's called "making shit up") in postulating a multiverse. Solely, they claim, to dodge the real explanation from nothing the philostofers and god-mullers expect. They misconstrue the multiverse conclusion as if it were a theory itself, more precisely an ad hoc hypothesis, posed to avoid finding the *"nothing"* ours came from. Again *"nihilo"* is assumed as an unquestionable entity because it is so entrenched in the cultural background they expect Krauss and the whole of cosmology and particle physics to find it. Krauss explains in his book, that the multiverse is not a theory someone made up, it's a prediction, a component of, a consequence of the early inflation of the universe. It is not a separate theory, or an ad hoc explanation pasted on, just made up, to explain where our universe came from, how our universe appeared. But the non-scientist crowd want *"nothing"* not multiverses because *"out of nothing, nothing comes"* therefore God. You need an intelligent agent of some kind to make something out of nothing. And you need real nothing. The Lateran Council proclaimed so

But that's all just made up. It's just an old idea that has become an accepted truism. It is merely a supposition. There is no theory or observation behind it, wholly unlike the gozillion observations, calculations and theoretical paths in cosmology and particle physics that lead to the multiverse conclusion. Ironically, the philosophers and the theologians through the centuries, sitting in their armchairs, actually did exactly nothing to get the ex nihilo idea. They did no systematic observation of the universe, they did no experiments, didn't arrive at any theoretical constructs built on observations, they did no calculations to lead them to the proclamation of the ex nihilo. They just made it up. It has no basis in the real world. It is pure speculation. Which is exactly what many philosophers and all theologians do, with the exception of some modern philosophers who take the empirical findings of science as their starting point. On the contrary, the multiverse conclusion and the observation that space is not really empty, is based on what we have discovered about the real world we find ourselves in. As Krauss says:

"While inflation demonstrates how empty space endowed with energy can effectively create everything we see, along with an unbelievably large and flat universe, it would be disingenuous to suggest that empty space endowed with energy, which drives inflation, is really nothing."

Science stresses the importance of our progress as a species in discerning our world, by actually going out into it and testing our conjectures. We can't sit back in our armchairs and ruminate, and then pontificate any longer. We have to test our ideas in reality. Oddly enough, some folks don't like that at all. So just what comes out of nothing, that is no observation, no experiment, no verification, no replication? Mostly bullshit. *"Ex nihilo...merda taurorum fit."* Loosely translated *"Out of nothing... bullshit comes."*

Pick a Story, Any Story

Forty three professors and employees of Murray State University, in Murray, Kentucky, where I taught for some time, placed an ad in the school newspaper proclaiming *"The Creator of the Universe Came to Earth for You"* suggesting students should access the Jesus Story as told by Josh McDowell, a well-known, longtime Xian apologist. I've read much of the Bible, compared its stories and read apologists like McDowell and others, but unlike most Xians, I've read the other side too: Biblical scholarship, the study of the origins and history of the Bible, how it was written, when and by whom. The ad lists statements about Jesus including:

"He remained on earth speaking to people for 40 days and then ascended to heaven."

There is no evidence of Jesus' deeds outside of the New Testament, so I grabbed my well-worn King James Bible in paperback with the duct-taped cover, which I've referenced for over 30 years, to see what it says about the 40 days and JC's Ascension into heaven. There are six different accounts of the Resurrection, and most of the details contradict one another irreconcilably. The 40 days claim, for example, as compared in Paul, Mark, Matthew, Luke, Acts, and John is no exception. Paul in his epistles says nothing of it, Mark, the first Gospel written, says clearly only one day passed before the Ascension into heaven, not 40, as does Luke, one of the Gospel rewrites of Mark. Matthew, the other rewrite of Mark says nothing, John, at least 8 days. Only in Acts does the period of 40 days appear. So was it one, eight, 40 or none? The Ascension itself is worse: Paul; no Ascension, Mark says Jerusalem, Luke; Bethany, Matthew; no Ascension, John; no Ascension and Acts; the Mount of Olives. So, was there an Ascension, and was it in Jerusalem, or a mile or so away on the Mount or specifically in Bethany? The accounts read like myths, like legend embellished over time, not like "reliable writing" as McDowell claims. This is but one example of many stories in the Bible, which sound plausible compiled into the composite story we were taught as kids, but for which apologists like McDowell, need to explain away the discrepancies and contradictions in the different accounts.

The point is this: when it comes to evidence, up to date knowledge, and lack of contradictory explanations that we demand in any other domain of human knowledge, religion gets a free pass. Most of us would be outraged if we sent our children to math or biology class and they got information 50-100 years out of date, like McDowell's composite Jesus stories. Imagine if your child took an astronomy course, and the knowledge gained in the last 100 years was conveniently glossed over, or plainly ignored: no galaxies, no quasars, pulsars, or black holes, no cosmic background radiation, no 13.5 billion year age of the universe, etc. We wouldn't stand for it.

But somehow it is OK when you send your child to Vacation Bible School, Catechism, weekly Bible study or religion class, and they get told the Gospels are eyewitness accounts by apostles, for example, when modern Biblical scholars, Xian and secular ones alike, know the Gospels were written anonymously, not by apostles, and that there are no eyewitness accounts in the Bible. None. Your kids aren't told that Paul never met Jesus or that nearly half of his epistles were not written by him, but are forgeries, written is his name. Or that the Resurrection story has six contradictory versions.

Imagine if your biology text had six different versions of the ATP cycle in successive chapters, and contradicted itself enough that your instructor would have to do the sort of verbal gymnastics that an apologist like Josh McDowell has to do, to make the Resurrection sound plausible. You wouldn't buy it for a second. But religious stories get a pass. What if your chemistry book had 6 different and incompatible structures for the benzene ring: one has 7, two have 6, one at least 8 carbon atoms, three are rings, but one is an open chain, and another account doesn't say how many carbon atoms there are. You'd be mighty skeptical and rightly so. The contradictions noted above are easily referenced and verified from dozens of sources of Biblical history and analysis, and you can examine them in the Bible for yourself. *Godless* by Dan Barker or any of Bart Ehrman's books provide readable introductions into Biblical history, where you can also source the original scholarship. Claiming you know things to be eternally true; like JC spending 40 days resurrected from the dead, chatting with his buddies and then ascended into heaven, when all the data show it is a hopelessly contradictory myth, passed down to us in multiple versions by unknown authors, and then teaching it to children as unquestionable truth, is hopelessly dishonest and in total denial of what we really know. How more arrogant can you get?

Only Bad, Bad Atheists

Pastor Rick Henderson published a piece in the Huffington Post in 2013 entitled *"Why There is No Such Thing as a Good Atheist."* To start straight off with an asshole statement like that is just breathtaking. Go for it Rick, step on your dick with both feet. Bring it on, pal. Proclaiming that us Unbelieving Scum are just that, scum, that we can't possibly be good, a good atheist has never existed, is just as dumb and arrogant a statement as it gets. One glance at Phil Zuckerman's *"Society without God"* will tell you just how good most of the non-believing inhabitants of Northern Europe are. Or read about someone like Bertrand Russell who despite his disbelief, won a Noble Prize in Literature in recognition of his varied and significant writings in which he championed humanitarian ideals. Not bad for a fucking atheist, huh?

Consider Bill Gates, another nonbeliever who just can't be good, despite giving 90% plus of his billions in personal wealth to charity, and spearheading stupendous humanitarian projects of incredible scope, all over the globe. What an asshole Gates is, huh? Fuckin' atheist. Or just go out and get to know a few non-believers, and you will find some pretty good people, some damn good ones even. Most of us disbelievers, who have jettisoned any idea of god or gods are just regular folks, not famous, not special, but nice common folks. We're your neighbors, law abiding citizens, generous, kind, polite, full of the same normal human empathy that believing folks have. We are as good as anyone else. So Rick's dead wrong from the start. *And everyone knows it.* Most believers know at least a few non-believers themselves, so they can vouch for us too.

But then Rick Henderson is a pastor. A Baptist minister who was trained in a Baptist seminary. So he knows. He's been trained that he has the ultimate truth already in his book and has no need of facts. Let's take a look at his reasoning which makes him so sure, that he cannot be refuted. At the very beginning of his HuffPo article, he does get it right that most atheists are also scientific materialists as well, and don't buy supernatural, wishful-thinking explanations of the world as we find it. So far so good. Additionally, he suggests most of us feel the universe appears rather indifferent to us, and there is no cosmic consciousness guiding it somehow. Once again, an accurate portrayal. However, after quoting a few nonbelievers on that indifference and lack of meaning we *find* in the universe, he skips the next part where most of us also feel our lives, all our lives, all human lives are not without meaning at all. As humans, as members of this species, we bring meaning to our lives in our interactions with others, in our pursuit of knowledge, in raising our kids, in helping our fellow man, in making the world a better place for us all. But he has to skip that part of course, because *"there is no such thing as a good atheist"*, remember?

Then Pastor Rick really goes off the rails. He rightly posits that atheists feel that our sense of morality is an evolved trait. But then he does his own "just so story" worthy of the worst misuse of evolutionary psychology ever, and decides that, wait for it: rape must be moral for atheists. You heard it right, atheists have to believe rape is moral. Yup, the only way our moral sense could have evolved is to include that rape was adaptive, it made us more fit, was a good way to produce offspring and therefore it is also moral. Got that? This is irrefutable, unassailable logic according to the mighty Pastor Rick. And get this; killing mentally handicapped kids or torturing diseased children, must have been adaptive too and therefore just as moral for atheists as rape. *Oh my.* Ludicrous, but he at least he tried to make an argument. The adaptiveness of *"torturing diseased children?"* Where the fuck did that come from? What sort of sick mind even thinks of that?

Worthy of another salute to the mighty mind, the staggering intellect of Pastor Rick! This is what happens when ministers attempt to do science, and conjure up how human evolution must have gone down. Because he can't think of any other way it must have happened, then that must be what atheists logically conclude, and he has got to be right. He warns all comers from the beginning: *"I contend that any response you make will prove my case... the deck is stacked, the odds are in my favor."*

Some spectacular ego, huh? Well, Rick, rape may not be all that adaptive, and it certainly isn't moral for anyone, despite your twisted logic and fantasy human evolution spiel. Most people, believers and non-believers alike, find it reprehensible. Nobody wants their mom or sister raped. Since the Enlightenment we have been extending our moral sense beyond our immediate family. Most folks nowadays, don't wish rape on anybody. If the good pastor studied a little human evolution, a little animal behavior, some anthropology, some real evolutionary biology (instead of the bullshit he made up), he might get a different perspective, having been appraised of some factual data from those disciplines. For example, it appears that pair-bonding, males and females staying together over the long term to raise human children together, may have been the adaptive strategy, probably not rape, sorry Rick.

Humans have the longest childhood of any species. The pre-adolescent body is immature in musculature and reproductive capability, and the adolescent brain isn't done with development until late adolescence, young adult hood. Couple this with the fact that the human infant is the most helpless of critters. Most other primates, like our chimp cousins, are fully adult in a third of the time as humans, and are developed in their motor systems enough to clamber around right after birth.

Human infants can't make a full fist for the first six months and can't support their weight until after their first year, and even then it is sketchy. They don't call them toddlers for nothing. Pair bonding is very common in species where it takes two to raise the offspring. Humans are consistent pair-bonders, and despite a little cheating, we stay paired or pair up again. It is universal and sanctioned the world over in the cultural practices of marriage. Especially in hunter-gatherer settings, two are really necessary to raise children and successfully propagate your genes. Outcomes of single motherhood children in difficult conditions are not good. It is tough enough in modern times, it may have been near impossible to raise children without a partner for most of human existence. Running around raping might not have done much for the species. So this unprecedented long childhood may have required pair bonding, consistent male and female commitment, and long term raising of children together to get this big brained child to maturity and teach it to survive in the human cognitive niche. Pair bonding and marriage is the norm for producing offspring in humans, not rape.

Rape might not have been so adaptive to spread your genes around for another reason: human females are the only primate that has concealed estrus. You don't know when she is fertile. When a polygamous male chimp copulates with a number of females during mating season, which is often coerced, it is often damn near rape, and he knows the females are fertile. Her obvious rump swellings of estrus are an unmistakable sign. You could say rape might be adaptive for chimps. Spread your seed and split whether she wants it or not. Chance of pregnancy couldn't be higher. Raping human females might not be such an adaptive strategy as you have only a small chance that any forced copulation might result in a pregnancy. Human females have no rump swellings or color changes to signal fertility. In addition, regular copulation throughout the woman's cycle, which is also unprecedented in any other animal, keeps the pair bond together, helps insure paternity and mediates the family unit that Xians like Rick are so ga-ga over. Yeah, Rick that likely evolved too. Long before the Adam and Eve story was written.

There is a vast literature in evolutionary psychology and anthropology on rape as well, and there is no consensus on the adaptiveness of rape in humans. I doubt if Pastor Rick's armchair musings have settled the score. But being a good Baptist, he gets to deny or ignore whatever science there may be, because as a man of god he already has the truth, all the truth. And whatever truth he doesn't have, like any good theologian, he will just make it up anyway.

Lastly, nonbelievers find rape to be as immoral as anyone else. You might have checked that data too. But no. Pastor Rick, you have proved nothing beyond your ego is as big as your propensity to make asshole statements. Besides, what the fuck do Baptist ministers, or any minister know about evolution? How many courses have you taken, how many books and published research articles have you read on evolution, paleontology, molecular biology, paleoanthropology, genetics, comparative anatomy, embryology, genomics and other related disciplines? Probably next to none, as Rick so aptly demonstrates by his complete ignorance of information from all these fields. Pastor Rick's claims just exemplify the arrogance of religious thought.

Don't Get Your Science from a Church

The earth is at the center of the universe, fixed, unmoving. Then the moon, inner planets, then comes the Sun, Mars, Jupiter and Saturn, then the stars fixed in the firmament, and beyond…the habitat of God. A decent, plausible, early model of the universe as one would observe it without instruments or space travel, or the benefit of meticulous observations like those of the 16th century Danish astronomer Tycho Brahe, all of which along with Kepler's laws of planetary motion, Galileo's observations of Jupiter's moons, and Newton's gravity, eventually led to the complete rejection of this geocentric (earth-centered) system and total modern acceptance of the Copernican heliocentric (sun centered) system. There is nothing inherently foolish or evil or repressive in the old geocentric system of Ptolemy as adopted by Holy Mother Church. But therein lies the problem. That earth-centered system was adopted and became unchangeable. When the Church decides to do science, a cluster-fuck is in the offing. Cuz ya see, the Church stands for everything that science is not: certainty, fixed-ness, faith, considering authority and scriptural claims as evidence in place of observational data and theory, and the threat of apostasy and eternal damnation should one dare to challenge orthodoxy. Denial of knowledge follows from faith.

The first 17 verses of Genesis describe a geocentric cosmos in agreement with the Ptolemaic-Aristotelian system described above. It was easy for the Catholic Church to adopt the earth centered model of the heavens and make it unassailable dogma. Significantly, there is one other thing the Biblical and the pre-Copernican depiction of the cosmos have in common. They are dead-nuts, flat-out, unequivocally, blind-fuck, douche-bucket wrong. And that's about as wrong as anything can get. Brahe observed supernovas come and go, Galileo saw moons around Jupiter, Venus had phases and the moon was not a perfect celestial orb, it was a mess of crags and craters. But the Church had to deny that science to save the adopted dogma that the heavens were perfect and unchanging with the earth at the center instead of the sun, and it only took them a few centuries to apologize.

God is Not Allowed in the Lab

God never shows up in the lab. When we really examine the world as it is, systematically observe it, and examine it employing theory and experimentation, there's no god to be found. We all tacitly acknowledge it, even the devout. They know better. It is pretty ridiculous that as soon as we put the fence of empirical discovery around a piece of God's creation, he's locked out. When we engage the world as we find ourselves in it, we find no god. And even if we believe in one, he doesn't ever show up in the lab and we don't let him in. Think about it, why not?

Why do even the most devout Xian scientists not pray in the laboratory, or expect a miracle to occur overnight so their experiment will have worked the next morning? What's so special about lab doors and walls, that even hard-core believers know God can't get in. He made every square inch of His Creation didn't he? The Red Sea parted at his whim, bushes burned, the dead rose (or at least they used to) and the locusts descended. He used to turn water into wine, a purely chemical trick, so why don't we pray to god to make our solution precipitate, or why don't we pray for him to make the complex pharmaceutical molecule we are trying to synthesize, just appear out of thin air? Because we know better. Every scientist, even believing ones, have enough experience with the world to know prayer doesn't work in the lab, miracles don't happen. God is not allowed. They know better. For that matter, why don't we pray for God, any god to re-attach an amputated limb or better yet, regrow one miraculously overnight? Why does our omnipotent god seem so impotent with basic science projects and medical repairs we can see?

Believers will pray for a remission of cancers hidden inside, so why not pray for him to rearrange complex molecules that we can't see either, to make our next "miracle" drug? Why? Because we know better. We all know better. Even Xians know better, scientists or not. They don't pray for a new finger, or even a paltry fingertip. They know deep down it is all bullshit. How 'bout an earlobe? Surely the master of the universe, the supreme intelligence who just had to be behind the Big Bang, creating all matter and energy, all our worlds, the land and plants and animals, surely a few measly earlobe cells would be a snore for Him. But we know better. Yes, the most godly of Xians don't pray for a new earlobe or a measly fingertip to grow back. They go see a plastic surgeon, even for paltry fixes such as these. Fact is, we all know better.

Think of it. If you believe, but you are also a scientist, you limit your omnipotent god's meanderings and heavenly influence to everywhere but in your lab, anybody's lab, all labs. You know it doesn't work that way. You know He won't show up. Deep down, I think everybody knows its bullshit but cultural inertia makes us retell the story that He raised the dead and turned water into wine and maybe snuck in a few miracles later on for a saint now and then, but all way back when. Not now. Never any miracles now, and certainly not in the lab. Any lab. Not ever. Try to publish a miracle. Go for it. We pay lip service to the scam that miracles occurred, but we really know better. And we betray that knowledge when we don't let god in the lab, or never pray for a new earlobe.

Maybe there's about 5,000 (50' x100') square feet in the average lab room. What's so special about that space, any lab space? Before the high rise research facility was built, and the space the lab occupies was just clear blue sky, God could look down and make the birdies sing or whip up one of his rainbows there, maybe answer that odd prayer every now and again as the Xians will tellya, but now that there are lab walls around that section of once heavenly sky, god ain't allowed in no more. He's locked out. Ludicrous, ain't it? Labs are off-limits to God, all gods, any gods. Isn't that interesting? Even when a scientist is so sure they are discovering, uncovering, the glory of their god and His handiwork in His creation through their science, they don't let Him interfere, He's not a factor, not a variable. He has no influence whatsoever. He's shunted aside, ignored. Even as devout a Xian as Issac Newton left Him out when doing his work: there's no god in the equations. All scientists leave their religion at the laboratory door.

Francis Collins and Science 10, Bible 0

The prominent scientist Francis Collins, director of the NIH (National Institute of Health), co-discoverer of the cystic fibrosis gene and head of the government effort that mapped the human genome, is a later in life born-again Evangelical Xian, who claims there is no conflict between religion and science. He claims unabashedly: *"God can be found in the cathedral or the laboratory."* I feature Dr. Collins, and two other prominent Xian scientists (Ken Miller and Theodosius Dobzhansky), in my special evolution lecture given in my Introductory Psychology courses every semester. Psychology textbooks refer to evolution regularly in explaining human behavior so I provide my students detailed information on evolution that most have never, ever, heard since many Xians in America do not share Dr. Collins conciliatory view of science and religion and make it very difficult for biology teachers to teach much "Evilution" in our high schools. Poll after poll, show nearly half of the US population denies evolution (and now some other modern scientific findings like the Big Bang), thanks to the well-funded efforts of conservative Xians. Sounds like a mighty big conflict of religion versus science to me. I show my students that denial of evolution is absurd given the oceans of data that we have and are continuing to accumulate exponentially with every passing day. I use Dr. Collins, and the other two respected scientists, as examples of devout Xians, as well as accomplished scientists, who staunchly defend evolution. Collins founded his own website "BioLogos" some time ago, to attempt to convince Evangelicals their religion must be interpreted in terms of modern science. Despite his characterization that there is no conflict, the fact that he needed a website to get his fellow Xians to stop denying whole chunks of science, is a blatant acknowledgment that there is an undeniable clash of religious and science claims; else he wouldn't need the website at all!

The only way to reconcile the inescapable conflict of religion and science is for religious ideas to yield to new knowledge. Religious claims are proven wrong by science, never the other way around. It has been going on for centuries (think Copernicus, Galileo, and others) and is now accelerating rapidly, due to the incredible advance of science in the modern age. For example, Collins' BioLogos website unequivocally supports the very new and damning genetic evidence that humans could not have evolved from only two people. The Adam and Eve story is metaphor at best, myth at worst. Modern human populations are descended from thousands of individuals, not two, and 10's of thousands of years ago, not a mere 6,000. As a nontheist, I wholeheartedly applaud Dr. Collins efforts, admire him greatly as a scientist, and have no issue with his rather deistic perspectives on God, which one encounters in his interviews or his book *Language of God*. If you believe that there must have been a Creator being, that some agent must have started it all, go for it, enjoy. Collins also believes in miracles, although he readily admits they haven't happened in his lifetime and are most likely incredibly rare, if they happen at all. More tellingly, as an accomplished, practicing scientist he knows miracles do not, have never, figured in the pursuit of knowledge anywhere, anytime. Like the other Xian scientists I feature in my lecture, in fact in company with all religious scientists, he leaves his religion at the laboratory door. God is not found in the lab.

No matter how devout he may be, and I don't doubt Dr. Collins' sincerity one bit, he doesn't expect prayers to be answered in his lab. He didn't hope for miracles to make the cystic fibrosis gene magically appear one day beside a burning bush, he didn't expect to beat the private attempt to map the human genome by having the 3 billion base pair sequence handed down to him inscribed on stone tablets. He knows the world doesn't work that way. If you are a religious scientist, let's take a Xian for example like Francis Collins, you believe in an all-powerful, omniscient god who made the entire universe and everything in it... no small feat!!! And you pray to him for some kind of intercession on matters of life and death, ill-health usually, hoping he will somehow intervene.

He could intervene, if your lab space wasn't a lab but a hospital room and your grandmother was dying of cancer and you would pray for him to stop her cancer. But within the same four walls, if converted later into the hospital medical lab, you wouldn't think to pray for your god to make a chemical analysis work to identify the same cancer. What if you move to another lab, or expand yours... suddenly god is locked out of an even bigger and wholly arbitrary chunk of the world that he fucking created?

Suppose, for example, your lab is scheduled to take over office space from a Xian charity organization that is moving out to better digs in the mega-church complex down the street (a not unlikely scenario). All the existing office staff in the charity organization begin their day with a prayer as part of their daily routine, and many feel strongly that on occasion, their prayers are surely answered. God is found throughout the entire floor and makes his presence known answering a prayer now and then, for the faithful in residence (or so they fervently believe). So they move out, and the genetics lab moves in, and God moves out with them. No miracle, no randomly answered prayers, no evidence of God's interaction to be found ever again. Or in any lab anywhere, at any time. And what if you have to do fieldwork? I'm fond of saying the arrogance of religious thought knows no bounds, but the absurdity of religious thought knows none either.

As a scientist Dr. Collins knows:

1. The earth isn't the center of the solar system,
2. Adam and Eve is a metaphor,
3. Females do not issue from males ribs,
4. Evolution happened: not Noah nor the Flood,
5. There were never giants in the human race,
6. The earth is 4.3 billion years old: not 6 or 10 thousand,
7. Human longevity was never hundreds of years,
8. Female humans don't have offspring in their nineties,
9. Language evolution is well documented without a Tower of Babel,
10. If someone hears voices in their head to slay their son with a knife for a burnt offering, they need medication, and quickly.

Francis Collins and Science, 10: Bible, 0... and we aren't even out of Genesis yet! And remember, this man considers himself an Evangelical Xian, and yet even he has to throw out so much of his very own precious Bible! That's how the conflict is settled; religious claims are reinterpreted or rejected outright in light of modern knowledge. There is no science in the Bible.

The Power of Prayer

Rain dances don't work. We know this. And sacrificing small animals will not grant us special favors from an unseen spirit. Such ideas nowadays are beyond laughable, not worthy of a moment's serious consideration. But the "power of prayer" remains as an unquestioned given for so many in our modern culture, that it is politically incorrect to doubt or disparage it, because the religious might be offended. So can we pray for rain and expect an answer? One of the Republican presidential candidates in the 2012 primaries evidently thought so. Rick Perry, governor of Texas, enshrined just such an expectation in an official state proclamation; *"...it seems right and fitting that the people of Texas should join together in prayer to humbly seek an end to this devastating drought..."*

Maybe he should have danced. That was in April of 2011 and the drought continued unabated for months. Undaunted, Governor Perry went for a grander request:

fixing a "Nation in Crisis" through a mass evangelical prayer rally that same August. Maybe praying for rain or a better economy makes some of us feel real good for a very short time, but don't we all know better, as far as what to truly expect from prayer, other than our own momentary feeling of satisfaction having prayed? We pray for survival from a heart attack, remission of cancer, the early end of sickness and pain. We pray only for hidden, ephemeral results: things we can never tell if prayer has any real effect upon. Nobody prays for a new limb, a reattached finger, not even a paltry earlobe. Instead we see a surgeon. As discussed above, should not a few measly earlobe or fingertip cells regrown in the night whilst we sleep be a trifling task for the Creator of the universe, who created every flippin' thing ex nihilo, down to every last elementary particle across the entire universe? Pretty obvious isn't it, the whole claim for any power of prayer is beyond ridiculous?

There's a whole website dedicated to exposing the absurdity of it all: *"Why Won't God Heal Amputees?"* One who is implored to rearrange weather patterns over hundreds of square miles of west Texas, or magically dissolve Obamacare at the Republican faithful's humble request, surely He could be called upon to whip up a few measly centimeters of earlobe flesh for us overnight? But nobody prays for that, or for a new amputated limb, or to start our car. Even the most devoutly religious get a jump from their neighbor or call a mechanic. They know better. We know better. So why keep up the delusion? Why continue to lie to our kids?

Consider this quick thought experiment. According to the CDC, over 150,000 US adults contract and die of lung cancer every year. Given that nearly 80% of us Americans are religious to some degree and believe in one god or another, one can safely assume that these victims of adult cancer: someone's mom, dad, aunt, uncle, sister, brother, were prayed for by any number of relatives, friends, coworkers, etc., on at least one if not many occasions. Even the non-believers among them, were likely included in the prayers of believing friends, relatives, and at very least in the general prayers "for the sick and dying" offered up in churches throughout the land every Sunday. So these 150,000-plus cancer stricken folks each conservatively had dozens of prayers for their survival submitted on their behalf. Besides being prayed for what do they all have in common? They're all dead.

That's millions of unanswered prayers for this one illness alone, in just one country. Extend that reasoning to the 6 million or so children who die every year before age five of disease, hunger, or mayhem worldwide; all prayed for by desperate parents and relatives to gods of all kinds. That's hundreds of millions, likely billions, of prayerful pleadings definitely left unheard, utterly ignored. Only on very rare occasions, when an unexplainable and hidden reversal or remission of a disease occurs, do some insistently claim credit for an answered prayer. But even then, if one maintains that such a case is really an example of the "power of prayer," one must also admit that this alleged "power", is so vanishingly small and altogether unprovable, as to be virtually nonexistent. And utterly useless.

Maybe prayer makes some of us feel better for a short time, but prayer doesn't make rain, cure cancer, fix transmissions, save children, regrow body parts or advance Republican agendas. Continuing this lie is what is offensive. Prayer to any god is useless. It doesn't work. We have this knowledge. We can prove it, with a quick back of the envelope calculation and thought experiment or refer to millennia of negative evidence that god, all gods, never answer prayers. Yet, religionists bluff and bluster and continue to deny this knowledge, except when they go in the lab, can't start their car or lose a finger. Their actions betray their acceptance of the knowledge. Such is the arrogance of religious thought.

9

INFORMATION KILLS RELIGION

"Traditional religious beliefs have been eroded, not so much by humiliating disproofs of their mythologies as by the growing awareness that beliefs are really enabling mechanisms for survival."

E. O. Wilson

"Religion is something left over from the infancy of our intelligence, it will fade away as we adopt reason and science as our guidelines"

Bertrand Russell

Ham on Nye

There is a subtle but effective argument that Xian apologists and Creationists, like the Ken Hams and Ray Comforts of this world are deathly afraid of: *"Appeal to the Intelligence of Your Audience"*... and Bill Nye used it during the infamous Ham-Nye debate over Creationism in early 2014. Bury them with evidence, and appeal to their intelligence and common sense of what's likely and what isn't. Even Ham's sympathizers all know and use science every day, and despite being hornswaggled by Creationist claims, they can still absorb new knowledge and hear things they have never heard before, and maybe eventually understand how unlikely it is all this science is wrong. It is getting harder and harder to deny the oceans of evidence for the age of the earth and evolution. Heck, even Pat Robertson is on board!

Consider Ham's audience, even if mostly hand-picked local Eastern KY die-hard Creationists: good Baptists, Church of Christ fundies, sympathetic Evangelicals of any stripe, they still are among the most scientifically exposed, if not the most literate generation on earth, due to modern technology and the constant barrage of scientific information and advances that make up our daily news. There's traditional media, the internet and in their hands: smart-phones. Scientific information, data is everywhere. Every word Bill Nye muttered, every data point, every fact, every explanation, anyone could verify in an instant or at very least look up later on their home computer, and read for hours. To date, there are over 5 million YouTube views of the official debate video, with countless other clips and stories of it in the public domain.

Rachel Held Evans weighed in with her preliminary comments on the Ham-Nye debate, at the behest of her readers:

"On the creation debate...Since I've been asked: I'm with Nye in that I don't be-

lieve young earth creationism is a viable model of origins in today's modern scientific era. I'm also a Christian who loves the Bible and believes it to be inspired by God and authoritative in the Christian life. My view is that Genesis 1, having emerged from an ancient Near Eastern context, assumes an ancient Near Eastern cosmology and addresses theological concerns, not scientific ones...And I believe that church leaders who teach that Christians have to choose between the Bible and science, faith and reason, are doing a huge disservice to the Church, essentially setting believers up for failure."

The "Great Debate" didn't do Creationism any good. The diehards had to hear about just the tip of the scientific iceberg that has to be denied to make Creationism work. They, at very least, heard that there are lots of reasons, and tons of data, that compel the rest of us to believe the science. Science didn't get hurt and Creationism certainly didn't win or buffalo anyone as expected, especially as feared by the secular community, some of whom really gave Nye a lot of heat for doing it. I think he gave science one helluva good hearing. Thanks, Bill! Bill was the right guy for a number of reasons. He was not recognized as one of the staunch evolution defenders prior to his comments on Big Think video, which irked Ham enough to get the whole thing started. Nor was he identified with the New Atheists. He's the Science Guy. So it wasn't like putting Dawkins or DeGrasse Tyson up there, whom the religious audience might already have an attitude about. Bill isn't an evolutionary biologist or scientist working in the field, who might easily have been tempted to provide too much information, and try to overwhelm the audience with more data than they could handle. Bill is an uncontroversial and generally loved figure, especially among the youth. I heard the Science Guy speak the night before the debate at Murray State University, KY, where I was teaching at the time, and he was received like a damn rock-star. He, being no stranger to the stage was obvious.

His 20 years of experience in front of the TV cameras really showed, and his ability to present science in an easy-listening and entertaining format made him the perfect man for the job. Consider this: even if none of Ken's audience of 900 plus supporters, or his thousands of minions eagerly watching at home changed their minds, they all heard more science in one evening than they might hear in one sitting anytime, anywhere. Bill may have planted a seed of discord or two, and for many they may yet realize just how much science has to be thrown away, how vast the web of science is that stands in opposition to Creationist claims. Appeal to their intelligence, what a concept.

There's only one source of all this delusion, and it needs to go. We can outgrow organized religion just like we jettisoned slavery, burning at the stake, and bloodletting. Primitive ideas eventually die from new information. This one may take a few decades or centuries longer, but we could put Xianity, Islam, and the rest in the dustbin of history where they belong. It won't happen overnight, or without concerted effort, but who in their right mind would have predicted, dared to predict 400 years ago towards the end of the Renaissance, just prior to the Age of Reason and the birth of modern science, that 80% of Northern Europe would now be non-believers? The bombast and blasphemy of a prediction like that, in the 1600's, would be outrageous (get you beheaded, after torture), yet here we are! Even the pervasively Xian US is at 23% "Nones" (no religious affiliation), in less than a generation and growing. People aren't stupid, and the only way someone gets sucked into the scam of Creationism is by child indoctrination, and later, not getting enough information to see what patent bullshit it truly is. Education is the key. Despite being raised evangelical, Rachel Held Evans and many others know too much.

Butthurt over *Cosmos*

Bob Berman, longtime *Astronomy* magazine columnist, in his "Strange Universe" column, in the August 2014 issue entitled, *Astronomy and God: Do anti-religious messages belong in science education*, took great exception to Neil de Grasse Tyson's refutation of religious behaviors and claims, in the recent Cosmos series. Anti-religious messages in science? Sorry Bob, they are inevitable. Nearly every finding of science refutes some prior religious conjecture: a 6 day creation, an earth-centered universe, a firmament, a world-wide flood, monkey or elephant headed gods, Adam and Eve, Tower of Babel, souls, reincarnation, humans living hundreds of years, etc., etc., There is not an ounce of evidence despite 2,000-3,000 years of wishful thinking for any religious claim and mountains of evidence against them.

The history of the world's religions is characterized by the continual disproof of their metaphysical conjectures and empirical claims. So every time we learn another detail of how the world works, and we teach it to the next generation in science class, it often contradicts a religious claim. Let's examine a couple of quick examples. There is no evidence for Zeus, or Osiris. The world's predominant ancient cultures, taught their children those gods and all their manifest attributes and behaviors were as undoubtedly real, as a Xian of today teaches their child of Yahweh, Jesus, the Holy Spirit and the resurrection. We don't teach about Zeus or Osiris, or hundreds of other gods in science class, precisely because there has been no evidence for their existence forthcoming, ever. Neither in high school earth science, nor in a college level meteorology class, do we instruct our students that Zeus, as head of an entire pantheon of mischievous and all too human gods, gathers the clouds for storms, and is the causal force of lightning and thunder. Both the empirical claim about Zeus's production of the earth's storms, and the overall metaphysical assumption that the ultimate reality of the world is governed by a whole panoply of gods, caught up in the intrigues and affairs of a celestial soap opera, have been humiliatingly disproved. Information kills religion. As Iggy Pop has said *"Nobody believes in the old gods anymore"*, and with good reason.

To modern day religionists of course, the Greek claims are nothing but primitive and quite silly myths, but they certainly weren't to the ancient Greeks. They took Zeus and his pal's existence for granted, as certain and as completely as Buddhists are sure there exists enlightened beings, who have reached nirvana, and our Xian friends unquestionably know baby Jesus was born on Xmas day. Ptolemy, when contemplating the mathematical precision of the planets and the heavens in his earth-centered model, proclaimed:

"I know that I am mortal by nature, and ephemeral; but when I trace at my pleasure the windings to and fro of the heavenly bodies I no longer touch the earth with my feet: I stand in the presence of Zeus himself and take my fill of ambrosia"

Ptolemy and the Greeks saw Zeus as easily and obviously in the clouds and thunder the way a Buddhist might see evidence for consciousness in everything. A Xian sees neither of those, but instead observes obvious evidence for God's grace and wisdom, that only a fool or a damn atheist like de Grasse Tyson and his ilk, could miss. The religious background of your culture greatly influences what you think you see. Science ignores all that, and reports only that which we actually do see. Berman continued:

"Fact is 74 percent of Americans believe in God, and very few abandon their faith just because host Neil de Grasse Tyson keeps suggesting the cosmos is all one big accident. Indeed the majority of the world regards the universe as suffused with overarching intelligence".

The majority of the civilized world for 3,000 years believed in Osiris too, but that didn't make him any more real than Zeus. Mass belief due to cultural teachings does not necessarily make for truth. The majority of the world, for nearly 5,000 years, believed in the inevitability and ethical acceptability of slavery, which was sanctioned by some of the world's main religions. That didn't make it right or true. Similarly, in the Xian Bible's OT, in the first 17 verses of Genesis, a geocentric universe with the earth fixed in the center is described, with the sun, moon and the stars stuck in a firmament rotating around it. The science taught in grade school, high school earth science, and college astronomy courses, presents the heliocentric model of our solar system, as proposed by Copernicus, which has proven to be true and directly contradicts the Biblical claims of how the universe is structured. Ever since the 1957 launch of Sputnik, the bazillion satellites and space junk in orbit, and especially the dozen Apollo missions to the moon and back, humanity has utterly disproved any notion of an Old Testament firmament. The new versions of the Bible the conservatives publish, conveniently leave out any mention of the firmament. Lying for Jesus knows no bound.

The fixed sphere of the firmament, which was said to hold the stars and planets, and held the waters of the heavens back unless its windows opened up to facilitate Noah's flood, was just another primitive and false religious explanation about the earth, its blue sky and how the heavens worked. The current fights over evolution are reflective of the same sort of underlying, unquestioned, and undisputed ideas of religion which remain in our culture solely because children are taught religious claims are eternally true.

We believe, based on evidence, in entities like quasars and pulsars, in the same manner that we believe in electricity and electrons, despite none of us mere mortals having ever observed or experienced electrons or pulsars directly. All the equations, theory, observations and evidence of their effects, leads one to believe in these entities, as we now believe in dark matter and dark energy. There is no similar evidence for the Trinity, or the Resurrection, or reincarnation, or enlightened beings. No observations, nor theory, lead to the existence of these religious entities or events. Like the existence of billions of galaxies, so much of this new information circulating in our modern culture is but a few decades old, and is competing to replace millennia-old religious assumptions, that permeate our worldview.

All the theories within science that we have developed over the centuries, which accurately explain how the world works, haven't found it necessary to employ any religious constructs. It could have been otherwise. 150 years of neuroscience may have led to the necessity of positing a soul to explain all sorts of neurological phenomena, but it hasn't. In fact, the lack of evidence for the existence of personality and intellect, separate from the functioning living brain, is overwhelming. All the evidence points to *"it's the brain, stupid."* Nothing like a soul is seen to emanate from large functioning neuronal systems that produce sufficient modeling, recursion, self-conception and episodic personal narrative to give us the human psyche. When the human brain dies, the mind, psyche, the "soul" dies. Period. Full stop. These processes appear to be solely instantiated in human brains. Other aware and alert mammalian and primate species, show varying levels of problem solving, self-recognition, emotion and certainly pain, but there is no evidence of anything resembling the rich experience of human consciousness and conception in the brains of other creatures on earth.

Like the luminiferous aether, phlogiston, caloric fluid, and N rays, the claims of religion, all religions ever, never seem to be supported or discovered to be true with the advance of knowledge. No Zeus, no Osiris, no Allah, or Yahweh, no enlightened beings, souls or reincarnation, no heaven nor hell. No-one gets all butt-hurt over Zeus being tossed into the dustbin of history (Ptolemy would have), but Intelligent Design, Creationism, Cosmic Consciousness, Adam and Eve, the Flood and God himself being questioned and discarded for lack of scientific evidence, really frosts some folk's asses.

"This view is neither right nor wrong" says Mr. Berman, referring to science finding only naturalistic processes, from the physics of the Big Bang to stellar chemistry and the production of the elements, to molecular biology and evolution producing life. All without any evidence of intelligent design. He calls it a view. Yet at the end of the very same paragraph he says: *"...Cosmos may be well intentioned but I fear they merely harden those who think science is a 'position' or 'view' of the world rather than an impartial portal to truth."* But, Berman, stated plainly, he himself believes science is a mere view in the opening sentence, that it is neither right nor wrong. He certainly didn't describe science as *"an impartial portal to truth."* Talk about your

doublespeak. What appears to be happening, is he doesn't like it when his "modern" religious claims and their metaphysical assumptions, appear to be as unsupported by current scientific knowledge, as Zeus and all of Greek mythology.

Consider Rep. Paul Broun, Republican from Georgia, who I discussed previously. The good US Southern Baptist legislator, extends the dislike of science to include the Big Bang, and even embryology, along with evolution, as *"lies from the pit of hell."* The conflict of religious and scientific ideas is expanding by the day as scientific info becomes more disseminated by the minute. Climate change is now in the cross-hairs of the conservatives as well. Berman suggests: *"And while we are discussing how to make science more attractive, a little less arrogance wouldn't be bad."* My first reaction to that sentence was "Bullshit." The arrogance is in the religion, Bob, not the science.

In *Cosmos*, de Grasse Tyson reports the science as we know it today, and readily admits what we don't yet know. Religionists, keep blathering on pissily, about what they have never known, but still proclaim vehemently they do. Maybe Berman, and others, can't handle it when de Grasse Tyson says we don't know anything about an Intelligent Designer, or consciousness, as a universal attribute of the cosmos, or the 7 day Creation story. It is religionists, making those claims, that are the arrogant ones, demanding an equal footing with evidence based knowledge, for their primitive and ancient conjectures. Religionists claim, that these are eternal truths: there is a god, a creator, a soul and an afterlife, a heaven and hell, or a reincarnation of that soul. All of these, are based on phony revelations and parochial claims to ancient wisdom from spiritual founders. That's what is arrogant as hell (pun not intended). There is no more proof of enlightened beings having escaped reincarnation, as the Buddhists would have you believe, than our Muslim friends have of Muhammad visiting heaven on his winged horse from the dome of the rock in Jerusalem. Complete myths all, as primitive and imaginary as Zeus and his buddies and their celestial exploits. More and more people on the planet aren't buying the old myths anymore. Even within stifling and threatening Islam, there are non-believers daring to speak out. Religion is losing ground, precisely because new information is killing it, slowly and inexorably.

The Lama Dumps Prayer

The Dalai Lama became enlightened. No shit. Truly, but not in the traditional Buddhist sense. Buddhist teaching claims that you can become an enlightened one, reaching nirvana through years of intense meditation, withdrawal from the world, and being devoted to monkish, repetitive, boring chants and rituals. You might lose the self, and become one with the universe, and break the endless cycle of reincarnations back into the unfulfilled desires and sufferings of this life, this despairing human existence. Seems almost nobody ever makes it, despite over 2,000 year's worth of efforts by millions of dedicated monks, nuns, Hollywood types, and humanities professors. Even Sam Harris, who is a bit of an apologist for eastern mysticism, admits there is absolutely no evidence anyone has ever achieved enlightenment. No one ever seems to get there, and neither did the current Dalai Lama himself. At least not in that way.

Tenzin Gyatso, the 14th Dalai Lama, became truly enlightened in rather a more mundane way. In one of his many books (he is a one man publishing house), *Beyond Religion*, he admits that other than some psychological benefit to the one doing the praying, the power of prayer is useless. The power of prayer is bullshit, basically, is his conclusion. He became enlightened in the true New Enlightenment sense of the word, through 70 years of observation, travel, learning, living in this world, gathering evidence here on earth and not in some imaginary, ethereal plane. Information killed that idea for the Lama himself.

Gyatso, has experienced how the world works, over a lifetime of travel and connection, with world leaders and people of differing cultures. As a result; he knows better. He has learned the power of prayer is useless, and that religious divisiveness is both wholly unnecessary and detrimental to human well-being. He readily admitted in the same book, that morality is not exclusive to religion. He has met too many moral people of all faiths, and of no faith, to realize there are good folks, habitually good folks, in all religions, and in all manner of secularism. That's why I love education and the secular university system, where folks of all cultures, ethnic backgrounds, genders and nationalities freely come together to learn anything and everything, free of religious restrictions. We can't all travel the world and get enlightened first hand like the Dalai Lama, but we can experience the knowledge we all share, of each other and how our world works. All religions work very hard to limit info to only what appears to agree with the particular religion. All anti-science and restriction of education, comes from religions. As people get educated, they figure out real quick what is unfair, unequal, and absurd, and don't buy into religious myths anymore.

Religious Pluralism, Scientific Consensus

How can there be hundreds of competing religions, each with up to thousands of different contradictory sects within them? Science on the other hand, has one version. Oceans of data, amassed in each of the main scientific disciplines, is verified and accepted worldwide. Disagreement is only over competing hypotheses, explaining or predicting new data, or new phenomena. There are no competing or contradictory sects by ethnicity or geography within any scientific discipline. As Sam Harris puts it: *"We all generate our electricity the same way."*

Water boils at the same temperature, iron melts the same way all over the planet. There is no: Muslim Chemistry, Jewish Biology, Hindu Psychology, Christian Physics, or Buddhist Mathematics. All science, works for all humans, anywhere on the planet. Religious thought relies on interpretation of claims of revealed scripture and reveres faith, which is belief without evidence. Science questions authority, and is egalitarian in that anyone can make a new discovery. There are no holy men with special knowledge. Scientific thought relies on evidence, not faith, and public peer review, and consensus of evidence and theory. It can discover which hypotheses are correct about how the world really works.

Once during a panel discussion I was on, with two Xian ministers, one of them made a claim that I'd heard before:

"Well, two theologians disagreeing over a point of doctrine is just like two physicists who can't agree on competing hypotheses."

Nonsense. Any two physicists agree on 99.9999% of the consensus of current physics, as described in the text books, because it is all verified data and proven theory. Two physicists may disagree on a new hypothesis of data or process, but one will be proven wrong, and one proven right upon further data collection and verification. There is a way to tell in physics, and in all of science, in any scientific discipline, who is right and who is wrong: how the world actually works.

The two theologians, on the other hand, have no way of determining who is right or wrong. There is no test in reality to determine which of their speculations could be correct. Like our examples of the innumerable ideas of Hell back in Chapter 3, speculation upon speculation over the years regarding theological issues of any kind, can build up and elaborate to infinity, as there is absolutely no way to determine who might be right. There is no test as to which religion, which denomination, which interpretation could be correct. For a book length treatment of this glaring issue, and the fundamental and irreconcilable differences between religion and science, see Jerry Coyne's *Faith vs. Fact*.

The inquiry into how our world works over the last two millennia, has shown there is no evidence whatsoever of any hell or heaven. It has been determined that all theologians, all theology is wrong about all their claims. They merely bluff and bluster, and indoctrinate another generation of children into the religions that still hang around. Zeus is gone. The river Styx and Hades went with him. Heaven, hell, Allah, and Yahweh are on their way out as well. It may take decades, but it may not have to take centuries to rid the world of these remaining fantasies.

Rachel Held Evans and the Effect of Information

Some might find it a bit odd that I'm promoting the book and blog of a once devoted Evangelical, and now a very liberal Xian. I have discussed Ms. Evans very honest quest for knowledge as expressed in her writings throughout this book. They are representative of what many all over the world experience, when they seek information outside the bubble of their faith. I not only follow her blog, I loved her book, *Evolving in Monkey Town: How a girl who knew all the answers learned to ask all the questions.* Despite living in the Bible belt, being raised within the Xian cocoon, daughter of a preacher, graduate of a Bible college, trained in apologetics, schooled in denying evolution, and taught that gays and heathens like me will burn in hell, she came to accept evolution with *"a sneaking suspicion the scientists might be right"*, and that gays and non-Xians don't deserve eternal fire. She believes firmly in the Xian faith, and that it must itself evolve: it must change in light of new information. The young, and even many middle aged folks in the US are seriously questioning or leaving Evangelical Xiansanity in droves. Why now? I think Rachel explained one key reason far better than I could:

"No previous generation enjoyed such easy access to information or experienced such a profound sense of connectedness to the rest of the world."

Getting to know unbelievers and gay folks personally, contributes as well. We do live in unprecedented times of instant information exchange, access to higher education and daily dialogue through social media, email, internet video, even TV and print news sources. The discussion of religion is constant and everywhere. Traditional religious ideas that promote division, repression, even hatred around the world are being questioned and jettisoned, due to the spread of information and connection with our fellow humans, all over the globe.

From inside Xianity, secular activists now have unlikely allies, like Ms. Evans and Francis Collins. Based in reason and compassion, humanistic values that transcend all faiths, questioners like Rachel are changing religion from within. Folks like me would like to push religion off the cliff as soon as possible, but being a realist, I will gladly take all the help I can get to diminish its grip in the meantime. Secularists are immensely glad, she and others are evolving in their faith back toward the normal human empathy and reason we all share, which is all too often pushed aside by the religious need of telling everyone else how they must live, to satisfy some deity. The history of Xianity is predominantly the elimination of belief in one Bible verse after another, as new knowledge and compassion for others makes supposedly inspired verses seem as cruel, primitive and man-made as they are. Like all religious folks I've ever met, Rachel is a smart person, who can change her views in light of new information. That sounds kinda scientific to me, and rational, and enlightened. I highly recommend reading her book now retitled as, *Faith Unraveled: How a Girl Who Knew All the Answers Learned to Ask Questions.* If I and the other unbelieving scum in the New Enlightenment secular movement, can't convince you to ignore more of the Bible and lighten up on your fellow man, maybe she can.

Many Xians feel, that since they change their beliefs by re-interpreting scripture due to new info from modern science, this should convince us there is no conflict between science and religion. Far from it, in fact it proves the point of the inevitable and recurring clash. For but one example, in the 1850's few educated people, if any, doubted the special, completely independent creation of all species by the Xian god as told in Genesis. Darwin's evolution by natural selection, coupled with mountains of data from comparative anatomy, biogeography, genetics, and now modern comparative genomics, the voluminous fossil and geologic record documented in every corner of the globe, and further the dozens of dating methods that document the age of the earth, human artifacts and fossils, have completely refuted the Genesis creation myth. Without all of these developments in science, the Genesis account, and other religious creation myths, might still seem plausible and remain unchallenged. But all this new information, garnered by science in the last 150 years, not only makes all the religious accounts of creation seem as primitive as they are, it provides an explanatory network so vast and comprehensive as to unquestionably validate Theodosius Dobzhansky's famous statement: *"Nothing makes sense in biology except in light of evolution."*

All this science negates the utterly wrong religious explanation of life on earth. If none of it had been discovered, the religious story would yet be accepted by all, even scientists, as it was prior to Darwin. As new information comes in, old ideas, especially primitive ones like fantastic and mythic religious explanations, are discarded. This is conflict and incompatibility. No amount of denial can change that. Information kills religion. End of story.

Too Savage

My Uncle Dan Savage, appearing on Bill Maher's *Real Time* back in 2013, didn't pull any punches and laid out the unfiltered reality of life as is usual for him, making Maher's conservative guests squirm, and look like they were about to vomit, when he expressed his hope for having another child along with his adopted son:

"Hey, anything is possible for god, so I'm gonna keep inseminating my husband and keep my fingers crossed..."

You can't get more matter-of-fact than that. That's a key to making homosexuality as accepted as apple pie, and Savage is so good at it. We have to normalize the facts of life in our everyday conversation without pause for apology. No defensiveness necessary. Dan does that better than anybody. We have to get the same way about all of science and human behavior, whether it conflicts with some entrenched religious nonsense or not. When asked about the significant progress made in gay awareness, Dan says he can't take any particular credit for it, instead it is all the LGBTI people who are "out" now, who made it happen. Coming out to friends, family, society does it, did it. Raising consciousness, changing perceptions, educating everyone, as up front and casually as Dan talking on TV about inseminating his partner, as if he were speaking of mowing the lawn, does it.

New information changes everything eventually. Savage reminds me of the early 60's with Lenny Bruce saying "dirty" words out loud, exposing that absurdity a generation ago. People would just cringe, or be "oh so offended", or angry as hell. But many were thoughtful, and many were supportive. Many more knew he was right. Dirty words was, and is, a silly idea, kept alive only by religious indoctrination. No-one is ever born afraid to hear the word "fuck." Bruce's envelope pushing displayed the idiocy for all to see, and made the debate over language and dirty words mainstream. It opened the way later, for George Carlin and HBO and the big change we saw in the 80's. Now, censorship is limited to small corners of media, and dirty words are a part of the culture, despite Xian cringing and wailing.

Dan is pushing the envelope by employing matter of fact talk about sexual practices and the idiocy of homophobia. That's how these ideas could become main stream in another generation or two. Remember when the first punk rockers started doing piercings and tats in the 70's? Earrings on a guy was way beyond respectable boundaries then, and so were sleeves. No-one, except those on the fringe, had them. Now, a generation later, they are a normal part of the culture. Tats and piercings are everywhere. You have to overcome that cultural inertia to get something accepted. Until then, the conservative element whines on how vulgar and improper the behavior is, like Lenny's dirty words, punk rockers body adornment or LGBTI sexuality.

As an example, how mainstream was anal sex a generation ago? Sure homosexuals, and a small element of heterosexuals did it, but no-one talked about it. It was even restricted to the dark corners of porn. It was not mainstream, even in porn! Now it is almost de riguer. It is so commonplace in porn, it's not even a novelty anymore. Even if many heterosexual couples still don't do it, a greater percentage of them surely do nowadays, and anal sex has become a regular part of our daily discussion. My, how things can change. It couldn't even be discussed a mere 40 years ago, you wouldn't dare bring it up. Sodomy is yet illegal in 70 countries worldwide, and its illegality was only struck down in the US by a Supreme Court ruling in 2003. Now you can mention it offhandedly, or make jokes about it in casual conversation. There has been a great deal of progress and social change on many fronts. But we can do more, we can do better. It is 2016. We just celebrated the tenth anniversary of the New Enlightenment. Along with the internet, we have an increased lessening of the social conventions against discussing once taboo subjects. It is the conservatives who are taking it in the ass on this one nowadays. (It was there I had to take it!).

Facebook, YouTube, Reddit, Tumblr, Twitter, Skype, Pinterest, email, blogs, etc., etc. Many of these information exchange platforms are even newer than the New Enlightenment itself. How fast can we turn things around with this instant and voluminous information transfer that is in full swing and increasing as I write? Smart-phones accessing the net really took off in 2007, with the introduction of the I-phone. In 2015, estimates are that half of the world's population is on the internet. That's over 3 billion humans, with nearly 2 billion of them holding smart-phones connected to information from the rest of the world, 24/7, and in the palm of their hands. Incredible.

Religionists, all over the world, are struggling with this exponential information explosion, but so many, to their credit, are "seeing the light." Do you think it likely we will be having the same discussion over butt-sex another 10 years from now? Gay marriage, in the US, is already a done deal. Dirty words are passe' thanks to Lenny Bruce's pioneering in the early 60's, and George Carlin's crusade after him. Homophobia, misogyny, religious divisiveness, and science denial are all untenable in light of modern knowledge. How long can these old ideas withstand the attack?

Many are falling off the Xiansanity wagon as we speak, and the un-predicted and courageous rise of ex-Muslims speaking out and calling for reformation is a very encouraging, very recent phenomenon. If religionists of any stripe, ultimately retain their faith for some time to come, I wager they will, at very least, question and modify so much of their beliefs, that the effect we secularists work for will be achieved. Religious ideas and practices will be modified as to be harmless, or jettisoned altogether. Getting rid of religion completely, won't happen in my lifetime, and maybe not the next generation's, but I'll take whatever modification we can get.

It is proposed, that Dan Savage's envelope pushin' pisses off a few people, offends some others, and that his matter of fact bluntness does his cause more harm than good, by alienating the people he's trying to reach. In a word: Bullshit. It worked with Lenny and dirty words, and anal sex, and tats and piercings. Progress happens by folks pushing the envelope. Some do get offended along the way, but not all. Whining conservatives get a lot of press, and play the persecution card: just watch Fox News. They bluff and bluster, but it doesn't hamper the effect at all. Stridency works. Making a loud noise, a clear no-holds-barred statement that can't be ignored, does the trick. Thnx, Dan!

Pope Frank

Pope Francis, Time magazine's 2013 man of the year, is considered to be doing a good job, by most Catholics polled (87%). However, 78% also disagree with him on the subject of contraception. Imagine that. The US based Spanish language network Univision, conducted a poll of over 12,000 Catholics across a dozen countries, which represent over 60% of the world's 1.2 billion Catholics. Those most likely to support the Church's teachings are married men and women, 55 years and older, who attend mass, and live in rural areas. Opposition to gay marriage is 99% in Africa (we can't blame it all on the Evangelicals), but only 40% in the US. The younger, the more educated, the more developed the country, the less likely you will buy into the dogma of the Catholic Church.

What does that say? It says that education is the key, information does kill religion. As the world turns, and becomes more educated, progressive, and secular, unfounded, arbitrary, religious ideas get rejected. A good many Catholics don't buy into the Pope and his Church's archaic and cruel stances. Poland and Italy both have 80% plus Catholic populations, yet they have very low birth rates. In those countries contraception is used regularly. We can outgrow this stuff, we can drop organized religion and its absurdities and cruelties, such as disallowing contraception. What is especially disgusting about the Catholic injunction on birth control is, what may be an inconvenience for someone in the developed world to have another child, can be a sentence to continued abject poverty, even an early death, to a child in a less developed country. The Church exerts more control over the lives of the uneducated, the poor, and already overpopulated, and condemns them to more of the same in service to made-up dogma. Pope Frank's job is to spread the influence and control of the declining Catholic Church far and wide, and put more of the uneducated and easily controlled into perpetual misery. Some man of the year. His influence is greatly diminished when people obtain enough education. Information loosens his death grip.

Outgrowing Religion

Consider someone living in Germany, France, or England in the mid 1600's (roughly 400 years ago), at the height of the witch trials, through the plague and the great fire of London, following 100 years of religious wars raging across Europe, and the equally religiously infused English Civil War. What if they dared announce the prophecy I suggested previously that by the 2000's, Northern Europe would be 80% godless, and that England would be 30% atheist/agnostic, and even the pervasively Xian US, following not far behind, would have 23% identifying as non-religious. It would be nearly certain, they would wind up tortured unmercifully until they recanted their heresy, and then beheaded (if one were lucky) or burned at the stake. Yet despite our bleak, ignorant, history of this smothering, crude, and cruel religiosity of post-medieval times, here we are, but a few centuries later, with religion incomparably diminished and in a continued steep decline. Even in highly religious countries, life proceeds daily in a predominantly secular fashion, with religion relegated to but one or two days per week brief observance. Only in Saudi Arabia, and a few other countries, does beheading, amputation, and torture for religious reasons still occur. The medieval western Xian world was as bad as Saudi Arabia is today. Most of the world has moved on to modernity, primarily through rejection of religion from most of our daily affairs.

Michael Shermer's answer to the annual Edge.org question "What scientific idea is ready for retirement?" was that the longstanding assumption that religion, and belief in a god, are innate to humans, needs to go. Religion and god-belief, may not be genetically programmed into the human brain. Poll after poll, in country after country, show the young to be the least religious as the questioning of religious beliefs has become more commonplace. As each generation becomes more and more educated than the previous generations, the world becomes less religious. Shermer:

"It is time for scientists to retire the theory that God and religion are hardwired in our brains. Like everyone else, scientists are subject to cognitive biases that tilt their thinking toward trying to explain common beliefs, so it is good for us to take the long-view perspective and compare today to, say, half a millennia ago when God beliefs were virtually 100%, or to the hunter-gatherer tribes of our Paleolithic ancestors who, while employing any number of superstitious rituals, did not believe in a God or practice a religion that even remotely resembles the deities or religions of modern peoples."

When you don't raise kids with a belief in god, most don't flock to find one. Many grow up utterly without the need for such belief, they display a benign indifference. Some may seek spiritual understanding of some kind, but it's often a mild form like the pacifism and mindfulness of Buddhism, often minus the reincarnation and supernatural realms parts. I raised four children, and didn't tell them about religion, and didn't wail against it in front of them either. In fact, I encouraged them to check out different religions once they were older. I even admonished one at age 13 or so, for claiming with a buddy from school, that they were atheists like many kids in his class, who thought religion stupid. I told him he was too young to know, and to check it all out when he got older and then decide. He might like one of the religions one day, for all he knew.

How's that for an Unbelieving Scum parent, huh? I respect my kid so much to make up his own mind, I refuse to push my disbelief upon him, upon any of them, the exact opposite of what the Xians and Muslims and Buddhists and many others feel is proper. Brainwashing your kid, under threat of punishment and ostracization is the norm. As discussed in Chapter 7, child indoctrination is one of the most accepted yet sleazy practices of religions. Youth ministry, praying (preying) on the cognitively immature and emotionally vulnerable adolescent, is the worst. Conning some defenseless 13 year-old into the monastery, the madrassa, the church or the temple, often with the specter of hell dangled in front of them, is the most reprehensible of acts. As I argued before, it is time to jettison this part of religious thought for good. Religions really would collapse under the weight of their own absurdity, without child indoctrination.

Shermer points out, that not that long ago, when religion ruled our thinking, we unquestionably assumed witchcraft and blasphemy, or somehow not pleasing some god in some way, was the cause of all misfortune in the world. Fire, famine and plague, must all be visited upon us by god because somebody sinned somewhere, someone must be to blame, their heresy and dancing with the devil must have brought god's wrath upon us. Somebody was evil. We all needed to pray more, and the heretics and witches must be rooted out and destroyed; and they were, in droves. Nowadays, we don't burn witches and heretics by the hundreds or thousands if there is a flu epidemic or earthquake. We have outgrown so much of what was normal in religious practice at the hands of better information. There is still more to jettison to be sure, but many of us have dropped all religious thought already. The billions of humans throughout history, and the few billion alive today, that live without any religion, prove Shermer's point. It is not innate. It is learned. It is a bad habit which we can drop altogether.

Giordano Bruno

Religion has been in the business of misinformation and even killing information for millennia now, mainly by threatening, torturing, and/or killing those who hold, or dare to disseminate information contrary to religious dogma. Heretics, apostates, heathens, blasphemers, etc., were so named because they dared to believe and to speak, of ideas different from what the dominant religion of a given time and place demanded allegiance to. Giordano Bruno was burned at the stake around the onset of the 17th century on behalf of the Catholic Church's Office of the Holy Inquisition, because he held ideas against the trinity, transubstantiation, and the like, but also for upholding heliocentric Copernican theory, thereby denying the earth centered universe of the Bible. He also presciently expressed the idea, that there may be many inhabited worlds orbiting stars like our sun. Pretty standard fare to consider nowadays but in 1600, it got you killed by religious authorities. Four hundred years later, thanks to Bruno, Copernicus, Galileo, Kepler, Newton, and countless other scientists and educators, the information has won. It is unchallenged, common, knowledge that the earth is not the center of the universe as the Book of Genesis and the Catholic Church maintained. A significant piece of religion has been killed by that bit of information. Information has been killing religion ever since Bruno. We have come a long way and still have a long way to go, but the progress made since those barbaric, ignorant times is formidable.

Four centuries ago, citizens of the civilized and developed world of Europe and England were incomparably more religious than the vast majority of us are today. Most people unquestioningly believed what the Church taught them (like Bruno, they didn't have much choice). The earth was the center of the universe, Creation took 6 days, Noah and the Great Flood, Adam and Eve, Babel, everything in Genesis and other parts of the Bible, were accepted literally by the Catholic and Protestant churches. Today, no-one believes in an earth centered universe (well, almost nobody), 1/2 of the US population doesn't buy Creationism, fewer still believe in the literal truth of Noah or Adam and Eve, and fewer still think we should stone adulterers on the edge of town. We have all become greatly less religious since the 1600's.

For example, back in those good old days, if one exhibited symptoms of a mental disorder: bipolar, OCD, schizophrenia, etc., it was for certain you were possessed by demons and an exorcism was in order, rather than mood stabilizers, anti-psychotics and compassionate therapy as is the norm in the modern world. Few today, believe in demonic possession as the causal factor of mental disease, despite the Catholic Church's insistence that exorcism, though rare, is a distinct possibility:

"According to the Vatican guidelines issued in 1999, 'the person who claims to be possessed must be evaluated by doctors to rule out a mental or physical illness.' Most reported cases do not require an exorcism because twentieth-century Catholic officials regard genuine demonic possession as an extremely rare phenomenon that is easily confounded with natural mental disturbances."

Even the cognoscenti of the mighty Catholic Church have had to back off due to better knowledge, and are now somewhat cautious about diagnosing possession, although they do still have hundreds of exorcists on staff, ready to take your call! Most sane folks, however, do not believe demons and possession are behind any mental illness, when 4 centuries ago everyone did. What happened to dispel this and other widespread notions, the previously undeniable articles of faith listed above? Information. Better information, real, true, factual information did the trick. The Catholic Church, and some evangelical Xians, still cling to some of these absurd archaic beliefs, but the majority of folks, Xian or not, don't swallow them hook line and sinker anymore.

In 1600, and in the subsequent years of the plague for example, nearly all believed horrific calamities like cholera, small pox and the dreaded plague, were undoubted acts of god. God's wrath was the unquestioned explanation of diseases and natural disasters. The populace has sinned and God is meting out just punishment. Nowadays, the vast majority of us don't give that explanation a first thought, much less a second thought, and why? Why has this centuries old explanation fallen by the wayside? We know better. People are better informed, and not under the thumb of religious explanations. Information kills religion now more than it ever did. Religion is still trying to maintain plenty of primitive explanations and succeeds all too well, with Creationism for example, bullshitting nearly half the US population. Wholly unlike the 1600's, today however, we have continual public debate across all media every day, over the Creationism/Evolution controversy, to the extent of nationally publicized events like the 2014 Ham-Nye debate. We now believe the germ theory of disease as Louis Pasteur first formulated it in the mid-1800's because we have learned new, real, factual information about germs: microbes, bacteria and viruses and the diseases they cause. We are incomparably less religious as a result. As with demonic possession, once assumed as the sole force behind aberrant mental behavior, we have utterly discarded "God's wrath" as the unquestioned cause of our diseases, and natural disasters as well.

Currently, though most folks still believe in some sort of an afterlife, it is only a watered down version of the graphic depictions of hell, once envisioned as undeniable fact centuries ago. Better information, in the form of a glaring lack of any evidence for the fiery pit, has diminished that belief significantly, despite the churches insistence on some version of an afterlife. Accordingly, most in the US also still believe in the existence of a soul. But back then, everybody did. There was an immortal soul, and the fires of hell were just a breath away for everyone.

After nearly 3,000 years or so of wishful thinking by most, if not all, of the world's major religions and 150 years of exponentially more investigative and delineating neuroscience, there is not one shred of evidence for either the existence of a soul, or an afterlife. Subsequently, many of us, even Xians when pressed, realize that when we die our personality and intellect disintegrate with the death of the brain, and no-one in all those centuries has ever come back from a visit to heaven of hell. So as dismaying as it may be, especially in the hyper-religious US of A, to see so many cling to medieval thinking promulgated solely by the Xian churches, we have to realize how far we have come in four centuries, for so many of us to be predominantly secular and scientific. Most people are quite realistic in our thinking today, when we all used to be unquestionably hyper-religious.

Tellingly, 33 years after Bruno's murder, burned at the stake at the behest of Xiansanity, they didn't kill Galileo. He was also convicted of heresy, but they merely showed him the instruments of torture and then confined him to house arrest. Maybe they fucked up, and should have killed him too. Galileo had significant connections with the Inquisitors and the Pope himself, which undoubtedly influenced his palpably less cruel treatment, but maybe the information itself may have had as great an influence, in sparing him from torture and a barbaric death. Bruno supported Copernican theory when it was not widely accepted yet, and promulgated his forward thinking theories of the cosmos without any new accepted information. He had no new data, no proof of his conjectures, his pure speculations. Galileo on the other hand, had information, proof, and lots of it. Maybe he had too much publicly available information in the form of the imperfections of the moon, the phases of Venus and the undeniable orbits of the moons of Jupiter, all perfectly accessible to anyone with a telescope, for him to be summarily executed.

How times have changed, since the death of Bruno and the sparing of Galileo. The conjunction of those two wholly opposite outcomes may have marked a real watershed. Education is the key. We can't stop exposing, ridiculing, and attacking religious nonsense. It works. And we can do even better. We've come a long way in 400 years. Given the current information explosion, driven in large part by the internet, and the effect of the New Enlightenment's insistence on the necessity and social acceptability of questioning religion, we can go even farther. By discussing, analyzing, and criticizing religious claims, I believe we can greatly accelerate such progress in the next few decades.

Looking Forward, not Back

Imagine not having to fight ISIS, not still fighting for woman's reproductive rights, not hoping against hope whether the Pope's conciliatory utterances toward gays will have any effect on the gaggle of bishops and cardinals, clinging to nearly two millennia of dogmatic bullshit, that vehemently and unequivocally opposes anything less than the condemnation of homosexual behavior. All this becomes reality when religion goes. For the gays, Romans 1, from "Saint" Paul says they deserve death, remember? Despite Elton John's gushing praise of the Pope's "make-nice" talk, it remains to be seen how long it will take to overcome 2,000 yr. old repressions ingrained in the dogma of the lumbering behemoth that is the Catholic Church.

"He is a compassionate, loving man who wants everybody to be included in the love of God," EJ said of the pope. Except there is no god and absolutely no reason to discriminate against homosexual behavior anymore. At the snap of our fingers, we could forever ignore every homophobic passage in the Bible. We already know they are no more the commands of some god, than those verses upholding slavery, promoting genocide, or not eating shrimp. Imagine (as John Lennon did), no religion. Think of it. What if we were past all this foot-dragging, completely retarded bullshit. No religion? No ISIS, no homophobia, no restrictions on woman's use of birth control anywhere?! No denial of science. No burqas, no pedophiles hiding out as clergy, and no TV preachers scamming millions.

Imagine, if we spent all of the energy that we now spend as a species, over 7 billion of us today, arguing about, combating against, discussing the "nuances" of, enduring the repressions of, rebutting the delusions of, escaping the persecutions of, religion..., on science, and charity, and education, instead. Imagine. Imagine redirecting all that utterly wasted effort, wrestling with all religions' wholly unnecessary absurdities and cruelties, towards the pursuit of new knowledge, the dissemination of information, and the improvement of living conditions for all. Imagine. The Pope and his minions look back to that nasty, shitty, little book that has caused untold suffering to gays and lesbians and women in general throughout all of modern history. The old boys in dresses waste all of our time and tears over primitive, cruel musings: deciphering the "nuances" of Pauline pronouncements or fanciful Gospel claims, or deflecting Old Testament ugly commands, while the secular world looks forward, moves forward. Let's put that ugly little book on the myth shelf where it belongs and put the Pope and his posse out of a job

Don't look back. The entire history of Xianity is the jettisoning of one verse after another, as better information, new knowledge of ourselves and the world we live in is acquired. Old, horribly outdated, primitive, and usually repressive, if not blatantly absurd, ideas are dropped for the amateurish and often cruel explanations and commands they are. The first Enlightenment and subsequent Age of Reason, along with the establishment of the business of modern science, and now the New Enlightenment, have been incredibly effective in loosening the stranglehold of religious thought, which once dominated the daily lives of all in the West, and still stifles progress all across the Islamic countries. Imagine if all that religious strife and obstruction of progress disappeared. How many more incredible discoveries and feats of technological success might we achieve, relieved of wasting voluminous time and energy combating religion's insanity?

The message of this chapter, and this book overall, is that we can win. Information does kill religion, and religion and religious thinking can be diminished much faster than most of us would otherwise anticipate.

10

THE NEW ENLIGHTENMENT

"The New Enlightenment is a movement. Its goal is to change society into a more free and compassionate place. Its method is to empower people to use reason for their own good. The first Enlightenment, a 17th and 18th century European movement, helped change society by advancing one key idea: that reason and observation are better than authority for figuring out how the world works. This lead to a move away from super-naturalism and the divine right of kings towards science and democracy. Despite the amazing progress that the first Enlightenment fueled, super-naturalism and arbitrary authority still hold far too much sway on our world. We seek to continue this important work with a New Enlightenment. The focus of the New Enlightenment is the same as the first, to spread the power of reason to more people and wean them off of authority. We believe that as we promote reason, and the courage to use it, people will build societies where they and others are free and empowered to find happiness"

August Brunsman, Secular Student Alliance

"Above all, we are in need of renewed Enlightenment..."

Christopher Hitchens

This chapter reviews the incredible explosion, of the critical examination of religion, which has become an everyday occurrence all across the globe, kick started by the publication of Sam Harris' *End of Faith* in 2004. The message of this chapter is that this New Enlightenment has been unpredictably effective, and can be even more successful in removing religious thought from daily life. In only a decade, compared to the nearly 2 millennia of domination by the worlds organized religions, the New Enlightenment is already giving religious thought the drubbing it deserves, slowly extracting its insidious underlying assumptions from within our modern culture, and replacing it with a growing emphasis on reason and tolerance. This paradigmatic shift is allowing our pragmatic and realistic search for knowledge, and our normal human empathy, to expand unheeded by the roadblock of religious thought. We may now have the ability to stick a fork in religion, with its arrogant and unfounded suppositions, a lot sooner than anyone might surmise. This chapter calls for a recognition and expansion of the New Enlightenment, and the end of religion; an idea whose time has come.

A Decade of Accelerating Enlightenment

Sam Harris's *End of Faith*, published August 2004 is considered to have ushered in the New Enlightenment movement. Just about one short decade, a brief 12 years ago, a mere 1/10 of a century back, and look how far and fast the secular advance has come. Sam's 1st book, along with Dawkins and Hitchens and other influential secular author's works following right after his, marks for many, the beginning of this growing 21st century secular movement, picking up where the first Enlightenment left off. A whole spate of books and their authors have come out in the last decade, which take a completely different tack on the human condition, than the unfounded fantasies and negative perceptions of man's sin and evil that religions dwell on.

The God Delusion, Richard Dawkins, 2006. It is possibly the most successful book of the "New Atheist" movement (as the Xians labeled it), with over 3 million copies sold, and having been translated into 35 languages. It remains the go-to book for justifying the rejection of religion and the source most often cited by many new unbelievers, who were once merely doubting their religion. For many, Dawkins' book gave them the permission and clear rationale to take the step away from their faith. In addition to the no-holds-barred critical examination of religion and its claims, like Dawkins, other New Enlightenment authors emphasize the "better angels" of our nature, and the incredible progress we have accomplished as a species through reason and tolerance, promoting our unlimited human potential, rather than dwelling on our supposed innate depravity, and wallowing in the claimed inevitability of the sin and suffering of all mankind. The perspectives of these authors is now part of our daily culture, and the conversation is becoming nearly as prevalent as religious thought. We're working on achieving "equal time", and burying religious thought as soon as possible.

God Is Not Great, Christopher Hitchens, 2007. This highly respected man of letters, and incomparably engaging speaker, left an indelible impression on those who read his books and were inspired by his as yet un-replaced polemic, exemplified in his many debates and speeches which left even his opponents, acknowledging the clarity and force of his exposition. He pulled no punches in damning religion, and could make his points with unparalleled eloquence, or merely by saying *"Fuck that"* when exposing religion's absurdities and repressions. Hitch, like Dawkins before him, went for the throat in calling out religion's cruelties and illogical claims. Their groundbreaking, straightforward, and unapologetic approach, legitimized the brutally honest critique of religion which has become an integral part of our daily discourse, with the claims and practices of the world's faiths being rehashed and wrangled over continually on TV, in the newspapers, in books, on social media, in blogs, and on videos. You name it, the conversation today is everywhere. Even Islam, is now being openly analyzed by a whole host of ex-Muslims, and courageous writers and bloggers, living within Muslim countries.

Breaking the Spell, Dan Dennett, 2006. The last of the "Four Horseman" of the New Enlightenment, along with Harris, Dawkins, and Hitchens. Dennett's calm, fatherly critique of religion from a philosophic and often Darwinian perspective, resonates with so many seeking to understand and break away from their religion. Many other works appeared in the same decade, by authors who aren't immediately identified as internationally recognized spokesmen of the atheist movement, but nonetheless, have played a significant part in the analysis of religion and its perspectives, which have become so mainstream and pervasive worldwide in such a short time.

Godless, Dan Barker, 2008. Dan and his wife, Annie Laurie Gaylor, co-presidents of the FFRF (Freedom from Religion Foundation), have done more to support secular causes, spread information and defend separation of church and state, than maybe any other two people on the planet through their speaking, books, debates, radio show and newspaper, and especially FFRF's constant vigilance and activities regarding 1st amendment issues nationwide. Dan's first book was another secular milestone in educating the public about the absurdities and contradictions in the Bible.

God, The Failed Hypothesis, Victor Stenger, 2007. The late physicist and author, analyzed the idea of what a world should look like had a god actually created it, maintaining that we can examine supernatural claims, and that the evidence for god is utterly lacking. Stenger pulled no punches as well, with regards religion. His direct confrontation of religion is sorely missed.

I Sold My Soul on eBay, Hemant Mehta, 2007. Hemant's blog entitled the Friendly Atheist (as he describes himself), is considered one of the go-to sources for current information on what is happening in the secular movement, along with Richard Dawkins Foundation for Reason and Science website. Hemant has become another very influential and prominent spokesman for the New Enlightenment movement.

Jesus Interrupted, Bart Ehrman, 2009. Professor Ehrman, a New Testament scholar, is not usually thought of as one of the "New Atheists." A professed agnostic himself, his ½ dozen popular books have brought Biblical history and criticism to the lay public like no-one else before, with four hitting the New York Times bestseller list, in the same decade as the New Enlightenment authors. Information kills religion, and Dr. Ehrman's efforts at educating the public about what we actually know about the Bible, and how it was written, has been an indispensable part of the secular movement.

Abundance, by Peter Diamandis, 2012, *Rational Optimist* by Matt Ridley, 2010 and *Better Angels of Our Nature*, Steven Pinker, 2011. I've included the first two books, by Diamandis, a space tech entrepreneur, and Ridley, a journalist and science editor for the *Economist*, along with Steven Pinker's *Better Angels* as examples of data-driven secular perspectives on our world and the human condition, past and present, that directly refute the religious perspective of inevitable sin, suffering and eternal pessimism. These authors are not generally thought of as part of the vanguard of the secular movement, but their books appeared in the same decade and presented formidable cases against the prevailing negative religious viewpoint.

Michael Shermer's *Moral Arc*, published late in 2015, is another addition to the growing secular viewpoint, which is orthogonal to religious claims and conclusions about our morality, its origins and its continued expansion. What all these works have in common, is an approach based on systematic observation and analysis of human experience, morality, human nature, and our destiny, once claimed to be exclusive to religious or philosophical consideration. These authors adopt an empirical approach, bringing to bear what has actually happened in human history, our progress, and our accomplishments in consideration of our moral behavior, and hope for the future, instead of a reliance on old scripture and the outdated and purely speculative viewpoints of theology.

Instead of proclaiming *"Life is all about suffering"*, or dwelling on the supposed *"innate depravity"* of man, or running around condemning one another to eternal torture in some omnipotent prick's fiery imaginary afterlife, New Enlightenment thinkers are concentrating on what we have accomplished, and can accomplish, especially by discarding the bleak outlook on our nature and our fellow humans. The depressing eventualities that religions promote, are but needless roadblocks to exercising our evolved intelligence and empathy in this life. In stark contrast to all religions, the New Enlightenment perspective unites us all in our hard-earned, shared, body of knowledge: science, and our formidable, evolved and expanding capacities for empathy and tolerance.

The Face of Non-Belief

"I am an atheist and that's it. I believe there's nothing we can know except that we should be kind to each other and do what we can for other people."

Katherine Hepburn

Xian propaganda says that non-believers, people who have no religion and no belief in god must be depressed, nihilistic, possess a bleak world outlook, are angry, angry at god, overbearing, and will most likely come to their senses and find god, usually on their deathbed. Many Xians I know, figure us Unbelieving Scum must be this way, because that's what they have been taught. *They couldn't be more wrong.* Try it for yourself. Go visit any local meet-up of secular, atheist, or freethinker groups that assemble in coffee shops, restaurants, and community centers all over America, any day of the week and see what unbelievers look like. You won't be able to tell them from the folks in any other sort of gathering. They won't look depressed, angry or despaired, even though that's what your minister might tell you about those godless, nihilist folks. For example, check out any of the Christian apologist Ravi Zacharias' books on the subject of us unbelieving scum and you will get gems like this on atheism: *"Its true nature-whether disguised in Eastern mysticism or American cynicism – is despair."*

Despair, right. No, your bullshit religion, your heroes, Calvin, Aquinas, Luther, and so many others, preach despair and depravity as the unchangeable elements of the human condition; not us. We secularists teach optimism and empathy. We don't preach original sin, that we are broken and hopelessly adrift without someone like Zacharias and his past taskmasters to set us straight with the saving grace of Jesus. We don't preach sermons like the infamous Jonathan Edwards' *Sinners in the Hands of an Angry God,* and the like; you do. According to one of his book overviews on the Barnes and Noble website *"... Zacharias exposes the hopelessness of Atheism..."*

The non-believing folks I know, don't look too hopeless to me. And the bazillions of non-believers I've met, or read about, or have seen on You Tube, or listened to in pod-casts or who make the news or write blogs and write books, who reside all over the planet aren't wallowing in religious guilt about their dastardly sinful ways. We don't have time for that demeaning, obstructive bullshit anymore. We are working on making life better for all, through the knowledge we have gained. For another real taste of what Xiansanity says, about those who dare to think for themselves and question religious and theistic claims, check out any of Albert Mohler's (President of the Southern Baptist Theological Seminary) pieces on the subject at his website. For a really enlightening discussion of such misinformation Xians are fed, peruse the questions and comments to Hemant Mehta's dialogue about us non-believers with Rachel Held Evans, published on her website. Once again, I just gotta give Ms. Evans, a serious Xian, mucho kudos for being a voice of reason and compassion from within the confines of Xiansanity. She is an unlikely ally to be sure. When asked: *"What is the biggest misconception that Christians have about atheists?"* Hemant replied:

"The biggest one that comes to my mind: Atheists are immoral because they don't believe in a god. That's absurd. On the whole, we are highly ethical. The atheists I know donate to charity, volunteer their time, donate their blood, help other people, etc. Why be good? Because it makes the world a better, happier place to live in. Wouldn't you want to live in a world where people were helping each other instead of hurting them? So why do people believe the opposite? I think a lot of pastors love to demonize atheists because they want you to believe that to be good, you need God... and since atheists don't have god, we can't *possibly* be good. It's just bad reasoning all around. To paraphrase something I've heard before, if your belief in god is the only reason you're not killing, robbing, or raping others, then maybe you need to see a psychiatrist...(For what it's worth, I'm aware there are good and bad atheists just as there are good and bad Christians.)"

Ravi Zacharias thinks he knows, Al Mohler also. They think they have us all figured out, they got it all down. Right. These two, and so many others like them, spread complete misinformation under the guise of religious authority and theological scholarship, due to having the respect of so many in our modern culture, who wouldn't think to question them, or their minister, their pastor, their priest or imam. How arrogant is that? They are allowed to lie, and lie to children, and then we have to clean up the mess. The billion or two of us on the planet today, who live free, secular, happy, fulfilled, moral lives unfettered by Bronze Age superstitions and repressive rules, prove these "authorities" utterly and completely wrong.

Unbelieving Scum Numero Uno

"Your petitioners are atheists and they define their beliefs as follows. An atheist loves his fellow man instead of god. An atheist believes that heaven is something for which we should work now – here on earth for all men together to enjoy. An atheist believes that he can get no help through prayer but that he must find in himself the inner conviction and strength to meet life, to grapple with it, to subdue it, and enjoy it. An atheist believes that only in a knowledge of himself and a knowledge of his fellow man can he find the understanding that will help to a life of fulfillment. He seeks to know himself and his fellow man rather than to know a god. An atheist believes that a hospital should be built instead of a church. An atheist believes that a deed must be done instead of a prayer said. An atheist strives for involvement in life and not escape into death. He wants disease conquered, poverty vanquished, war eliminated. He wants man to understand and love man. He wants an ethical way of life. He believes that we cannot rely on a god or channel action into prayer nor hope for an end of troubles in a hereafter. He believes that we are our brother's keepers and are keepers of our own lives; that we are responsible persons and the job is here and the time is now."

Madalyn Murray O'Hair

The above quote was her opening statement to the 1959 Supreme Court, in her case against compulsory Bible reading in schools. I was 5. What a depraved worldview, right? No wonder she was branded the "most hated woman in America." What a depressing, angry, bleak, outlook huh? No wonder the Xians, then and now, despise us Unbelieving Scum. We don't believe in an afterlife and concentrate on this one and making it better, for all. We prefer a hospital to be built that all can use and benefit from, regardless of faith or lack thereof instead of erecting another exclusive clubhouse of "worship", where useless rituals to the benefit of no-one are conducted, and misinformation and divisiveness is preached under the guise of sanctity. We believe in evidence and reason over scripture, superstition, authority, and faith. We believe we are all our brother's keeper, and denounce the false divisions and negative view of humanity ensconced in religious beliefs. We are the people your minister warned you about: the godless, the un-churched. We must be immoral, right? Madalyn's manifesto above, speaks for all non-believers.

O'Hair followed Robert Ingersoll's lead, who crusaded against religion a century before her, in having the 24 karat audacity to stand up against the overwhelming cultural inertia of the time. The 1950's and '60's were not an enlightened time. The *"Rights Revolution"* we all take for granted: civil, woman's, gays, and now the one decade old secular rights movement, weren't even whispered of yet. This lady had balls. I was 10 when Life magazine referred to her as *"the most hated woman in*

America." I think she would be more than pleased to know that there are more and more of us Unbelieving Scum coming out and being counted, 50 years after her heroic efforts to end having the Bible shoved down our throats in schools. Her lawsuit helped accomplish that, a year after another court case struck down officially sponsored prayer in schools.

O'Hair's reputation as an arrogant and irascible person, may explain some of the over the top vehemence saved for her. Like Galileo, it is said she may have brought much of it upon herself. Be that as it may, the words in her Supreme Court appeal are not those of a hateful zealot, someone fuming and angry with god, but relay the reasoned perspective of the empathetic secular humanist. In building hospitals instead of churches, in doing science instead of praying, jettisoning our superstitions in pursuit of a better life through our wits, for the betterment of our fellow man, she yet speaks for all secularists today.

Changing of the Guard

Time magazine's special edition: "100 Most Influential People of 2015" featured Malala Yousafzai, and Pope Francis together, side by side on the last page of their "Icons" section. They demonstrate truly, a telling contrast on a number of levels: young vs. old, female vs. male, East (Pakistan) vs. West (Argentina), Muslim vs. Xian. These comparisons seem largely superficial at first glance, but more intriguing and enlightening, is the contrast in titles given to the short biographies which accompany their images. This young female is heralded as a "Champion of Education" and this old man as "The Humble Pastor." Education vs. religion. New ideas vs. old ideas, female vs. male. It is no accident that a male, an old male, represents religion and a young female, though also raised in a religion herself, (one that had her shot for going to school) represents education, especially education for girls and women all over the world.

Malala stands in stark contrast to her religion, about as diametrically opposed as one could get, as a survivor of a religiously motivated assassination attempt by a male committed to a religion that not only condemns women to second class citizenship (like the Pope's religion), but to ignorance and subservience. She was shot by the Taliban in 2012 for attending school, and for being a very visible and outspoken activist for woman's education. Malala's activism goes far beyond promoting education of women and girls worldwide. In talking to another old male world leader of some influence, Malala attempted to educate him as well to a pressing situation in her home country:

"Innocent victims are killed in these acts, and they lead to resentment among the Pakistani people. If we refocus efforts on education it will make a big impact."

Malala was expressing her concerns to Barack Obama, that US drone attacks may be fueling more terrorism.

The Pope, on the other hand, stands for his very old patriarchal church, an organization that embraces an archaic misogyny. Women can't be priests, bishops, cardinals, or Pope. They can't rise to run the organization, they can't control it. Worse still, they are denied their reproductive rights by the Catholic Church's ridiculous and deadly dogma which may be one of the most heinous commands of any religion, responsible for more suffering and deaths than even the religion which needed Malala to be killed. Both Malala and Pope Francis are heralded as icons of our modern age by Time magazine, yet one is pushing for modernity and the end of millennia-old thinking that restricts women to religiously approved behaviors in dress, sexuality, education and status as formulated by men centuries ago, and the other is head of the largest institution on earth that maintains such repressions. Education eradicates those restrictions. Worldwide, the more women become educated and the more they take back their reproductive rights and gain status and economic power, they leave the religious restrictions on their behavior, written and enforced by men, far behind. Educated women, even in predominantly Catholic countries, utterly ignore the Pope and his Church's absurd ideas about birth control. Malala represents new freedoms for women, and change. The Pope represents old repressions, and the status quo.

The fact that it is time for a change with women coming to the forefront, finally becoming equal to men with access to all endeavors, is most eloquently stated by the anthropologist, Melvin Konner, in his new book: *Women, After All: Sex, Evolution and the End of Male Supremacy.* From the introduction:

"...women are fundamentally pragmatic as well as caring, cooperative as well as competitive, skilled in getting their own egos out of the way, deft in managing people without putting them on the defensive, builders rather than destroyers. Above all, I mean that women carry on the business of a complex world in ways that are more focused, efficient, deliberate, and constructive than man's, because women are not frequently distracted by impulses and moods that sometimes indirectly lead to inappropriate sex and unnecessary violence. Women are more reluctant participants in both. And if they do have to be drawn into wars, these will be wars of necessity, not of choice, founded on rational considerations, not on a clash of egos escalating out of control"

Science tells him this. Konner makes a rather strong case in 310 pages of data and findings from anthropology, sociology, psychology and biology, that women and men are not the same. Furthermore, the differences women bring to the table, may be superior to those of men, and those skills could be just what is needed to make a better world. It is a great read, and a scientific tour de force, do give it a look. I could not agree more. We need more women senators, representatives, business leaders, scientists, world leaders and courageous champions of education like Malala. We do not need any more Popes, imams, ministers, monks, pastors (however humble), or priests of any kind. We need less of all these bastions of male rule-making and phony authority, that keep the world divided and women repressed. The New Enlightenment calls for an end to all religious "authority" and their disabling ideas. Malala represents the changing of the guard that Konner argues for.

Why We Fight, Why I Write

I have two audiences for my writing, and finding that fine line between emboldening one, and not pissing off the other (too much), while attempting to enlighten and prod them both, may determine how successful a writer I become. As for the first, I challenge the religious audience to think of what they have been taught, unquestioned since they were little, in a very different, very critical, and often glaring light. There is no time to pull punches. My liberal Xian friends think everything is fine because they live within a faith that is neither demanding nor demeaning of others, and can't understand why all this "religion bashing" is necessary. They wonder what the fuss is all about. Would that every religionist in the world be as considerate of others. But they are not, most are not. There is a strong, very vocal and repressive, religious minority in this country, and incredibly cruel and overwhelmingly repressive religious factions in other countries around the world, that impose their beliefs and behaviors daily, without letup, on everyone they can, especially women and gays. Millions of lives are ruined every day at the hands of the religious.

Militant theism is widespread, and accepted as a normal component of having religious faith, even in our own country. In this country militant theism may be on the surface less apparent, and thankfully less damaging (though not always), than in Islamic countries for example, but it is no less insidious. The USA Today published an article a few years back, covering the Evangelical response to Obama's coming out in favor of gay marriage. In the accompanying photo, was a black Baptist minister waving his Bible, very upset that Obama was obviously going directly against Scripture. The sort of nonsense the good minister sincerely believes, needs to be questioned, and ridiculed, and eliminated, from modern culture as soon as possible. Why should the rest of the country, and the majority of us who are not Evangelical Xians, be compelled to live by his religious standards? He is certainly free and welcome to never marry a gay in his church. He is free to be as ignorant and intolerant as he chooses. But the other 85% of us non-Evangelicals, don't need or want, laws based on his or anyone else's intolerant and ignorant interpretation of old, outdated, horribly primitive, and just plain wrong scripture.

Liberal Xians of course aren't quite like this, but they participate in the belief in the same scripture which legitimizes the Conservative Xian logic. As I reported in the previous chapter, I took part in a panel discussion about LGBTI issues, at the college where I taught, with two very kind ministers, definitely members of the liberal Xian camp. Yet, there they were, apologizing from the very beginning, in their opening remarks, about the treatment and perspectives accorded to gays by their respective churches. Gays couldn't be ministers in either of their churches. They are second class citizens from the start. The gay lifestyle, whether their particular churches go along with the absurd evangelical propaganda of it being a choice or not, isn't condoned in the least. The tired, old, "love the poor sinner, hate the sin" hedging is portrayed as somehow kind. Not surprisingly, the ministers dragged out the word "nuanced" to describe the ongoing theological debate on the gay issue, as they tried to explain that their respective churches were certainly hard at work on the problem, of reconciling modern societal acceptance of varying sexual orientation, based on science, with wholly arbitrary selection and interpretation of the Bible "clobber" passages, which condemn homosexuality. *"We're working on it, and we'll get back to you"* was the upshot.

Isn't that just special? Well gee, come on over to the secular non-religious camp. There is no gay problem here. You are not a problem for us non-believers. We know modern science says sexual orientation varies in hundreds of species, mediated by multiple genetic and hormonal prenatal developmental processes. It is as normal as variation in any other physical or behavioral trait. End of story.

As for my second audience, the vast (and may I co-opt and reverse the meaning of an old term) "silent majority", of people who value reason and tolerance and compassion for their fellow humans, over religious dogma any day of the week, I attempt to express what they may be thinking. Militant theism has got to go. The arrogance of religious thought has had its run. We need to push it over the cliff as soon as possible. Personal religious freedom should be protected, as always, in every country, but the supposition that you may then impose your beliefs on anyone else, including your children, has got to go, abandoned like the bad habit that it is. Keep and enjoy your comforting rituals, and sense of community and whatever cosmological speculations you entertain about a particular deity. Just leave everyone else alone. Leave the rest of us alone, including your children.

We don't want to live by Baptist attitudes toward sex and gays. We don't want to live under Catholic attitudes toward birth control and abortion. We don't want sharia law. We would like every religious person worldwide to be just like the Amish, the Mennonites or the Jains; completely unobtrusive in their beliefs and rituals, wholly respective of every other human's space and rights on the planet. The Amish may not like zippers, internal combustion engines or electricity, but they don't attempt to legislate against anyone else employing and enjoying them. If only the Baptists, Muslims, and Catholics would keep their conservative, repressive and absurd ideas on sex, porn, stem cell research, gay rights, woman's rights, evolution, birth control, and abortion to themselves. Folks, like the Amish and Jains, very kindly, leave the rest of us alone. If we can get the Baptists, Muslims and Catholics to do the same "what a wonderful world it would be." Imagine no guilt over sex or birth control. No absurd denials of science. No homophobia, no misogyny, and a diminished mess in the Middle East. The political and economic problems would remain, but just imagine if religion were taken out of the equation. No Xiansanity, no Judaism, no Islamic thinking, to muck up the works of solving the Palestinian problem. I'll risk tiptoeing off that fine line now and then, for that. I'll dare to be called strident, or offensive any day.

There's a Whole Lotta Norms Out There

Kudos for my polemics on religion have come from unexpected fronts regularly, and for a couple of years now, since I began my editorials and column in the college newspaper and later published my weekly blog posts. One of the first, and most memorable instances of unsolicited support, was received in a bar while chatting with a few students. In the midst of conversation, someone brought up one of the first editorials I'd written long awhile back. His name was Norm, and he had been in one of my classes a few years earlier. He thanked me for writing on religion as I did, really liked what I had to say, felt my pieces were inspiring and really hoped I'd continue and looked forward to the next installment. Needless to say I was flattered, and pleased to find I had reached someone enough for them to speak up and give me a pat on the back as it were. Since then, similar encouragement has been offered enough times, from out of nowhere, and equally unsolicited, that I put an entry in my journal "TAWLNOT." I use acronyms as reminders of things I need to develop into daily routines or habits of mind and *"There's a Whole Lot of Norms Out There"* (TAWL-NOT), has been one of my mantras ever since. You never know who is listening and appreciating your work.

Not long ago I read an interesting article about comedians developing their act, their persona, patter, and presence. Back in the late 60's at the height of his stand-up career, Bill Cosby was advising a young Joan Rivers, who was just starting out, not to alter her unique, but sometimes rather abrasive style. Not to edit herself, but to plow ahead as he said *"If only 1% of America likes you, you'll fill stadiums."* That has stuck with me ever since. I've never had a goal to fill stadiums, but anyone that writes obviously wants to reach an audience, and I took away the important point that you will not please everybody, and you may not please most, but if you are getting such positive feedback as I have received, you are connecting with a good portion of folks, so press on. I subsequently put labels saying "Don't Edit Yourself" on my laptop and my office computer. Cosby, it has recently come to light, had a perverse dark side, apparently engaging in the regular drugging of women for unsolicited sex, but he did know his comedy and the mechanics of popular appeal.

Besides the random emails of thanks and approval from folks I've never met, or the someone I do know looking up at me over the sandwich counter, while they wrap my burrito saying *"Hey, I read your column now, awsum, keep it up"* or words to that effect, the best and most unique praise and encouragement has been over the bumper stickers on my car. They get a lot of eye-traffic. The latest incarnation includes:

"Got a Revelation for ya, there is no such thing"

"Misogyny, Homophobia and Science Denial all go away when Religion does"

"Everyone else's Prophets heard voices in their heads...but yours REALLY talked to god, right"

"Information Kills Religion"

They have been on there for a few years now and I've had numerous people come up to me and go *"Wow, those are great!"* or *"Your bumper stickers rock!"* A few, were friends of my kids who dug them. One guy was a stranger at a local bar, in a rural area up here in Northern Illinois, who came up to me after having a smoke out in the parking lot and asked, *"Is that your little vehicle out there?"* It was the only non-pickup truck in the parking lot and I said, "Yes-sir" not sure where he was going to go with this. I half expected to get reprimanded by a Xian of some sort, but he proceeded to tell me how he had no use for religion, and it was high time people came out and said what needed to be said as my bumper stickers did, gave me the thumbs up and split. He was 50 something I'd guess. Ya just never know. *"It is high time someone came out and said what needed to be said."* He nailed the entire motivation for this book.

I've had a few notes stuck on my car, most of them positive: *"Love your stickers"* or *"You made my day."* Once, however, a concerned good Xian person left me a very heartfelt message, a full page, saying that if I just open my heart, stop being angry at god and let Jesus in, god will still love me and my soul would be saved. Uh huh. One other time a guy on a motorcycle pulled up alongside of me to inform me *"Jesus loves you."* Now, normally I'd shake that off and just smile back *"Yeah, yeah"* and let it go, but I was in a foul mood for one reason or another and was thinking *"Oh, bite me"* and flipped him off and said: *"Fuck you."* Sometimes you just get tired of the bullshit ya know? It is everywhere, and obnoxious.

To say so out loud that religion is a bunch of hooey, still isn't that easy for anyone, and my bumper stickers are but one more way to legitimize what so many people are thinking about the religion they grew up on, that is all around them, that still surrounds all of us even today, in our modern culture. And they say *"Right On"* when you diss religion clearly, straightforward, and without hesitation. The few folks that take the time to say something, or feel compelled to write me a note, represent just the tip of the iceberg. There's so many more that feel the same way, but many remain quiet to avoid confrontation. There's many more than the religionists dare to admit. I especially like watching the minivans full of nicely dressed families, inch closer to my bumper on Sunday mornings at the stoplight, as the occupants peer over their dashboards, and I watch their lips move. Many smile and chat and comment, some however recede back, heads shaking. One lady pulled up alongside of me in the summer. As our windows were both down, she shouted out she would pray for me. By the look on her face, I wasn't sure exactly what direction she might be asking her deity of choice to send me. Not a day goes by that I don't notice folks reading my bumper stickers at stoplights, or pausing to read as they walk by my car in the parking lot. It is but one more way I can spur people into thinking, questioning their beliefs, even if some take offense.

A van once followed me into the parking lot at school, and as I opened my door a middle aged guy gets out, totally non-threatening and says *"Hey, I followed you into the parking lot just to tell you how much I like your bumper stickers!"* Unreal. I thanked him of course, and he asked if I got a lot of heat for them down here in western Kentucky, where I was teaching at the time. I said *"No, not really"* and that I hadn't been beat up yet or yelled at or anything, but that I do get a lot of positive comments like his. He said *"That's surprising"* and *"It's about time this kinda stuff was said."* That is a common refrain.

Most secularists: atheists, agnostics, freethinkers, deists, even liberal believers, feel this way. They're pretty much fed up with the churches on every corner, the politicians, the TV preachers, and the often obnoxious church signs that offer a daily reprimand of religious proscriptions, condemnations, and just plain absurdities that we have quietly endured for years. No more. Nowadays many of us are expressing more of a *"Yeah, yeah, blow it out your ass"* kinda mentality. Hitch did that so well, but in such erudite language. We secular activists feel like we are just warming up, and religion is finally getting the rebuttal it has deserved for millennia. We are nowhere near up to equal time yet. So, offensive sometimes or not, providing a thought provoking message is what it is all about. Many are challenged, but so many more are relieved, glad to see somebody speaking out. There are a whole lot of Norms out there.

A Nonbeliever Leaves the South

Last class, last exam, last final of the semester, of the school year, of a 5 year stint at Murray State University, Murray, KY never to return, passing out my 60 multiple choice question test... and a student asks: *"Hey Dr. Z, what's the shirt for... 'Unbelieving Scum', what's that all about?"* I hesitated for a moment, thinking about it...*"Pride."* You get tired of being told you're a sinner all the time. You get tired of hearing this claim or that, about the wrongness of gays or how woman's bodies are surmised to work. You get tired of all the strained euphemisms that are just so clever and cute yet carry a dastardly message. On every street corner in America, on TV, by street preachers on campus, by Republican Baptists that don't know shit, but think they do because they get their science from a Church, you get the same message; how somebody is gonna burn in Hell because we are all so lucky to have a god out there that really loves us. How science must be wrong, since it doesn't comport with their nasty little book. How everyone needs to live the way one arrogant blatherer or another tells us: Mark Driscoll, Franklin Graham, Ted Haggard, all the Popes, priests, all the imams, the monks, and all the ministers.

Pride, and a bit of throw it right back in their face 'cuz I'm the guy your minister warned you about. Yup, there's lots of us, and we don't buy an ounce of their horseshit. Then when you get to know me or any one of a bazillion of other non-believers of whatever stripe and we don't fit the sinister stereotype you've been told, you realize the crap you learned about atheists is as much bullshit as any of the other Xian propaganda you have heard your whole life. So yes, I wear my *"Unbelieving Scum"* shirt with pride. Come get to know me or any non-believing freethinker and find out for yourself just how reasonable, empathetic, tolerant, and, sure, flawed a bit, we all are. In a word, normal. Just like you, or the vast majority of us wandering around the planet, trying to figure it all out and making it up as we go along. Grow up in a faith? You've been hosed. Such is the absurdity and arrogance of religious thought and we're fucking tired of it. It doesn't get a free pass anymore. *"Yeah, it's pride."*

"Come Out Come Out, Wherever You Are...."

All my gay friends are brave as hell, by comparison to us non-believers as a whole. Though there are a lot of prominent exceptions, especially as far as Islam is concerned, we secularists haven't had it nearly as tough as the gays. The LGBTI folks deal with real discrimination, ostracization, even hatred. Some might say it is as bad as the racial discrimination many minorities face, depending on how un-enlightened a country they live in. We non-believers, of all stripes need to take another page from the civil and gay rights movements, and be even more vocal, upfront, and open, about our non-belief. Consciousness raising is what it is all about. For some, it is not easy at all. The loss of family, friends, maybe even a job is a real possibility. De-conversion books, like Jerry DeWitt's *Hope after Faith*, contain a good exposition of how damaging it can be for some to come out as unbelieving scum in a hardcore community of obnoxious belief. Losing your job, family, or your friends is usually the extreme end of consequences for a non-believer but it does happen, and all too often. Like Jerry, and so many others, we all need to come out. We need to challenge the underlying, unquestioned religious assumptions that pervade our culture such as: *"Morality is exclusive to religion,"* or *"Non-believers are desperate, hopeless, nihilistic, lost without a moral basis."*

The discussion of religion and secularism is everywhere and it is allowing more and more of us to dare say what we have been thinking for some time now. As I've pointed out, in 2014 Pew Research reported that the number of Americans identifying as *"Nones" ("having no particular religious affiliation")* has risen to nearly 23% of the population. That's nearly as big a voting block as the Evangelicals, already bigger than the Catholics. That is a lot of non-religious folks, many of whom, are non-believers of various kinds (atheists, agnostics, non-theists) and minimalist believers (deists, pantheists). Many of us know more than a few others, who still identify with a given religion, yet when pressed, believe very little of its tenets, but who, for various reasons, can't come out. Don't you wonder what that number of non-believers really is? If everyone who suspects or has figured out religion is bullshit "came out," would those numbers be 30%, 40% or more?

I'll go out on a limb here and suggest that like Northern Europe we are already in the majority, over 50% secular here in the US, but with a sizable number of folks, yet unable to be open about it, or dare exercise what they are really thinking. We need to make it easier on them. It works. *It is working.* We may not be in Kansas, Toto, where they actually installed little prayer booths in some of the empty old telephone ones, but I betcha just like the Munchkins in OZ, there's a whole lot of Unbelieving Scum out there in hiding, still in the closet, just waiting for permission to speak their minds. *"Come out, Come out, Where ever you are!"*

The more we come out, then the more we raise consciousness about the legitimacy of non-belief, just as the civil, gay and women's rights movements have done before us. The more people realize they know a non-believer, the quicker the stereotypes promulgated by the Xian faiths disappear, just as has so recently and quickly occurred with gay marriage approval. Too many people, young and old, but especially the young, know too many gay and lesbian folks to even think of treating them as less than equal human beings. And LGBTI folks make up less than 10% of the population! The *"Nones,"* non-religious at least, with many of them full blown non-believers of some kind, make up at very least 23% of the population, and 36% of the 18-24 year-olds! We secularists make up a huge portion of society. We could possibly be in the majority. Everyone in America knows someone who is not religious, and most likely also knows more than a few complete non-believers as well. They just don't know they do. We gotta come out.

Non-belief is Not a Religion

From dictionary.com: re·li·gion [ri-lij-uhn] noun

1. a set of beliefs concerning the cause, nature, and purpose of the universe, especially when considered as the creation of a superhuman agency or agencies, usually involving devotional and ritual observances, and often containing a moral code governing the conduct of human affairs.

2. a specific fundamental set of beliefs and practices generally agreed upon by a number of persons or sects: the Christian religion; the Buddhist religion.

3. the body of persons adhering to a particular set of beliefs and practices: a world council of religions.

4. the life or state of a monk, nun, etc.: to enter religion.

5. the practice of religious beliefs; ritual observance of faith.

On occasion, I'll receive a comment on my website objecting to my blog posts that are critical of the Dalai Lama's Buddhist beliefs claiming I really shouldn't couldn't go after Buddhism because it isn't really a religion, as it has no "creator god," no supreme being, big kahuna, big cheese, Yahweh, Allah, or similar stern, demanding Omnipotent Prick. Since I'd heard this objection before I thought it would be good to address it. The above definition of a religion was a good start to which we could include:

6. multiple supernatural entities

7. moralizing

8. explanation of the universe

9. rituals

10. rules of membership

11. reliance on faith, that is, belief without evidence

12. devotional practices

13. a hierarchy of authority: priesthood, monks, imams, usually celibate.

14. an uncritical reliance on ancient ideas

15. a sacred scripture(s) to be consulted and interpreted

16. a negative, restrictive attitude toward sex

17. a negative attitude toward reason

18. purpose of human beings

19. exclusive paths and claims to truth

20. reliance on authority over evidence

21. patriarchal in outlook, relegating women to 2nd class citizenship

22. more rules for women than men

23. holy places

24. houses of worship: temples, churches, monasteries.

25. afterlife beliefs: souls, heaven, hell, reincarnation, nirvana, etc.

So even without a specific single creator being, which even the dictionary definition is flexible on, I'd say Buddhism hits the last 20 attributes spot on. We could also add "often homophobic" and "internally and externally divisive." That divisiveness comes from many competing sects that are generally hostile or at least demeaning to non-believers. I'd say Buddhism hits them all, including belief in supernatural entities, just not the Big One.

In direct contrast, consider non-belief, which some Xian apologists claim is just another religion (as if to bring secularism down to the same level). Well, non-belief, that is atheism, non-theism, deism, agnosticism, secular humanism, what have you, does not instantiate most of the above 25 attributes. Nothing is sacred. There are no rituals. There is no moralizing, supernatural, scripture or authorities, no priests or monks, temples or churches. Non-belief has no worship of anything, no afterlife, no restrictive attitude on sex, no misogyny, no homophobia, no divisiveness, and a reliance on reason and evidence, with a commitment to tolerance and the well-being of all, focused on this life, this world, not some afterlife, ethereal realm or ultimate reality beyond this one.

Based in science and reason, non-belief does have an explanation for the universe and a path to truth, which many would argue is exclusive to the scientific method. The creation story we do have, for example, is based on science that all humans share, not some exclusive cultural set of primitive myths, that display a child-like explanation of the world, that is millennia old, hopelessly out of date, and just plain wrong. So if some DB starts telling you atheism or some other form of non-belief is just another religion, you got the goods on them. Atheism, non-belief of any kind is not a religion. Non-belief does not employ faith (belief without evidence), in unseen deities and old myths. Enlightenment into non-belief, identifies a lack of religion. It is not a retreat into another one.

The Myth Shelf

The picture that makes up the banner across the top of the opening page of my website and blog, *Dispatches from the New Enlightenment*, says it all. It depicts the Bible and Koran retitled "Hebrew Mythology" and "Arabic Mythology" respectively, placed on a bookshelf where they belong, sandwiched between all the other cultural myths that have come and gone from cultural acceptance, as once true religions. It epitomizes exactly what the New Enlightenment is all about. The Bible and the Koran both belong on the shelf along with all the other ancient cultural myth collections: Greek and Roman Mythology, the Egyptian Book of the Dead, Norse Mythology and others. No one believes in Mars, Zeus, Osiris, Ra, Wodin, or Thor anymore. No one should believe in Yahweh, Jesus, or Allah either, and for the same reasons. They're myths. And no-one should believe an ounce of the utterly absurd modern mythologies of Mormonism and Scientology, 19th and 20th century science fictions respectively, each written by megalomaniacs bent on inventing a religion.

One day, we humans won't believe this nonsense anymore. These book's claims to divine authorship, will be rightly tossed into the dustbin of history, as Hitch proposed. They will be placed alongside all the other collections of fantasy, and regarded as cultural myth, history, and literature, but nothing more. They won't be regarded as scripture. They will no longer be considered as true accounts of gods, containing directives from the gods, to be heeded or ignored, at one's peril. They will no longer absurdly proclaim to be revelations from some god or gods on high, just like all the other religions of the past. They will not even be falsely respected, as divinely inspired works to live one's life by. The Hebrew myths and the Arabic myths, need to take their place along with the rest as soon as possible. That is what the first Enlightenment began, by questioning the morality, authenticity, veracity, and authority of stories of the divine. The New Enlightenment, armed with 21st century knowledge of the abject, fanciful, and often ugly, inhumanity of these books, intends to take the endeavor to its conclusion, by eliminating any faith in these books, eliminating any respect for these books, other than as mythic histories of their respective cultures. It is time we dropped the absurd contention of all religions; that their scriptures are revealed. Religions are intellectually and empirically bankrupt from the git-go. The claim to revelation is wholly unsupportable and the biggest, most dangerous mistake in human history.

Krauss and Lennon

At the American Humanist Association Meeting, May 7-10 2015, in Denver, Colorado, Lawrence Krauss, physicist, cosmologist, and tireless promoter of secularism and science, in a very moving 30 minute presentation, proposed something once thought completely impossible; the end of religion, and sooner than anyone might have thought. Krauss:

"Is it naive to believe that we can overcome centuries of religious intransigence in a single generation through education?"

Quoting Nelson Mandela, who languished in prison from 1962 to 1989, and went from prison to the presidency of South Africa in less than a generation, he continued: *"It always seems impossible until it is done."*

I've been singing this same tune for 10 years now and for nearly 2 years on my blog. End religion now. It is not the least bit crazy. Shoot for the moon and you get the stars, and sometimes the whole, full, moon. Religion is not needed, natural or necessary. Religion as it is practiced today by 2/3's of the world's population is just a bad habit, a historical accident of civilization that can be dropped like other bad habits we have outgrown, especially in developed countries. Information kills religions and education is the key. Racism, witchcraft, routine torture, the divine right of kings, regular child beatings, gladiator competition, burning heretics at the stake, prophecy, astrology, slavery; all of these have been eliminated or marginalized, from once being unquestioned everyday practices and beliefs, considered normal and indispensable aspects of the human condition. Remnants of these practices linger, but only on the fringe of modern society, driven underground or to the margins, as empty mindless repetitions, that no longer dominate our daily life.

Over 1/3 of the world's population, in the neighborhood of 2 billion people, have dropped the bad habit that is religion already and become irreligious. Krauss ain't crazy. It is doable. We can live without it. So many of us have dropped it completely, and live utterly without religion. Claiming humans can't live without religion is religionist hype, and nothing more. Krauss notes that the "question" of gay marriage which rolled through the US State legislatures, and finally the Supreme Court in 2015, is now a "done deal" and is a prime example of how fast we can jettison religious thinking. It's over, there is no question for the current and coming generations, despite the pleadings and pronouncements from older leaders, both religious and political, that it is the doom of mankind or some such shit. The game is over, gay marriage is here to stay and to young people of Krauss's teen daughter's age, it isn't even an issue.

I've been observing, and promoting, the same viewpoint for years now, having watched my own students aged 18–mid 20's, even the hard-core Xian ones, become more and more liberal on the once religious non-negotiables of their parent's, and grandparent's generations. All of them, whether identifying with a religion or not, know gay people. They know friends, couples, acquaintances, celebrities, family members, who are gay and have no compulsion to limit their rights in any way, much less due to interpretations of the same old scripture that upholds genocide, rape, animal sacrifice, and slavery. The verses in support of which have been completely ignored for some time now. Just add the homophobic "clobber passages" to the list of now passe' Bible instructions. They are now being ignored as they should be. As Krauss says, *"it is a done deal."* with the young. There is no counterargument to the illogical picking and choosing of what verses from the Bible modern culture should follow, and which to ignore, given their obvious status as primitive rules of ancient date, from an ignorant and cruel era of human history, and nothing more.

The youth of today who remain religious, do not practice their grandparent's religion. They are utterly unconcerned with race, sexual orientation, sex behaviors, or religion itself, as reasons to divide and discriminate against other people. The consciousness raising of the civil and gay rights movements have changed society dramatically, in much of the West at least, in but a generation. This is not the 60's anymore. And with the global and immediate transfer of information driven by the net, and the relaxing of social restrictions to communication, that consciousness raising is spreading to all corners of the world. So how crazy is it to imagine as Krauss does, the end of not just the fight over gay rights, but the end of religion itself? Is it any crazier than Mandela languishing away in prison, imagining he would be free one day, and president of the very country in which he lay imprisoned under a life sentence, in less than 30 years? Absurd, ridiculous, improbable, impossible, but it happened.

Imagine if you could have tapped on the shoulder of one of the French Resistance fighters, during the bleakest of times in the midst of 1943, more than 3 years into the occupation of France by the Nazis, French citizens murdered daily with impunity by the occupying regime, the Allied invasion of D-Day barely past the proposal stage, in what seemed an eternity of suffering, that had no hope of an end…if you could have leaned-in from the future and said: *"Don't worry, France will be liberated in but another year and the Nazi's defeated utterly, Don't give up hope, Don't give up the fight."*

It happened. And if you could have sidled up close to one of the 1960's civil rights marchers, stuck in an Alabama jail after being hosed, beaten, put on by dogs, surrounded by white folk, who would love to see them lynched, if you could have whispered to them: *"Don't give up, in another 45 years a black man will be president."*

These things happened. In less than a generation, in a few short years, or a few decades of long, seemingly interminable time, they happened nonetheless. As Krauss notes, things of this magnitude can happen, have happened in less than a generation. Complete cultural shifts of thinking through education. So why not educate everyone to the evils of religion we too often let pass unchallenged in our modern culture? Like the absurd cruelty of homophobia that is being demolished worldwide, not just in the US, or irreligious Northern Europe, but even in uber-religious countries such as Ireland. I hear all the time: *"It's so impossible to convince a religious person, they will never change",* or *"The direct attack on religion is so counterproductive, it just hardens the fundamentalists to be even more extreme."*

In a word: Bullshit. Richard Dawkins' website alone has over 2,000 testimonials listed in his Convert's Corner. And that would represent just the tip of the iceberg. The vast majority of those who may have been helped along the path to skepticism, by Dawkins' and others' writings probably did not take the time to write in to thank the "strident" and "militant" atheist, as he is often described. On the contrary, it works, it is working, it has worked, yes, it does work, and will continue to work! No person is ever changed in one dramatic conversation, won over in one victorious confrontation. That fantasy only happens in the movies. But skepticism and secularism are on the rise, precisely because the information is out there, it is near impossible to ignore, and it slowly eats away at the absurdity of faith. The questioning of religion is everywhere. Education is the key. With even the most hard-core believers, seeds of doubt are being planted every time their flimsy faith claims are confronted. It just takes repeated exposures, often over years.

Consider also the spate of de-conversion books published by once hard-core religionists, the very sort of fundamentalists that people often despair will never convert. Bullshit, they do all the time, just not in one conversation, nor with the first contesting of their beliefs! Dan Barker, Bart Ehrman, John Loftus, Mike Aus, Jerry DeWitt, Seth Andrews, and so many others who are so prominent in the secular movement, were once born again, hardcore believers, and for years, some even preachers for a decade or two, but all are no longer Xians, but are decided non-believers. From as fundamental, conservative, and as evangelical as it gets, to full on secularists. The Gateway to Reason Rally, in St. Louis in 2015, featured a slate of newer de-converted Xians on its speakers list: Theresa McBain, Nathan Phelps, Vyckie Garrison (former Quiver-full, how much more hard-core Xiansanity can you get?), Sarah Morehead, Matt Dillahunty, Tracie Harris and Dave Smalley... former hard-core Xians ALL!

Of course confrontation of ideas works! It just takes time. You can be direct, yet polite, forceful, yet not ad hominem, pull no punches, while still being respectful. You can respect the person and their intellect while not giving an ounce of respect to their undeserving beliefs. Education is the key. It takes time and a lot of information to overcome years of indoctrination into the religious cocoon. It doesn't happen overnight, but it does happen, regularly, to the moderates, and yes, just as often to the most hardcore. Krauss has a lot of valid reasons to imagine the unthinkable, and he is in good company with so many others, along with John Lennon in imaging a world without religion.

Why I Write II

I don't wanna hear about one more gay high school kid who commits suicide, because they have been hearing from their Baptist, Pentecostal, or Church of Christ minister, or their Catholic priest, that they will surely burn in hell for a "lifestyle they have chosen." The suicide rate for gays down in the American South is twice that in the North. That keeps me writing and talking. Until pastors no longer exercise what they think is their God-given right, to spread misinformation in pushing their archaic and utterly wrong ideas about homosexuality, and other moral issues in the public square, I won't shut up. When kids brainwashed into Conservative Xiansanity, stop witnessing to other kids, bullying them with why they are going to Hell, all because their parents and ministers taught them this shit is right, then I'll have a lot less to say. When Republican politicians, the majority of them male, and most of them Baptists, stop spewing their unscientific and stupid claims about rape, conception, masturbation, libido, climate, evolution, etc., all bullshit they learned from their conservative Xian church, and stop introducing bill after bill to limit woman's rights, then I'll shut up and stop writing. When the Pope, and all the old white guys in dresses in Rome, admit they are wrong and reverse their archaic, cruel, illogical and unfounded stance on birth control and stop condemning millions of poor children to a life of misery, and many an early death, then I'll shut up and stop writing. When no-one like Pastor Jamie Coots kills themselves, convinced by Bible passages somebody taught them were true, that they can handle venomous snakes because god will protect them, then I'll stop. When no-one is conned into harming or killing others in order to do some cockamamie idea of "god's work", then I can quit.

Religion is not natural, needed, nor necessary. We function during 99% of our daily life in non-spiritual, practical reality mode. We trust our fellow humans, our scientific authorities and teachers. We trust that our car will start and that electricity is real and works, though few of us could actually explain the flow of electrons through a wire. We go to a hospital for treatment, not to shamans and witch doctors. Religion can't know, but proclaims to anyway. All theology of contemporary Islam, Xianity, Buddhism, Hinduism, or what have you is as silly as discussing the attributes of Zeus, or interpreting the nuances in the directives from the oracle at Delphi. All are complete and utter fantasy, yet we coerce our children into becoming another generation of Jesus followers and submissives to Allah. It must stop.

People the world over have their lives ruined by religion. The young girl in Nepal, stuck in her cramped menstrual shed for another cold, wet, sleepless night, the Saudi blasphemer languishing away in prison fearing another near-fatal lashing, the gay kid in Alabama raised Pentecostal and contemplating suicide, the millions of starving infants and toddlers of uneducated Catholic parents, in developing countries having even more children than they can feed, because their arrogant spiritual leader assures them they must not use birth control, the women raped and beaten into sex slavery by the latest incarnation of Islamist purity...all this can end.

Religion is not natural, but a historical accident. It is merely a bad habit of our developing civilization, which, like slavery, can be terminated in a generation or two, for the good of all. It is not needed, longed for, not missed in any way, by billions who have walked away from indoctrination. They live completely without desire to worship the non-existent, or condemn their brothers and sisters to eternal pain. And religion is completely un-necessary for a person to have a moral, fulfilled, productive, compassionate, and completely whole human life. In fact, its delusions and degradations merely get in the way. Whatever good religion engages in, can be duplicated through any number of secular activities, without the delusions, divisiveness, misogyny, homophobia, condemnation, sexual repression, and denial of knowledge and progress, which our patriarchal religions promote to so many at their peril.

End religion now. All of them. Information kills religion, and education is the way to diminish if not outright eliminate religious thought. The New Enlightenment has put one hell of a dent in religion in but a decade. Imagine if we had another two or three decades, or a full century of clear-headed rebuttal of religious nonsense and arrogance. It is more than merely possible, but an imperative. We owe it to our fellow humans crushed by religion, now and in the future. The human race must get rid of the idea that there is any sort of god's work to be done. We must drop the last ideology that puts mere ideas ahead of human rights.

"And I think it should be, religion, treated with ridicule, hatred, and contempt and I claim that right."

Christopher Hitchens

ACKNOWLEDGMENTS

There are so many people to thank, for helping make this dream of becoming a writer come true, throughout all the stages: the editorials, the weekly column, the 2-1/2 years of my blog (350 website posts) and now, the first book. It is actually difficult to write this without tearing up a bit.

First of all, a huge thank you to all the folks at MSU, many of whom I've never met, who sent me words of thanks and encouragement for my letters to the editor, and later my weekly columns, which questioned religion from within the smothering, highly religious culture of Western Kentucky. That kudos was the initial boost I needed to finally pursue this lifelong dream. Thanks to Evan Hannan and David Villers, who helped me design and setup my website, which put me on the path to this book. Thanks to Kim Vogler, for support and friendship, and setting the example on the level of BAMF-ness (Bad-Ass Mother Fucker) needed to persevere in a successful speaking and writing career. Thank you also to all the former students, who still stay in touch on Face book. Your compliments and continued support for the attack on religion are yet so rewarding. A special thanks to Ben Shelby, for his example of tireless advocacy of secular and science education.

A shout-out goes to Jim Leonard, my editor, who allowed me free reign to bend the grammar and indulge in my run-on sentences, while clarifying the excesses of same. Thank you to my pen-pal in Australia, Anita Spinks, who was first to read the manuscript, pronounced it a "good read", and who has been a source of sound advice and a supporter of my writing for some time. I'm very grateful to all the secret admirers of my bumper stickers, who have bothered to leave me notes on my windshield over the years, saying that my upfront anti-religious slogans made their day. Big thanks goes to my supporters Ron and Cheryl Toth, who also sent me my most excellent book designer, Heidi DeMarco. Her graphic skills made my vague ideas come to life. Much appreciation goes to Combo, audiobook recording engineer extraordinaire, whose skills as a producer made my vocal performance incomparably better. If it still sucks, it is not his fault. Thanks to my son Will, who one day called me out of the blue some years ago, and said: "Pops, When did you learn to write?" To my oldest son Anthony, a special note of appreciation is in order. He reviewed and critiqued the entire manuscript, along with his wife, Franci. Anthony pushed me to reconsider, re-arrange, clarify, and rewrite, when I didn't realize that I needed to, and provided unparalleled encouragement and direction throughout this massive project, more than anyone. Lastly, love and thanks to my darling bride, Kimmy, and our kids, and grandkids...it is all for them.

REFERENCES AND RECOMMENDED READING

Chapter 1 Divisiveness

1. Campbell, Joseph. *Masks of God*. New York: Penguin, 1976.
2. Labarre, Weston. *The Ghost Dance*. Illinois: Waveland Press, 1990.
3. Dawkins, Richard. *The God Delusion*. New York: Houghton-Mifflin, 2006.
4. Hitchens, Christopher. *God is not Great*. New York: Hachette Book Group Inc., 2007.
5. Harris, Sam. *The End of Faith*. New York: W.W. Norton, 2004.
6. Dennett, Daniel. *Breaking the Spell,* New York: Penguin, 2006.
7. Boyer, Pascal. *Religion Explained*. New York: Basic Books, 2001.
8. Atran, Scott. *In Gods We Trust*. New York: Oxford University Press, 2002.
9. Internet Infidels. http://infidels.org/
10. Ehrman, Bart. *Misquoting Jesus*. New York: Harper Collins, 2005.
11. Richard Dawkins Foundation for Reason and Science. https://richarddawkins.net
12. Coyne, Jerry. Why Evolution is True. https://whyevolutionistrue.wordpress.com/
13. Statue of Liberty. http://www.nps.gov/stli/index.htm.
14. Dennis Terry Introduces Rick Santorum https://www.youtube.com/watch?v=B2emBxDOY7g
15. Thomas Jefferson's Letter to the Danbury Baptists. http://loc.gov/loc/lcib/9806/danpre.html
16. Shahada. https://en.wikipedia.org/wiki/Shahada
17. John F. Kennedy Assassination. https://en.wikipedia.org/wiki/Assassination_of_John_F._Kennedy.
18. Apollo 11 moon landing. https://en.wikipedia.org/wiki/Apollo_11.
19. Bronowski, Jacob. *The Ascent of Man*. New York: Little, Brown, 1973.
20. Jacob Bronowski at Auschwitz. http://www.youtube.com/watch?v=JlDumTPyn00
21. Gospel of Mark. https://en.wikipedia.org/wiki/Gospel_of_Mark
22. Shia Islam. https://en.wikipedia.org/wiki/Shia_Islam
23. "HS. Story, An ex-Muslim and and ex-Hindu in love." http://exhijabifashion.tumblr.com/post/92562117185/hs-story-an-ex-muslim-and-an-ex-hindu-in-love

24. "Religious Hostilities'"
    http://www.pewforum.org/2014/01/14/religious-hostilities-reach-six-year-high/

25. Thomas Jefferson.
    https://www.monticello.org/site/jefferson/superstition-christianity-quotation

26. PEW Research. https://en.wikipedia.org/wiki/Pew_Research_Center

27. Sam Harris and Dave Rubin Talk Religion, Politics, Free Speech (Full Interview).
    https://www.youtube.com/watch?v=zQqxlzHJrU0

Chapter 2 Misogyny and Homophobia

1. Judges 19: 25-30 King James Version, World Bible Publishers.

2. Brother Dean Stanton ASU preacher profiled on VICE NEWS:
   http://samuel-warde.com/2014/11/brother-dean-profiled/

3. Women in the US Senate.
   https://en.wikipedia.org/wiki/Women_in_the_United_States_Senate

4. Femen:https://www.youtube.com/watch?x-yt-ts=1421914688&v=RF6rBjTbmO0&x-yt-cl=84503534

5. William James and Mary Calkins: https://en.wikipedia.org/wiki/Mary_Whiton_Calkins

6. Steve Neumann, a contributor to Salon magazine; "Cut it out atheists, Why it is time to stop behaving like Bill Maher and Richard Dawkins." http://www.salon.com/2014/09/20/cut_it_out_atheists_why_its_time_to_stop_behaving_like_bill_maher_and_richard_dawkins/

7. Malala Yousafzai: http://www.biography.com/people/malala-yousafzai-21362253

8. Ziauddin Yousafzai: http://www.ted.com/talks/ziauddin_yousafzai_my_daughter_malala

9. "Muslim Statistics (Education and Employment)"
   http://wikiislam.net/wiki/Muslim_Statistics_-_Education_and_Employment

10. "Fatima's Story." http://exhijabifashion.tumblr.com/post/98513150815/fatimas-story

11. "S's Story" http://exhijabifashion.tumblr.com/post/98505000325/ss-story

12. "Femen world outlook." http://femen.org/about-us/

13. "Commonwealth Policy Center Letter to the Editor", MSU NEWS
    http://thenews.org/2014/03/28/letters-to-the-editor-3-28-14/

14. Pew Research "Gay Marriage." http://www.pewresearch.org/data-trend/domestic-issues/attitudes-on-gay-marriage/

15. USA Today "Modern Family in High Court." http://www.usatoday.com/story/opinion/2014/05/29/modern-family-supreme-court-gay-marriage-column/9732813/

16. Dan Savage. https://en.wikipedia.org/wiki/Dan_Savage1

17. "Students Walk Out on Dan Savage" http://www.citizenlink.com/2012/04/18/students-walk-out-on-dan-savage/

18. "Rick Wiles Claims Ebola Could 'Solve' Homosexuality and Other Issues in America." http://www.huffingtonpost.com/2014/08/07/rick-wiles-ebola_n_5658481.html

19. "Bishop: UNESCO Plans to Turn ½ the World Gay." http://www.rationalskepticism.org/news-politics/bishop-unesco-plans-to-turn-1-2-the-world-gay-t28342.html

Chapter 3 Eternal Damnation

1. "Number of Christian Denominations." http://christianity.about.com/od/denominations/p/christiantoday.htm

2. Bell, Robert. *Love Wins: A Book about Heaven, Hell and the Fate of Every Person Who Ever Lived*. New York: Harper One, 2011.

3. "We Have Seen This All Before: Rob Bell and the Re-emergence of Liberal Theology." http://www.albertmohler.com/2011/03/16/we-have-seen-all-this-before-rob-bell-and-the-reemergence-of-liberal-theology/

4. Alexander, Eben. *Proof of Heaven*. New York: Simon & Schuster, 2011.

5. "Death is not Final" Intelligence Squared Debate. Sean Carroll and Steven Notella vs. Eben Alexander and Raymond Moody. https://www.youtube.com/watch?v=h0YtL5eiBYw

6. Real Time with Bill Maher "Heaven is Real" https://www.youtube.com/watch?v=1zpYn3aha7E

7. Dalai Lama website. http://www.dalailama.com/

8. Brodie, Fawn. *No One Knows My History*. New York: Vintage, 1995.

9. Naraka. https://en.wikipedia.org/wiki/Naraka

Chapter 4 Creationism

1. Hugh Ross website. http://www.reasons.org/about/our-mission

2. Science Daily website. https://www.sciencedaily.com/

3. Science News website. https://www.sciencenews.org/

4. F.A Macdonald et al. "A newly identified Gondwanan terrane in the northern Appalachian Mountains: Implications for the Taconic orogeny and closure of the Iapetus Ocean" http://geology.gsapubs.org/content/42/6/539.abstract?sid=e65ce902-b1cb-4eb0-863e-1b3241c8a0adGeology journal Taconian orogeny 2012,13 14

5. Answers in Genesis (AiG) website: https://answersingenesis.org/

6. Meteor Crater wikipedia. https://en.wikipedia.org/wiki/Meteor_Crater

7. Niagara Falls wikipedia. https://en.wikipedia.org/wiki/Niagara_Falls,_Ontario

8. Mississippi Delta wikipedia. https://en.wikipedia.org/wiki/Mississippi_Delta

9. Yellowstone wikipedia. https://en.wikipedia.org/wiki/Yellowstone_National_Park

10. Grand Canyon wikipedia. https://en.wikipedia.org/wiki/Grand_Canyon

11. Mt. St. Helens wikipedia. https://en.wikipedia.org/wiki/Mount_St._Helens

12. Yosemite wikipedia. https://en.wikipedia.org/wiki/Yosemite_National_Park

13. Great Lakes wikipedia. https://en.wikipedia.org/wiki/Great_Lakes

14. Devils Tower wikipedia. https://en.wikipedia.org/wiki/Devils_Tower

15. Badlands wikipedia. https://en.wikipedia.org/wiki/Badlands_National_Park

16. Hawaii wikipedia. https://en.wikipedia.org/wiki/Hawaiian_Islands

17. Eyjafjallajkull wikipedia. https://en.wikipedia.org/wiki/2010_eruptions_of_Eyjafjallaj%C3%B6kull

18. Toba wikipedia. https://en.wikipedia.org/wiki/Lake_Toba

19. Klein, Richard. *The Human Career: Human Biological and Cultural Origins*. Chicago: University of Chicago Press, 2009.

20. Interactive Tree of Life. http://itol.embl.de/

21. Bill Nye Debates Ken Ham. https://www.youtube.com/watch?v=z6kgvhG3AkI

Chapter 5 Evangelizing and Moralizing.

1. Roulston, Helen. Personal Communication.

2. Pinker, Steven. *The Better Angels of Our Nature: Why Violence has Declined*. New York: Penguin, 2011.

3. Mitt Romney biography. https://en.wikipedia.org/wiki/Mitt_Romney

4. Ten Commandments wikipedia. https://en.wikipedia.org/wiki/Ten_Commandments

5. "Remarks by Obama at the National Prayer Breakfast" https://www.washingtonpost.com/local/remarks-by-obama-at-the-national-prayer-breakfast/2015/02/05/e9374b70-ad53-11e4-9c91-e9d2f9fde644_story.html

6. "This Week' Panel: Are Evangelicals out of Touch with Mainstream Views" http://news.yahoo.com/week-panel-evangelicals-touch-mainstream-views-180648088--abc-news-topstories.html;_ylt=A0LEVjohstFWVoMA.KQnnIlQ;_ylu=X3oDMTEycTQ2MzBxBGNvbG8DYmYxBHBvcwMxBHZ0aWQDjE3NDVfMQRzZWMDc3I-

7. Ray, Darrel. *Sex and God: How Religion Distorts Sexuality*. Bonner Springs: IPC Press, 2012.

8. "Max Lucado: Husain Abdullah Needs our Company in Prayer." http://www.usatoday.com/story/opinion/2014/10/01/husain-abdullah-nfl-prayer-column/16528619/

Chapter 6 Conservatism

1. Common Ground "USA Yesterday." http://www.usatoday.com/story/opinion/2014/07/16/common-ground-usa-yesterday/12759389/
2. "101 Sins I Commit During Ramadan." http://exhijabifashion.tumblr.com/post/91863969390/101-sins-i-commit-during-the-world-cup-and-ramadan
3. Embryology wikipedia. https://en.wikipedia.org/wiki/Embryology
4. Gaza Strip wikipedia. https://en.wikipedia.org/wiki/Gaza_Strip
5. Ismail Abu. *Islam in Nutshell*. IBQI Media, 2011.
6. Garrison, Vyckie. "What is Quiverfull" http://www.patheos.com/blogs/nolongerquivering/what-is-quiverfull/
7. Military Budget of the United States. https://en.wikipedia.org/wiki/Military_budget_of_the_United_States
8. Diamandis, Peter. "Abundance is our Future." http://www.ted.com/talks/peter_diamandis_abundance_is_our_future
9. "A New Science of Morality" http://edge.org/events/the-new-science-of-morality
10. "Why Giving Away our Wealth has Been the Most satisfying Thing We have Done" http://www.ted.com/talks/bill_and_melinda_gates_why_giving_away_our_wealth_has_been_the_most_satisfying_thing_we_ve_done

Chapter 7 Child Indoctrination.

1. Richard Dawkins Foundation for Reason and Science Converts Corner https://richarddawkins.net/community/convertscorner/
2. Buddhism wikipedia. https://en.wikipedia.org/wiki/Buddhismbuddhism wiki
3. Mohler, Albert. "And Then They are All Mine." http://www.albertmohler.com/2010/08/18/and-then-they-are-all-mine-the-real-agenda-of-some-college-professors/
4. Zingrone, William. Response to Al Mohler's "And then they are all mine" MSU NEWS.
5. "Snake That Killed Pastor Jamie Coots will be in Church Again Saturday." http://www.charismanews.com/us/42852-snake-that-killed-pastor-jamie-coots-will-be-in-church-again-saturday-his-son-saysjamie coots
6. Gospel of Mark. https://en.wikipedia.org/wiki/Gospel_of_Mark
7. "Post-Evangelicals and Why We Just Can't Get Over It." http://rachelheldevans.com/blog/post-evangelicals-and-why-we-cant-just-get-over-it?rq=Post%20Evangelicals
8. Dewitt, Jerry. *Hope after Faith*. Boston: DaCapo Press, 2011.
9. Neil Carter Godless in Dixie blog. http://www.patheos.com/blogs/godlessindixie/

10. Dawkins, Richard. *The God Delusion*, New York: Houghton-Mifflin, 2006.

11. Harris, Sam. *End of Faith*. New York: W.W. Norton, 2004.

12. "Stop Saying that Creationsim is Child Abuse." http://www.patheos.com/blogs/godlessindixie/2015/07/08/stop-saying-that-teaching-children-creationism-is-child-abuse/

13. Andrews, Seth. *De-Converted*. Parker, CO: Outskirts Press, 2013.

14. Dillahunty, Matt wikipedia. https://en.wikipedia.org/wiki/Matt_Dillahunty

15. Loftus, John. *Why I Became an Atheist*. New York: Prometheus, 2008.

16. Barker, Dan. *Godless*. Berkeley: Ulysses Press, 2008.

17. Madalyn Murray Ohair wikipedia. https://en.wikipedia.org/wiki/Madalyn_Murray_O'Hair

Chapter 8 Denial of Knowledge.

1. Evans, Rachel Held."Privilege and the Pill" http://rachelheldevans.com/blog/privilege-and-the-pill

2. Rep. Paul Broun Says Evolution, the Big Bang and Embryology are "Lies from the Pit of Hell." https://www.youtube.com/watch?v=ZBy3MbP4WDo

3. "Ben Carson Apologizes for Comments on Gay People." http://www.cnn.com/2015/03/04/politics/ben-carson-prisons-gay-choice/index.html on Homsexuality in Prison.

4. Ben Carson wikipedia. https://en.wikipedia.org/wiki/Ben_Carson.

5. 7th day Adventists. https://en.wikipedia.org/wiki/Seventh-day_Adventist_Church

6. US Prison Statistics. wiki: https://en.wikipedia.org/wiki/Incarceration_in_the_United_States#Men

7. Todd Friel, "What Happens When You Apply Bill Nye's Worldview" https://www.youtube.com/watch?v=Ce-bS7YBPsY

8. C14 wikipedia. https://en.wikipedia.org/wiki/Carbon-14

9. Beta-Analytic website. http://www.radiocarbon.com/?utm_source=bing.com&utm_medium=cpc&utm_campaign=radiocarbon&utm_term=carbon%2014&utm_content=Radiocarbon%20Dating

10. Carpintieri, A., G. Lacidogna, and O. Borla. 2014. Is the Shroud of Turin in relation to the Old Jerusalem historical earthquake? Meccanica. doi: 10.1007/s11012-013-9865-x

11. Krauss, Lawrence. *A Universe from Nothing*. New York: Atria, 2012.

12. Zingrone, William. "Religious Ideas Must Yield to New Knowledge." http://thenews.org/2013/11/01/zingrone-religious-ideas-must-yield-to-new-knowledge/

13. Barker, Dan. *Godless*. Berkeley: Ulysses Press, 2008.

14. Henderson, Rick. "Why There are No Good Atheists." http://www.huffingtonpost.com/pastor-rick-henderson/why-there-is-no-such-thing-as-a-good-atheist_b_4442287.html

15. Francis Collins wikipedia. https://en.wikipedia.org/wiki/Francis_Collins

16. Biologos website. http://biologos.org/

17. Collins, Francis. *The Language of God*. New York: Free Press, 2006.

18. Rick Perry 2012 Texas Prayer for Rain Proclamation. www.gov.texas.gov/news/proclamation/16038

19. Lung Cancer Statistics. http://www.lung.org/lung-health-and-diseases/lung-disease-lookup/lung-cancer/learn-about-lung-cancer/lung-cancer-fact-sheet.html

Chapter 9 Information Kills Religion

1. Bill Nye Debates Ken Ham. https://www.youtube.com/watch?v=z6kgvhG3AkI

2. Held Evans, Rachel. "On the Creation Debate" http://rachelheldevans.com/blog/creation-debate-nye-ham?rq=creation%20debate

3. Berman, Bob. "Astronomy and God: Do Anti-Religious Messages Belong in Science Education?" http://www.astronomy.com/magazine/bob-berman/2014/06/astronomy-and-god

4. Gatsyo, Tenzin. *Beyond Religion*.New York: Houghton Mifflin Harcourt, 2011.

5. Coyne, Jerry. *Faith vs Fact*. New York: Penguin, 2015.

6. Held Evans, Rachel. *Evolving in Monkey Town*. Nashville: Zondervan, 2011.

7. Rachel Held Evans blog. http://rachelheldevans.com/

8. Dobzhansky, Theodosius. "Nothing in Biology Makes Sense Except in the Light of Evolution" *American Biology Teacher* 1973 volume 35, pp. 125–129.

9. Dan Savage makes Maher's Guest's Squirm Hard with Talk of Inseminating His Husband for God https://www.youtube.com/watch?v=7X01i6hyvic

10. Univision Catholic Poll. http://corporate.univision.com/2014/02/landmark-univision-poll-finds-that-majority-of-catholics-worldwide-disagree-with-church-doctrines/

11. Michael Shermer's Answer to Edge Annual Question. http://edge.org/response-detail/25333

12. Giordano Bruno wikipedia. https://en.wikipedia.org/wiki/Giordano_Bruno

13. Catholic Church exorcism. http://www.slate.com/articles/life/faithbased/2014/05/exorcism_in_catholic_church_pope_francis_says_satan_the_devil_is_real.html

14. Dolnick, Edward. *The Clockwork Universe*. New York: Harper Collins, 2011.

15. Galileo Galilei. http://www.galileo.usg.edu/welcome/?Welcome

16. Elton John on Pope Francis.

http://www.cbsnews.com/news/elton-john-pope-francis-is-my-hero/

Chapter 10 The New Enlightenment

1. Harris, Sam. *The End of Faith*. New York: W.W. Norton, 2004.
2. Dawkins, Richard. *The God Delusion*. New York: Houghton-Mifflin, 2006.
3. Hitchens, Christopher. *God is not Great*. New York: Hachette Book Group Inc., 2007.
4. Dennett, Daniel. *Breaking the Spell*, New York: Penguin, 2006.
5. Barker, Dan. *Godless*. Berkeley: Ulysses Press, 2008.
6. Stenger, Victor. *God, The Failed Hypothesis: How Science Shows that God Does Not Exist*. New York: Prometheus, 2007.
7. Mehta, Hemant. *I Sold My Soul on eBay*. Colorado Springs: WaterBrook Press, 2007.
8. Ehrman, Bart. *Jesus Interrupted*. New York: Harper Collins, 2009.
9. Diamandis, Peter. *Abundance*. New York: Free Press, 2012.
10. Pinker, Steven. *The Better Angels of Our Nature: Why Violence has Declined*. New York: Viking Press, 2011.
11. Ridley, Matt. *The Rational Optimist*. New York: Harper Collins, 2011.
12. Shermer, Michael. *The Moral Arc*. New York: Henry Holt and Company, 2015.
13. Zacharias, Ravi. http://www.barnesandnoble.com/w/real-face-of-atheism-ravi-zacharias/1103065927?ean=9780801065118&quickview=true.
14. Edwards, Jonathan. "Sinners in the Hands of an Angry God." http://www.biblebb.com/files/edwards/je-sinners.htm
15. Mohler, Albert website. www.albertmohler.com
16. Mehta, Hemant. http://rachelheldevans.com/blog/ask-an-atheist-questions?rq=hemant%20mehta blog
17. Madalyn Murray Ohair. http://atheists.org/about-us/history
18. Malala and Pope Francis in Time Magazines "100 Most Influential People 2015." http://time.com/collection/2015-time-100/
19. Konner, Melvin. *Women After All*. New York: W.W. Norton, 2015.
20. PEW Research Religious Landscape Study 2014. http://www.pewforum.org/religious-landscape-study/
21. Dispatches from the New Enlightenment. wearedone.org
22. Krauss, Lawrence. American Humanist Association Humanist of the Year Acceptance Speech 2015. https://www.youtube.com/watch?v=yShIt-jHmi4
23. Richard Dawkins Convert's Corner. https://richarddawkins.net/community/convertscorner/